Advocacy, Outreach, and the Nation's Academic Libraries: A Call for Action

edited by

William C. Welburn
Janice Welburn
Beth McNeil

Association of College and Research Libraries
A division of the American Library Association
Chicago, Illinois 2010

The paper used in this publication meets the minimum requirements of American National Standard for Information Sciences–Permanence of Paper for Printed Library Materials, ANSI
Z39.48-1992. ∞

Library of Congress Cataloging-in-Publication Data

Advocacy, outreach, and the nation's academic libraries : a call for
action / by William C. Welburn, Janice Welburn, and Beth McNeil,
editors.
    p. cm.
Includes bibliographical references.
ISBN 978-0-8389-8549-6 (pbk. : alk. paper) 1. Academic libraries-
-Public relations--United States. 2. Libraries and colleges--United
States. 3. Libraries and scholars--United States. 4. Academic
libraries--Information technology. I. Welburn, William C. II.
Welburn, Janice. III. McNeil, Beth.
Z675.U5A4145 2010
021.7--dc22
                            2010018611

Table of Contents

Acknowledgements

We would like to thank all of our contributors for their willingness to be a part of this project. The thought that they have given to advocacy as related to their respective areas of expertise is well appreciated. We also to acknowledge Elizabeth Wawrzyniak for her assistance in organizing and editing much of the work submitted to us. Finally, very special thanks to Evelyn and Edward Welburn, Grace Moore, Lorene Brown, Joan Gieseke, and Wes Welch for always believing and lending their support.

Preface

Mary Ellen K. Davis

Accountability. Assessment. Return on investment. Performance indicators. Now more than ever these terms are heard in higher education. The financial pressure brought about by "the great recession" has intensified the culture of accountability in postsecondary education. According to a recent OCLC report, "Research Libraries, Risk and Systemic Change," (www.oclc.org/research/news/2010-03-25.htm) the two greatest threats to academic libraries are the availability of online information resources (e.g., Google) and the erosion of our user base.

In the face of these very real challenges, librarians must be able to clearly articulate their value to the teaching, learning, and research mission of the institution. It is imperative that all academic librarians embrace advocacy as a core responsibility and develop greater fluency in communicating and demonstrating value, worth, impact, and influence.

The Association of College & Research Libraries has long recognized that advocacy is a critically important issue for the profession. Indeed, advocacy is a key goal in the current strategic plan. Our recent advocacy efforts include participation in national and international collaborative partnerships such as SPARC, CNI, and the Library Copyright Alliance. We have also developed toolkits for practitioners. ACRL has been a strong advocate on behalf of the profession on many issues including protecting the fair use doctrine, ensuring public access to federally funded research, experimentation with new publishing models, embedding information literacy in the general education curriculum, and increasing funding for libraries.

Advocacy, Outreach, and the Nation's Academic Libraries: A Call for Action explores the many opportunities for advocacy and helps us as librarians to better understand our role in the world of civic engagement as well as our role as an advocate for the library on campus. These essays also highlight the collaborative nature of advocacy and the importance of seeing opportunities for effective advocacy in challenging situations.

This volume provides essential ideas, theory, case studies, and much more to help us become more effective and fluent advocates.

I am confident that *Advocacy, Outreach, and the Nation's Academic Libraries: A Call for Action* will help us to advance our collective goal of demonstrating the value of academic libraries for our most important stakeholders—those who use libraries and those who can provide needed resources to meet the challenges of the 21st century academy.

Mary Ellen Davis
Chicago, April 2010

Introduction: Libraries and the Practice of Advocacy in Postsecondary Education

This book addresses aspects of advocacy in college and university libraries in the United States. Over the course of the first decade of the new millennium, leaders in the Association of College and Research Libraries (ACRL) and, more broadly, the American Library Association (ALA) have placed emphasis on advocacy in their organizations' strategic platforms. In ACRL, advocacy has also emerged as a key value in planning and envisioning future scenarios for both libraries and working professionals.

Despite the preponderance of advocacy in the public discourse of our professional associations and among our leaders and working practitioners in academic libraries, the very term *advocacy* continues to evoke a feeling of ambiguity as an explicit roadmap for gaining influence and support. Even those within academic librarianship who feel versed in advocacy may also find themselves struggling to implement it on college and university campuses. The collection of essays in this volume further defines, explores, and contextualizes advocacy across the topography of college and university libraries, especially in service and resource development, adoption of information and communication technologies, enacting governmental policy and legislative action, governing campuses, and in the everyday practice of management and decision making.

This collection also stems from a collaborative research project by the editors that sought to examine the way that academic library directors perceived the values of advocacy defined by influence strategies and tactics. Using the *Kipnis-Schmidt Profiles of Organizational Influence Strategies* (POIS), the editors surveyed library directors at four-year institutions across the United States to gain insight into perceptions of lateral influence they had with peer group campus administrators. In our study, evidence suggested that while influence strategies and tactics vary somewhat, there is also clear indication of a need for library administrators to exert influence among peers—whether through assertiveness, coalition building, or by seeking consensus—to gain support for libraries in campus-level decisions. Yet the editors also became painfully aware of the dearth of literature reaching down below the surface of understanding about advocacy, even though advocacy had become a part of our nomenclature. Moreover, we recognized that our understanding of advocacy-in-practice was further limited by the lens of library directors, missing the perceptions from the frontline as encouraged by advocacy leaders Camila Alire and Julie Todaro.

In the chapters that follow, the editors challenged a group of librarians from different walks of life holding a variety of professional responsibilities and appointments to relate advocacy as they understood and defined it to their respective areas of expertise. What emerged from the careful thought given by each author is a form of *meta*-advocacy, one that transcends otherwise disparate aspects of the academic library agenda and different communities of academic librarians.

Advocacy, Outreach, and The Nation's Academic Libraries: A Call for Action begins with a comprehensive review of the concept of *engagement* as applied to higher education by Scott Walter, Associate University Librarian for Services and Associate Dean at University of Illinois at Urbana-Champaign. According to Walter, engagement in its contemporary usage can be sourced to Ernest Boyer's concepts of "scholarship of discovery"…and "application," referring to "the activities or programs that an institution of higher education pursues in order to serve the needs of communities outside its campus." In higher education, public engagement has historically been accomplished through outreach and extension into various communities. Walter provides a pragmatic assessment of opportunities and challenges for librarians to engaging in building platforms for advocacy.

D. Scott Brandt, Associate Dean for research at Purdue University, explores the role of advocacy in developing collaborative relationships in the research enterprise, drawing a clear distinction between librarians' support for research and actively engaging in research endeavors, particularly in an environment shaped by interdisciplinarity and the pursuit of governmental research funding. Beth McNeil, Associate Dean for Academic Affairs at Purdue University Libraries, surveys different ways that the concept of scholarly communication has been institutionalized in both professional associations and organizations. She links these developments with opportunities to recast or re-envision the importance of individual leadership, identifying the most relevant leadership styles that are fundamentally associated with new and emerging roles of librarians.

Ray English, Azariah Smith Root Director of Libraries at Oberlin College, and Heather Joseph, Executive Director of SPARC, The Scholarly Publishing and Academic Resources Coalition, examine how library advocacy has been placed in practice for public access to federal government-sponsored research. Their review of more than ten years of advocacy and active efforts in Congress demonstrate the capacity and effectiveness of librarians' decisions to form coalitions with other entities to advance open access. Camila Alire, American Library Association President for 2009-2010, argues for the efficacy of advocacy as strategy-in-action from frontline librarians with direct contact with academic library user subcommunities, including students and faculty. Using scholarship from education and the social and behavioral sciences, Alire places advocacy as a strategic imperative within the academic milieu when she writes, "When both library groups (library administrators and library faculty) work on library advocacy, their efforts enhance the academic library's chances for receiving its fair share of campus resources and they contribute to the long-term credibility of the academic library throughout the academy." Her proposal reaches across levels of administrative hierarchy to broaden responsibilities for carrying forward the priorities of libraries.

Jean Zanoni, Associate Dean, and Scott B. Mandernack, Head of Research and Instructional Services, both of Marquette University Libraries, explore the need to understand campus environments as a prerequisite for integrating advocacy into strategic planning processes. Their essay identifies a broad spectrum of stakeholders that are internal and external to the campus that have an effect on libraries' strategic directions.

Paul Bracke, Associate Dean for Information Technology and Resource Services at Purdue University, discusses an association between advocacy and outreach opportunities and information technology development in academic libraries. Bracke develops a sociotechnical framework to understand libraries and IT development, particularly in the broader IT community, as opportunities and challenges are presented for partnership and collaboration. Kim Leeder and Memo Cordova, both Reference and Instruction Librarians at Boise State University, argue for greater adoption of interactive information and communication technologies—"the need to become more active in the very forum that has overshadowed us"—as a form of digital advocacy that responds to a widely held assumption that the broader public gets their information from easily accessible search engines and wiki resources. By adding interactive contact to Web sites and adopting blogs, chat services, media sharing devices, Web-based answer boards, and many libraries are shifting their roles from gate-keepers to open gateways. Susan Vega-Garcia, Head of Instructional Programs at Iowa State University, begins her essay with full acknowl-edgement that "advocacy and outreach are the bread and butter of in-struction librarians," and that information literacy affords an occasion for partnerships and coalitions within academic environments. Her review of issues and trends in instructional positions, including job requirements, stresses the importance of expectations for successful faculty-librarian collaborations.

Janice Welburn, Marquette University's Dean of Libraries, gives an overview of the affinity between advocacy and diversity, specifi-cally examining how groups of librarians and others within the university can position themselves to support campus-level diversity initiatives. These initiatives are exemplified in employment, services, and access to resources. William Welburn, Senior Advisor to the Provost on Diversity Initiatives at Marquette University uses his past experience as a graduate college administrator to explore common interests of graduate education and libraries in preparing the next generations of academicians and professionals. The congruent goals between libraries and graduate schools form an opportunity to create coalitions to advocate for resources to support students.

Julie Todaro concludes the volume by juxtaposing excuses given for shying away from advocacy with assertions on the benefits of ad-vocacy processes. Her thesis is predicated upon the need to bring the centrality of libraries to the foreground in educational settings.

The editors hope that *Advocacy, Outreach, and the Nation's Aca-demic Libraries: A Call for Action* will equip librarians with an under-standing of issues that will help them to have informal and formal discussions among colleagues within the library and across their respective campuses. We also hope the content of this volume will aid in opening a new level of discussion about advocacy in practice. These discussions may take the form of a 30 second elevator conver-sation, a 30 minute formal presentation, or a quick interaction at a service desk. They can be practiced by an administrator working with peer campus administrators or a front line librarian with firsthand knowledge and expertise. Having the right tools in one's toolbox—and learning from others in similar situations—will strengthen and enable advocacy efforts and allow for those important conversations.

I. Advocacy and its Publics:
Critical Issues for College and University Libraries

Advocacy through Engagement: Public Engagement and the Academic Library

Scott Walter

Introduction

The last few years have been challenging ones for library users in Macomb County. Macomb is one of the most populous counties in Michigan, with over 825,000 residents living in its corner of the Detroit metropolitan area.[1] The Macomb County Library (MCL) serves as "an information and reference center for all of Macomb County," and its collections in popular fiction and children's literature are complemented by subject emphases in public policy information, consumer health information, business information, and career information.[2] MCL provides Internet access to school children and job hunters, and its ongoing programs as a federal depository library, a center for literacy education, and a resource for library users with disabilities ensure that "[there] is something for every age at the Macomb County Library!"[3] "Something for every age," that is, as long as it doesn't require significant funding because the Macomb County budget—like the budget of many state and local governments—is in trouble.

For the library, the trouble began in 2005, when only an intense lobbying effort by its users convinced the Macomb County Board of Commissioners to reject a proposed plan to "cut or eliminate" the library budget as part of a larger plan to address shortfalls across the county. By 2006, the library budget was back on the table, when the Board voted to reduce its allocation by $166,000—a change designed to reduce service hours by several hours each week.[4] Budget reviews and reductions continued over the next 18 months, and, by 2008, the county and the library budget were in dire straits with no clear path ahead to maintaining library services in Macomb County.

The Macomb County Library story is a familiar one—so familiar, in fact, that it could have served as a model for the description of broader problems facing public library funding found in a recent study by OCLC, *From Awareness to Funding: A Study of Library*

Support in America (2008). Public libraries, OCLC argues, play a unique and critical role in their communities: a role defined by their "[provision to] every resident of the United States the opportunity to thrive through access to information and lifelong learning."[5] Public libraries are funded primarily by local communities, but the leaders of those communities are increasingly challenged to meet a variety of needs with shrinking resources, including emergency services, health care services, educational services, and recreational services. The Macomb County Board of Commissioners saw this challenge grow between 2005 and 2008, and its members may have appreciated the stark picture of this increasingly difficult budgetary balancing act painted by Bill Finch, Mayor of Bridgeport, Connecticut, when he proposed significant cuts to his own 2008 library budget: "We are getting back to basics: police, fire, and education… Libraries are not essential services."[6] Recent news stories have demonstrated precisely how essential public libraries can be in times of economic hardship, and many of the long-time advocates of the Macomb County Library might disagree with Finch's conclusion, but, as OCLC suggested, the way in which public libraries are funded is a mystery to many of their patrons, and the options available for addressing budgetary shortfalls in ways that do not pit one "essential service" against another are not always clear.[7]

OCLC proposes to address the problem of public awareness of the role of the public library in the community, and the question of whether increased awareness might result in support for increased funding, through a concerted program of "marketing and advocacy" (an approach also embraced by the American Library Association through its "Visibility @ Your Library" campaign).[8] Perhaps this approach would have benefited the Macomb County Library, and, if it had, we might find the current essay in a collection about advocacy for public libraries, rather than one concerned with academic libraries. Where Macomb County and the broader picture painted by OCLC diverge, however, is precisely where Macomb County and academic libraries overlap: it was not "marketing and advocacy" that promised to save the Macomb County Library from budget reductions as drastic as those announced in Bridgeport; it was the university.

In June 2008, a "surprise plan to save the Macomb County Library…emerged"—MCL would become part of Wayne State University.[9] The university, based in Detroit, proposed to lease the library building from the county, and to manage the library, in part, as a means of supporting the Library and Information Sciences (LIS) program housed at the nearby Macomb Community College University Center. If accepted, this proposal would lead to the rise of a library serving a diverse group of users drawn from the community college, the university, and the broader public. While surprising to Macomb County residents, perhaps, there is ample precedent for this type of partnership. In California, for example, San Jose State University operates the Dr. Martin Luther King, Jr. Library in collaboration with the San Jose Public Libraries; in Washington, a single library serves the students of both the University of Washington at Bothell and Cascadia Community College; and in Iowa, the Russell D. Cole Library serves both as the Cornell College library and as the public library of the City of Mount Vernon.[10] Alternately referred to as "joint-use" or "dual-use" libraries, partnerships of this sort are widely seen as a means of maintaining library services in difficult budget times, fostering collaboration across our professional communities, and enhancing services to library users.[11] The global scope of the joint-use library model has been noted before, and, were this simply the story of another such library, we might end a brief essay here with the long-hoped-for promise of continued support for library users in Macomb County realized.[12] The partnership proposed between Wayne State and Macomb County, however, is different; it is representative of a broader strategy employed at Wayne State—and at universities across the country—to foster "engagement" between the university and the community.

"Engagement"—alternately referred to in the literature as "public engagement," "civic engagement," or "community engagement"—refers to the activities or programs that an institution of higher education pursues in order to serve the needs of communities outside its campus. The School of Architecture at the University of Illinois at Urbana-Champaign—home of the university's East St. Louis Action Research Project (ESLARP)—defines public engagement as "the application of new and existing knowledge to address real world problems and improve local communities."[13] Kelly Ward, Associate Professor of Higher Education Administration at Washington State University, and former Service Learning Director for Montana Campus Compact, describes the "engaged campus" as one that is "committed to its students and faculty and fulfilling its traditional role in teaching and training students and citizens, but also…to serving the communities and constituencies that surround and support it."[14] President Robert Bruininks of the University of Minnesota refers to public engagement as "an institutional commitment to public purposes and responsibilities intended to strengthen a democratic way of life in the…Information Age."[15] Unlike earlier notions of "outreach" that focused on the simple provision of campus resources to community members, "engagement" is defined by the application of campus-based expertise to issues of public concern, and by the notion of a "partnership" between the university and members of the community that allows mutual benefit to accrue to each side.[16] The mutually beneficial nature of public engagement programs is highlighted in the vision articulated at Illinois, one in which "faculty, staff, and students collaborate with external audiences to address the needs and opportunities of society."[17] Through public engagement programs, the unique resources and expert knowledge that reside on campus are placed in service to the community, especially as those resources may further the goals of civic responsibility, cultural awareness, lifelong learning, or other locally-defined needs.

If approved, the Macomb County Library may join other Wayne State "community partners," in "[providing] faculty with the tools necessary to strengthen their course content; students with the opportunity to give back and apply classroom theories in a hands-on way; and community organizations with the chance to receive assistance from some of Wayne State's most dedicated citizens."[18] As in other public engagement programs, the resources and expertise housed in the university, including the library, may be deployed to meet a community need. By making a commitment to engagement, the university demonstrates its value to the community, and by taking part in engagement programs, faculty, staff, students, and community members become the university's advocates. While the OCLC study provides valuable clues toward a broader strategy for enhancing support for the public library, it was not "marketing and advocacy" that provided a foundation for the future of the Macomb County Library, it was "advocacy through engagement."

Academic libraries have provided a wide array of services to members of their local communities for years, including access services, reference services, instructional services, and public programs.[19] Derek Bok, then-President of Harvard University, recognized the value of outreach programs when he identified the provision of access to campus-based cultural heritage organizations, including museums and libraries, as evidence of the commitment of the university to the public good.[20] The purpose, direction and scope of library outreach programs, however, have been challenged over the past decade by increasing attention to the concept of engagement—a vision of collaboration between campus and community that goes well beyond traditional notions of outreach.[21] In making a commitment to public engagement, for example, the library might give the same priority to collaboration with campus public engagement programs as it does to collaboration with traditional academic programs. The library might move beyond the provision of community borrowing services and public programs toward the sponsorship of partnerships across library types, with civic and community organizations, and with professional communities at the local, state, regional, national, or international level. It might also focus on the ways in which the professional expertise housed within its organization—expertise related, for example, to the location, retrieval, evaluation, and management of information, the preservation of artifacts, or the creation, description, and management of digital collections—might be deployed in ways that address community concerns.

Service to the community beyond the campus walls through a strategic commitment to engagement is widely seen as a means by which institutions of higher education may advocate for their needs in an environment marked by decreasing public support for higher education.[22] The proposed partnership between Macomb County, Michigan, and Wayne State University—an institution that has recently received formal recognition of its commitment to engagement through a new classification process offered by the Carnegie Foundation for the Advancement of Teaching—provides a landmark opportunity to demonstrate how academic libraries can contribute to broader campus efforts at public engagement.[23] There are, however, many other paths to this same end that might be pursued by academic libraries not presented with the singular opportunity presented to Wayne State.

The University of Maryland Libraries, for example, have provided a variety of traditional public programs as part the annual "Maryland Day" celebration at the university (including programs on government information, children's literature, local history, digital collections, and preservation and conservation); an event that, according to University of Maryland President Dan Mote, promotes among its attendees (over 75,000 strong in 2008) "a greater appreciation of the

University and higher education."[24] The University of California—Irvine Libraries have supported the "School Partnerships in Research and Information Technology" (SPIRIT) program for the past decade in order "to reach out to the community and enrich the lives of area junior high and high school students," and to contribute to campus efforts to serve the local community's need for access to higher education by providing programs that support the recruitment and retention of a diverse student population.[25] Finally, the Kansas State University Libraries have worked in collaboration with the United States Army since 2005 to improve services provided to soldiers (and their family members) based at nearby Fort Riley.[26] The question is not whether there are opportunities for the library to play a substantive role in campus public engagement programs, but whether academic librarians will choose to pursue these opportunities, and whether their campuses are attuned to the ways in which the resources and expertise housed in the library may become part of the institutional commitment to advocacy through engagement.

However well versed they may be in strategies for outreach, academic libraries have been slow to adapt to the challenges and opportunities provided to them as part of the public engagement agenda on their campuses. Lynn C. Westney concluded that libraries have been "conspicuous by their absence" from public engagement programs, and Nancy K. Herther has noted the lack of involvement by academic librarians in service learning, one of the hallmark programs in any public engagement initiative.[27] While not related to service learning (although the connection to the Wayne State LIS program provides an obvious opportunity), the Macomb County Library example highlights other ways in which academic libraries might add their resources and expertise to those deployed across the campus in support of public engagement programs. There are many examples of academic libraries engaging community members outside the campus—K–12 students and teachers, health information professionals, and local arts and cultural heritage groups, for example—which leads one to ask why academic libraries are rarely discussed as part of the public engagement agenda, or, if they are discussed, why the vision of their contribution to the broader program seems relatively limited.

What factors limit the involvement of academic librarians in public engagement activities? How might academic library leaders better support the involvement of libraries and librarians in campus public engagement initiatives? Most importantly, in an age marked by the dual imperatives of the library to advocate for its significance to the campus, and of the campus to advocate for its significance to the community, how might academic libraries make a strategic commitment to public engagement equivalent to those made in recent years to information literacy instruction and scholarly communication? The library is a critical resource for any campus striving to demonstrate its commitment to public engagement, and a commitment to designing, delivering, and assessing public engagement programs provides librarians with an opportunity to add a valuable new facet to their efforts to advocate for the ongoing importance of the academic library to the university mission.

Literature Review

There is a rich literature related to public engagement in academic libraries, but it is largely hidden. The most familiar aspect of this literature relates to service learning, but library involvement with K–12 schools is also evidence of the library contribution to the public engagement agenda on campus, as is library involvement with academic programs aimed at fostering the success of first-generation college students or students representing racial and ethnic minority groups historically under-represented in institutions of higher education.[28] Studies of library involvement with Cooperative Extension programs offer another example, as do studies of library involvement with cultural heritage organizations.[29] There are studies of academic library collaboration with public libraries, school libraries, and state libraries, as well as studies of collaboration between academic libraries in the United States and libraries in the developing world. Taken separately, these studies are interesting; taken together, they demonstrate the impact that academic libraries and librarians can have on the public engagement agenda on their campuses. Like the public libraries that OCLC reminds us must focus more attention on their marketing efforts, academic libraries must weave these disparate stories of service together into a narrative of the library contribution to the campus commitment to public engagement. Owing to the broad scope of that narrative across the literature of academic librarianship, this review will touch only upon selected resources for further study. The purpose of this review is not to provide a comprehensive introduction to the literature of outreach and public engagement in academic libraries, but, rather, to identify the "corner pieces" that may allow others to continue putting the puzzle together.

Outreach

Outreach is the foundation for any public engagement program, but it is how one builds on that foundation that determines the degree to which the library contributes to engagement initiatives on campus. In the library context, "outreach" has traditionally been defined as service activities designed to meet the information or instructional needs of an underserved user group.[30] Historically identified as a function of public libraries, it has become common in recent years for academic librarians to discuss efforts to communicate and collaborate with campus colleagues as "outreach," as well as to identify library services aimed at off-campus students and faculty as "outreach services."[31] Most recently, efforts to "embed" librarians in academic departments, residence halls, and other campus facilities have been discussed as a feature of outreach services.[32]

Outreach activities of this type are critical to the academic library mission, and this use of the term in consistent with what Louise Phelps referred to in the broader campus context as "internal outreach," i.e., "where faculty members serve as expert consultants and advisors to other faculty or administrators, applying professional expertise within the institution."[33] Critical though they are, however, efforts to communicate with, and to improve service to, core academic library user groups (whether resident on campus, or participating in academic programs through distance learning programs) are not what is meant by "public engagement." Public engagement relates to those activities that allow the faculty member (or librarian) to apply his or her professional expertise outside the traditional academic context. Given, however, that these internal outreach activities often embody precisely the collaborative and mutually-beneficial approach to service development associated with public engagement initiatives, we may justifiably refer to them as "campus engagement." Studies of traditional outreach services, as well as campus engagement programs, are staples of the library literature, and these studies provide the starting point for understanding the potential for public engagement programs in academic libraries.

Tina Schneider, for example, identifies a variety of outreach services housed in academic libraries, including community borrower programs, programs aimed at local high school students, consumer health information programs, and business information services. A review of programs such as these may identify opportunities for academic librarians to contribute to public engagement programs on campus. Likewise, some of the issues that Schneider identifies as germane to the study of academic library outreach, e.g., establishing a library-wide commitment to supporting these "non-traditional" users, and aligning the outreach agenda with the broader mission of the library, are essential to any attempt to integrate the library into campus public engagement programs.[34]

Colleen Boff, Carol Singer, and Beverly Stearns provide an overview of the range of academic library services associated with campus engagement programs through their analysis of position descriptions in areas such as distance library services and multicultural library services.[35] Their study suggests that library positions focused on campus initiatives that go beyond that which has become associated with the work of traditional subject specialists—i.e., communication with, and provision of services to, faculty and students associated with established disciplines and academic programs—may require the library to recruit professionals with different sets of skills and experiences than has been the case in the past. If this is true of the positions identified by Boff, Singer, and Stearns, how much more might this be the case if the academic library were to pursue substantive involvement in public engagement programs? Just as the commitment to public engagement has led to changes in the research agenda and pedagogical practices among campus faculty, so, too, may it require changes to some of the practices and priorities of academic librarianship.

The relationship between a commitment to campus engagement initiatives and the future of traditional public service programs is also the subject of the study by Phyllis Rudin of new approaches to liaison services. Rudin demonstrates how advances in information technology have allowed librarians to take their expertise to the point of need for students by establishing "outposts" in facilities including student unions, residence halls, and elsewhere. Likewise, she shows how changes in the ways in which faculty make use of information in their research and teaching (and, one might argue, broader changes in the information landscape across many disciplines) have given rise to opportunities to re-envision services to academic departments through models that allow librarians to become "embedded" in the physical (and virtual) spaces associated with those departments or disciplines.[36] Like Boff, Singer, and Stearns, Rudin demonstrates that campus engagement continues to be a major focus of concern, and a major source of innovation, in academic librarianship. While not public engagement programs, per se, the efforts made over the past decade by librarians to re-envision core public service programs in order to address new challenges and opportunities have led to the rise of new positions and new approaches to the delivery of library resources and services. Innovation in support of campus engagement opens the door to future discussions of the role of the library professional in public engagement programs situated in the academic department, the student union, or elsewhere on the campus or in the community.

Service Learning

If outreach is the foundation for engagement programs in libraries, then service learning is the foundation for engagement programs on campus. Service learning is an approach to teaching and learning that "incorporates community work into the curriculum, giving students real-world learning experiences that enhance their academic learning while providing a tangible benefit for the community."[37] According to Campus Compact, a network of over 1,000 institutions of higher education offering campus-based service programs, almost 50% of its members incorporated service learning into their academic majors in 2007, and almost 40% incorporated service learning into the core curriculum.[38] John S. Riddle provides a theoretical framework for library involvement with service learning through information literacy instruction, and outlines ways in which information literacy learning objectives might complement the objectives associated with service learning programs.[39] Westney and Herther provide descriptions of the opportunities provided to libraries by campus service learning programs, but, as noted above, they conclude that pursuit of those opportunities by librarians has been limited.[40]

Interestingly, while the literature suggests that the integration of information literacy instruction into service learning programs has been limited, there is ample evidence that service learning models have been adopted within the Library and Information Science (LIS) programs through which most academic librarians enter the profession. Nancy J. Becker, James K. Elmborg, Loriene Roy, Lorna Peterson, and Mary Alice Ball, among others, have written about the integration of service learning into LIS education.[41] Ball has even written about the academic library, itself, as the site for service learning in LIS education (although we must leave aside for the moment the distinction between "service learning" and "clinical education," which I would argue is a more appropriate way of describing field-based components of LIS programs).[42] At the University of Illinois at Urbana-Champaign's Graduate School of Library and Information Science (GSLIS), the Community Informatics Initiative focuses squarely on the question of how expertise in fields related to information and communication technologies may be deployed to meet the needs of local communities for technology centers, library services, etc.[43] If service learning is so popular and powerful an approach to professional education for librarians, one wonders why relatively few academic librarians appear to have built more effective collaboration with faculty taking part in service learning initiatives. Why have academic librarians not pursued service learning programs as partners to the same degree that they have pursued programs such as Writing Across the Curriculum and First-Year Experience?[44] If they have, why does it appear that their attempts to connect with service learning initiatives have been less successful (or, at least, less well documented)?

Cooperative Extension

"Extension" is an essential component of the mission of over 100 "land-grant" institutions of higher education in the United States.[45] According to the U.S. Department of Agriculture, which administers the Cooperative State Research, Education, and Extension Service with which these institutions are associated, contemporary extension programs find their roots in the commitment to the provision of agricultural, vocational, and other "applied" educational programs made by the federal government through passage of legislation such as the Morrill Act (1862) and the Smith-Lever Act (1914).[46] Today, Cooperative Extension supports research and educational programs in areas including agricultural science, natural resources and environmental studies, family and consumer sciences, nutrition and consumer health, and community and economic development.[47] At land-grant institutions, Cooperative Extension is typically the "flagship outreach effort," and the multidisciplinary approach to public engagement taken by extension programs provides rich opportunities for collaboration with academic libraries.[48]

The greatest emphasis in the study of library involvement with extension programs has been on the provision of information and instructional services to extension agents who serve as the link between the campus and extension offices across the state.[49] Betty Rozum and Kevin Brewer describe a survey of extension agents conducted by Utah State University to determine their information needs, and to design and deliver useful library services to this distributed network of library users. They found that extension agents were largely unaware of the resources to which they had access. Based on these findings, they developed Web and print-based information resources to help guide extension agents to useful services, including access to digital content, interlibrary loan and document delivery programs, and digital reference services.[50] Kornelia Tancheva, Michael Cook, and Howard Raskin describe the development of a similar set of resources aimed at extension agents at Cornell University, and how the establishment of a formal liaison program led to the development of information literacy programs designed to meet the needs of extension agents, "as well as the needs of end users who contact Extension offices for information and documents."[51]

It is in the dual nature of the extension agents' information needs that one may see opportunities for further library involvement in extension activities as an aspect of public engagement. Extension offices around the state are not only the workplaces of extension agents, but also the sites through which members of the public go for assistance from the university with their information needs. To members of the public, the extension office may be the classroom, the research laboratory, and, yes, the university library. Library services for extension agents are a critical feature of any public engagement program in academic libraries, but imagine the impact of library services—information literacy instruction, for example, or government information services—delivered by librarians to members of the public *through* extension offices and education centers. With public engagement in mind, academic libraries at participating institutions can, and should, make better use of the statewide opportunities made possible through Cooperative Extension.

K–12 Education

Finally, there are the schools. There are few areas in which more evidence of opportunities for public engagement with the academic library is available than in connection with K–12 education. The Association of College & Research Libraries and the American Association of School Librarians recognized the potential for collaboration between their members in support of common concerns for the information literacy instruction of K–12 students and teachers in the establishment of the AASL/ACRL Task Force on the Educational Role of Libraries (now the AASL/ACRL Interdivisional Committee on Information Literacy). The Task Force's "Blueprint for Collaboration" noted that school librarians and academic librarians "share the goals of fostering lifelong learning and ensuring that students at all educational levels are prepared to meet the challenges of the 21st century," and that these goals were likewise shared by K–12 teachers and administrators (and, one assumes, the parents of K–12 students).[52] Work in the State of Ohio over the past 20 years demonstrates that opportunities exist for meaningful collaboration between academic librarians, K–12 teachers, and school librarians committed to meeting the shared goal of a "K–20" approach to information literacy instruction.[53] In an earlier essay, I referred to education librarians housed in academic libraries, school librarians, and children and young adult librarians housed in public libraries as a network of professional support for K–12 teachers and students, and that network continues to provide opportunities for academic librarians committed to public engagement.[54]

Melba Jesudason describes library involvement in "precollege programs" at the University of Wisconsin-Madison (UW) in the early 1990s. While the instructional approach she used may seem dated to many reading her essay today, her description of the library's integration into the broader "precollege programs" at Madison remains valuable. Focusing on their contribution to university outreach to students from historically underrepresented groups and to students identified as academically gifted, the UW libraries were part of a campus-wide approach to providing services to K–12 students. Among the benefits of participation in this campus-wide approach identified by Jesudason were: 1) better communication and collaboration across library types; 2) more effective networking and communication between academic librarians and other campus groups; 3) enhanced "town-gown" relationships; 4) increased opportunities to market library services; and 5) increased opportunities to integrate the library into campus efforts to enhance diversity among the student body.[55] While the UW program described by Jesudason pre-dates the recent focus on public engagement, one can see how attention to the design and delivery of academic library services to K–12 students might provide multiple opportunities for highlighting the library contribution to related efforts, e.g., programs aimed at supporting the recruitment and retention of students of color to the university.[56]

While Jesudason described the provision of library services to K–12 students, Janet Nichols and Janet Martorana, et al., describe the development of instructional programs aimed at K–12 educators. Nichols describes a program jointly designed by librarians at Wayne State University and their counterparts at several Detroit-area schools, while Martorana, et al. describe the development of "train-the-trainer" workshops aimed at K–12 teachers in California. In both cases, the programs were designed to meet the information literacy needs of K–12 students, and to address the need for continuing professional education for K–12 teachers expected to provide information literacy instruction to their students. In both cases, the connection between the academic environment in which K–12 teachers and administrators receive their own professional education, and the academic environment in which they prepare their own students for the Information Age is highlighted.[57]

Finally, Kenneth Burhanna and Mary Lee Jensen provide a programmatic view of engagement with K–12 education through their description of "Informed Transitions", a "formal library outreach program to high schools" at Kent State University. Burhanna and Jensen describe an academic library that has made a broad commitment to engagement with K–12 schools based on common instructional goals and on the shared commitment among K–20 educators in Ohio to support student success. Their discussion of the challenges that any library considering a similar program will face is especially useful, e.g., establishing a sustainable model of human resource allocation to this effort. Providing services to K–12 students and educators seems a popular choice for library-centered public engagement programs, they conclude, but even a popular choice is difficult to make, and to sustain, in an era of constrained financial and human resources in academic libraries. This lesson from the history of K–12 engagement in academic libraries must be remembered in regard to any public engagement program, and the question must be asked if your library has the capacity to add this dimension to its public service portfolio.[58]

Outreach efforts, service learning programs, extension networks, and K–12 schools provide opportunities for library involvement with public engagement initiatives on almost any campus. These programs, singly or together, should be considered closely related to the service missions of land-grant institutions, regional state institutions, private institutions, and community colleges. As Ward wrote: "The service mission of higher education is most strongly associated with the land-grant movement…[but examination] of the history of higher education through the lens of service shows how firmly embedded service is in the mission and actions of most colleges and universities."[59] Many of the examples highlighted in this essay are drawn from the ranks of public research universities, but engagement activities may be found on campuses (and in libraries) of all types.[60] Indeed, the institution of higher education in America today that does not recognize the need to engage the public, to demonstrate its value to the community, and to pursue outreach and engagement activities designed to enhance its efforts to recruit and retain a diverse pool of students is a rare one! There are many other facets of the public engagement agenda in higher education, but these four were highlighted owing to the fact that most librarians will find at least one of these programs on campus. With these programs as the "corners," let us turn next to some illustrative examples of current practice that further demonstrate both the complexity and the vitality of public engagement programs in academic libraries today.

Public Engagement in Academic Libraries—Case Studies

The preceding literature review identified areas in which academic libraries might invest effort in order to make an immediate contribution to public engagement programs on campus. Any such investment will likely build on programs already found in the library, e.g., tours for K–12 students. My argument is not that academic libraries have not been involved in public engagement activities, but, rather, that they have not been as strategic as they might be in identifying those activities as central to the academic library mission. There are numerous opportunities in the contemporary higher education environment for academic libraries to contribute more effectively to institutional efforts to promote advocacy through engagement, and we must pursue them with the same vigor that we pursue opportunities to collaborate with classroom colleagues on the identification of student learning objectives, or with researchers on plans to describe, disseminate, and preserve datasets and other digital content. Having identified some of the broadest opportunities for public engagement in academic libraries through the literature review, let us turn now to a trio of brief case studies that further illustrate the potential for library-based public engagement programs. As with the literature review, the goal of presenting these case studies is not to be comprehensive, but to illustrate both what is possible in terms of making a commitment to public engagement in academic libraries, and what some of the major challenges to making that commitment may be.

Washington State University—Central Washington REACH Program

Washington State University (WSU) is a public research university serving over 25,000 students at its flagship campus in Pullman, at regional campuses in Spokane, Richland ("Tri-Cities"), and Vancouver, and through a variety of distance education programs.[61] Established in 1890 as the state's land-grant institution, WSU maintains not only its four academic campuses, but also ten learning centers located around the state, as well as extension offices in each of Washington's 39 counties.[62] For almost a century, WSU has provided service to the State of Washington through its Extension programs, which "[engage] people, organizations, and communities to advance their economic well-being by connecting them to the knowledge base of the University and by fostering inquiry, learning, and the application of research."[63] From its origins as a resource for agricultural and home economics education, WSU Extension has grown into a network of programs encompassing community development, sustainable agriculture, and research on alternative forms of energy.[64] While Extension remains the primary sponsor of engagement programs at Washington State, the university's public engagement agenda is also served through programs provided through the College of Veterinary Medicine, the College of Education, and the Division of Student Affairs, Equity, and Diversity.[65]

The Washington State University Libraries include six libraries on the Pullman campus, as well as libraries on each of the regional campuses.[66] Library support for engagement initiatives is provided both through Pullman campus libraries associated with academic programs that sponsor engagement activities, e.g., the Education Library, and through the Library Instruction Department, which has developed an active program of liaison and instructional services for campus programs affiliated with the Division of Student Affairs, Equity, and Diversity, and others.[67] While the WSU Libraries have a history of successful involvement in a variety of public engagement programs, one initiative is notable for the way in which it demonstrates the potential for library leadership in this area: the Central Washington Resources and Education for Achieving Community Health (REACH) Program.

The Central Washington REACH Program was designed "to improve access to health information for health care providers in central and eastern Washington, especially those who serve the migrant and seasonal worker community." The need to improve access to high-quality health information, both for health care professionals and for community members, provides not only an opportunity for the academic library to develop instructional service programs, but also to develop partnerships with community health organizations and other social service providers. In this case, the WSU Libraries collaborated with partners such as Washington State WorkSource, Wenatchee Valley College, Columbia Valley Community Health, and Yakima Valley Memorial Hospital, to develop instructional materials, training programs, and Web-based resources aimed at enhancing access to health information for members of an underserved community. Funded by a grant from the National Network of Libraries of Medicine (Pacific Northwest Region), the Central Washington REACH Program provided 19 training sessions to members of the target communities during 2003–04, and sponsored a poster session at the annual Western Migrant Stream Forum, a professional conference that offers workshops and other programs "designed to meet the needs of clinicians, administrators, educators, advocates, researchers, and students dedicated to serving migrant and seasonal farmworkers."[68] While not sustained past the conclusion of its grant funding, the Central Washington REACH Program demonstrated how the academic library can partner with a variety of community-based organizations to promote a public engagement initiative founded on professional expertise held in the library—the ability to identify, access, evaluate, and manage health information—and how the library can contribute based on that expertise to the public engagement agenda on campus.

University of Kansas—Territorial Kansas Online
The University of Kansas (KU) is a public research university serving over 30,000 students on its campuses in Lawrence, Overland Park ("Edwards"), and Kansas City (KU Medical Center).[69] Established in 1866, KU is not the land-grant institution for the State of Kansas, but recognizes "Service to Kansans" as a core component of its institutional mission, and identifies a number of teaching and research programs essential to meeting its commitment to public engagement.[70] Among these programs are K–12 and lifelong learning opportunities provided through the Lied Center for the Performing Arts, public programs offered through the Hall Center for the Humanities, health and wellness programs for community members provided through the KU Medical Center, and research activities coordinated through

the Kansas Geological Society and the KU Natural History Museum and Biodiversity Research Center.[71] One of the programs contributing regularly to "service to Kansans," at the university, however, is one that does not appear as part of the campus overview of its engagement activities—the University Libraries.

The KU Libraries include six libraries on the Lawrence Campus, as well as a branch library on the Edwards Campus. "Community Outreach" is identified, alongside more familiar programs in information literacy instruction and scholarly communications education, as a core component of the Libraries' instructional services program.[72] Bringing the concepts of "lifelong learning" and "community engagement" together under the programmatic rubric of "community outreach," the KU Libraries identify instructional service commitments to programs aimed at K–12 students and teachers, adult learners, and students associated with a number of programs sponsored by academic colleges, including the College of Liberal Arts and Sciences and the School of Engineering.[73] While the KU Libraries are notable for the degree to which outreach and engagement are recognized as essential to the instructional services program, one of the Libraries' most significant engagement initiatives can be found outside the instruction unit: Territorial Kansas Online.

Territorial Kansas Online (TKO) is a digital repository of primary source materials related to the turbulent period leading up to Kansas Statehood in 1861. Funded in 1999 through a grant from the Institute of Museum and Library Services (IMLS), and with work continuing through 2004, TKO represents a collaboration between the Kansas State Historical Society and the KU Libraries to provide access to "government documents, diaries, letters, photographs, maps, newspapers, rare secondary sources, and historical artifacts" held in the two collections.[74] While providing enhanced access to materials of public interest in collaboration with another state-sponsored cultural heritage organization might be notable, in itself, the significance of this project for demonstrating library contributions to public engagement programs is most apparent in its attention to how the materials will be used, especially in the K–12 environment. The need to assist K–12 educators in designing inquiry-based learning activities attuned to state and federal guidelines provides an opportunity not only for instructional service initiatives in libraries, but also for initiatives designed to foster increased use of primary source materials and other special collections. In this case, the staff of the KU Libraries'

Kansas Collection collaborated not only with the collection curators in the Kansas State Historical Society, but also with the staff in the Society's Education and Outreach Division, which sponsors a variety of programs and resources for K–12 teachers, students, and community members.[75] In collaboration with these museum educators, KU librarians contributed to the development of lesson plans that demonstrate how primary source materials can be used to support student learning consistent with the Kansas Curricular Standards for Kansas and United States History.[76]

In collaboration with TKO partners, KU librarians provided instructional sessions across the state in 2003-2004 to promote use of the site, including programs at the Shawnee Mission (KS) School District, Kansas History Center, Kansas Territorial Chautauqua, and a number of course-integrated instruction sessions on campus.[77] Heavily-used throughout the project period with over 40,000 "hits" on the Web site, Territorial Kansas Online was recognized by the American Association for State and Local History with an "Award of Merit" in 2004.[78] While no new material has been added to its Web site since the conclusion of the grant-funded program, the TKO project demonstrates how digitization projects—dependent on library collections and the expertise of library staff in the application of digitization standards, metadata, and digital preservation strategies— can complement broader K–12 engagement initiatives on campus, and provides another example of how the university can contribute to public education.

University of Illinois at Urbana-Champaign—American Music Month

The University of Illinois at Urbana-Champaign is a public research university serving over 40,000 students on the Urbana campus, and through a variety of distance learning programs.[79] Established in 1867 as the state's land-grant institution, Illinois "has a long record of commitment to public engagement and to the discovery and application of knowledge to improve and serve the greater society in which we live."[80] In addition to its Extension program, which encompasses programs in agricultural education, economic development, early childhood education, and health and wellness, Illinois supports an array of engagement activities, including those housed in units such as the School of Labor and Employment Relations, the College of Fine and Applied Arts, and the Graduate School of Library and

Information Science.[81] With its commitment to public engagement woven throughout campus teaching and research programs, Illinois provides innumerable opportunities for the provision of service to the community, including in the area of "cultural engagement," which is recognized by the campus as including not only programs sponsored by fine arts venues such as the Krannert Art Museum, performing arts venues such as the Krannert Center for the Performing Arts, and cultural heritage organizations such as the Spurlock Museum, but also those sponsored by the University Library.[82]

The University of Illinois at Urbana-Champaign Library is one of the largest public research libraries in the world with more than 30 departmental libraries housed in buildings across the Urbana campus.[83] Built around a traditional model of subject specialists serving faculty and students associated with one or more of its departmental libraries, the University of Illinois at Urbana-Champaign Library has pursued public engagement activities as an adjunct to traditional public services such as reference and instruction, and in a highly decentralized fashion. The Education and Social Science Library, for example, provided resources for student teachers in local schools through its "Take Us to School" program, while the Applied Health Sciences Library spearheaded the development of a Web site designed to provide enhanced access to health information both to health care providers and to other health information consumers.[84] The Rare Book and Manuscript Library provided public programs highlighting special collections and rare materials available in the library collection, and sponsored a club for book collectors on campus and in the community.[85] Recently, the campus attention to "cultural engagement" has provided an opportunity to bring a number of library-supported activities together under the umbrella of the "Preservation Working Group," a group that includes representatives of the University Library, the Krannert Art Museum, the Krannert Center for the Performing Arts, and WILL-AM (a National Public Radio affiliate).[86] The Preservation Working Group has sponsored a number of public engagement programs over the past few years, including "Home Movie Day" and the "Preservation Emporium."[87] While each of these programs is worthy of note, the one that has had the greatest sustained success has been a campus-wide effort coordinated through the library's Sousa Archive and Center for American Music (SACAM): American Music Month.

American Music Month is an annual celebration of America's diverse musical and cultural heritage that has taken place at venues throughout the Champaign-Urbana community each November since 2004. With a unique theme each year—"Stars, Stripes, and Sousa" (2004), "Lifescapes of America's Music" (2005), "An Illinois Chautauqua" (2006), "Music Without Borders" (2007), and "Lincoln and his Music" (2008)—American Music Month activities have included lectures, exhibitions and public programs at fine and performing arts venues on campus, as well as at SACAM and other library units, lecture demonstrations at local public libraries, concerts at campus and community venues, and educational programs for K–12 music students.[88] American Music Month programs have also been coordinated with other innovative library programs, including the Fall 2007 "Gaming Night" at the Undergraduate Library.[89] Supported through grants from the Illinois Humanities Council, the Lincoln Bicentennial Committee, and the Office of the Chancellor of the University of Illinois at Urbana-Champaign, and sustained through ongoing partnerships with campus and community groups such as the Krannert Center for the Performing Arts, the University of Illinois Alumni Association, the Community Center for the Arts, and the Champaign Park District, American Music Month has demonstrated the integrative role that the library can play in campus public engagement programs.[90]

A growing and ongoing program, American Music Month has fostered partnerships not only between campus and the local community, but between the local community and national cultural heritage organizations, including the Library of Congress, the U.S. Marine Band Library and Museum, and the Smithsonian Institution (which named the University of Illinois at Urbana-Champaign as an "affiliate organization" in 2005).[91] American Music Month is also notable for the recognition its has garnered for its sponsoring partners, including a 2008 "ACE Award" presented to SACAM Director Scott Schwartz (in his role as coordinator of American Music Month programs) by the Champaign County Arts, Culture, and Entertainment Council, and Schwartz's recognition as a 2008 recipient of the "Campus Award for Excellence in Public Engagement."[92] American Music Month is only one example that demonstrates how the library can contribute to "cultural engagement" initiatives on campus and how, by complementing efforts made by programs in the fine and applied arts, and by other cultural heritage organizations, the academic library can embrace opportunities to benefit from advocacy through engagement.

Each of these case studies demonstrates different ways in which the academic library may contribute to public engagement programs on campus, and each demonstrates different ways in which the resources and expertise housed in the library may complement those housed elsewhere on campus. As noted above, these case studies are meant to be initial and exploratory; like the literature review, they present pieces of a very large puzzle. The complexity of this puzzle is evident in the Illinois example where multiple engagement initiatives across campus have come together to be recognized as an important part of the broader campus commitment to "cultural engagement," and where a number of independent public engagement activities housed in different library units are becoming increasingly coordinated through the efforts of a newly-established Public Engagement Working Group (Appendix 1). While this introduction to public engagement programs in academic libraries cannot hope to provide a true picture of the breadth and depth of engagement activities, there are lessons that may be learned to help us to better recognize both the opportunities for advocacy these activities may represent for our libraries, and how to help foster the development of public engagement programs from what may now only be a disparate set of individual activities.

Fostering Success in Public Engagement Programs

While a tradition of public service can be found throughout the history of American higher education, the contemporary interest in public engagement may be traced back to *Scholarship Reconsidered* (1990), the landmark work in which Ernest Boyer articulated an understanding of scholarly activity designed to encompass not only the traditional "scholarship of discovery," but also scholarly approaches to teaching and service.[93] Boyer's definition of the "scholarship of application" would lead to over a decade of inquiry into the question of how one might define scholarly approaches to working with members of the community, as well as how one might recognize and reward scholarly approaches to service—approaches that would be referred to throughout the 1990s as "professional service," "outreach," and, finally, as "public engagement."[94] Providing an overview of the development of what we now refer to as the "scholarship of engagement" is beyond the scope of the current essay, but our understanding of the challenges and opportunities for public engagement in academic libraries may be informed by what studies have shown about how to foster a commitment to scholarly approaches to public engagement across the campus.

Perhaps the greatest challenge to fostering success in public engagement programs can be found in the professional reward structure, both on campus and in the library. As Ward wrote: "Faculty are unlikely to engage in meaningful service if they are uncertain as to where it fits in larger schemes of work and how likely it is to be rewarded."[95] Faculty asked to identify what would motivate them to increase their commitment to public engagement programs regular identify the established system of professional recognition and reward, especially as these are related to decisions about appointment, promotion, and tenure, as a critical component in their decision-making.[96] In February 2009, the University of Illinois at Urbana-Champaign implemented a new set of tenure and promotion guidelines that recognize the value of public engagement as a dimension of faculty work.[97] Illinois joins a number of universities that have modified promotion and tenure guidelines over the past decade to allow for recognition of service activities, and to allow for the rigorous review of scholarly engagement activities, but this remains an ongoing challenge for faculty members and academic librarians interested in pursuing public engagement programs—will these efforts be recognized in a fashion equivalent to efforts resulting in more traditional forms of scholarly output?[98] To address this challenge, academic libraries that provide for tenure-system appointments, or other "continuing appointments," should investigate the degree to which public engagement is recognized as part of the campus promotion and tenure guidelines, and should make an organizational commitment to supporting librarians taking part in public engagement programs that may likewise be recognized as a valuable dimension of the scholarly and professional work.

A second challenge to fostering public engagement programs lies in the sometimes vague (and often shifting) definition of what we mean by public engagement and the scholarship of engagement. Ernest Lynton, Barbara Holland, Kelly Ward, and others have noted that "service" has been defined in many ways in institutions of higher education over the years, and that this makes it all the more difficult (and all the more critical) to define more precisely the sort of work that is representative of true public engagement.[99] As David J. Weerts and Lorilee R. Sandmann wrote, "the concept of engagement is still emerging and is not uniformly understood"; and, as Ward concluded: "Because service is vaguely understood and defined, it is often viewed as less meaningful and important than the more easily defined (and rewarded) roles of teaching and research.[100] To address this challenge, academic librarians must join campus colleagues in identifying the core characteristics of their public engagement programs, and should distinguish these programs from the more familiar approaches to library service found in outreach programs and campus engagement programs. All academic libraries provide public service, and many provide public access, but how many support public engagement? This is an important question for future research.

Third, fostering public engagement programs lies in planning for their sustainability—both in terms of financial resources and in terms of human resources. Burhanna and Jensen noted this as a key challenge to any academic library considering making a commitment to engagement with K–12 schools, and Holland identified both the time required to cultivate partnerships, and the lack of resources to sustain new activities as key obstacles to faculty involvement in public engagement.[101] Certainly, there is ample evidence from the case studies presented in this essay that even successful programs have difficulty finding the resources to continue following the conclusion of grant projects. To address this challenge, the academic library must articulate a strategic commitment to public engagement as a core feature of its mission, identify library services that have the greatest potential for impact on complementary public engagement programs (or commitments) on campus, and create the funding structures and personnel framework that will allow public engagement to thrive as a feature of academic librarianship similar to information literacy instruction and scholarly communications. Many academic libraries have created positions for instructional leaders and for innovators in digital library and scholarly communications programs, but how many articulate public engagement as a key organizational capacity, and how many have functional leadership for public engagement similar to that found in many public libraries, museums, and other cultural heritage institutions? This, too, is a question for future research.

But the final challenge is the one that complements all the others—leadership. If there is one finding common to every study of public engagement and the scholarship of engagement, it is that leadership at the campus, college, and departmental level is essential to supporting faculty work in this area. Academic leaders establish the sense of mission at every level that includes public engagement as a core commitment for the institution and the academic units. Academic leaders can provide support for faculty undertaking public engagement programs through the provision of supporting infrastructure and professional development opportunities. Finally, academic leaders may influence the system of professional incentives and rewards that may encourage a faculty member to dedicate his or her time to public engagement and to the development of scholarly approaches to engagement activities.[102] To address this challenge, library leaders must articulate the library commitment not just to providing public access, but to pursuing public engagement. Library leaders must support librarians dedicated to collaborating with campus public engagement programs and to focusing their work on the information needs of many "non-traditional" users who are not part of traditional academic programs.

There are many challenges to fostering public engagement programs in academic libraries, but perhaps the greatest is the need to help librarians articulate both their connections to campus public engagement programs and the professional expertise that they can bring to issues of concern to the public beyond the campus. In an Information Age, an academic library should be a valuable community resource—not for the services that it cannot share (e.g., access to licensed electronic content), but for the expertise that it can. Expertise is what distinguishes public service from public engagement, and commitment to sharing that expertise through public engagement programs may provide new opportunities for advocacy.

Conclusion

Why are academic libraries so often forgotten during campus discussions of public engagement? We are forgotten because we have historically associated service to "community users" with the simple question of access, and because we have looked at programs such as instruction for K–12 students as an addition to our core programs (or, at best, as an adjunct to the core programs aimed at faculty and students in teacher education programs), rather than as essential programs in their own right. Over the past decade, academic librarians have made powerful arguments regarding the contributions they can make to instructional programs, the support they can provide to faculty facing a new landscape in scholarly communication, and the expertise they can lend to projects related to the creation, description, dissemination, and preservation of digital content, but the challenge of public engagement remains before us—how can we weave the disparate stories of the many public programs we routinely provide into a narrative of public engagement that will be recognized by the campus as contributing to this strategic concern of the institution, and how can we support librarians in engaging in scholarly approaches to this work that will allow them to be recognized and rewarded for the time and commitment such efforts require?

The challenges are many, but the potential return is great. There are few traditions that run deeper in the history of American higher education than "service." As Adrianna J. Kezar, Tony C. Chambers, and John C. Burkhardt noted in their collection of essays on the contemporary service movement: "The idea that higher education exists to serve the public good has been at the heart of the enterprise since its inception in the United States almost five hundred years ago."[103] Over the past decade, academic leaders have come to appreciate service not as an important historical artifact, but as "[the hallmark] of the university of the future."[104] Pennsylvania State University President Graham B. Spanier led a national discussion of how to foster the development of the "engaged university" by arguing that "successful universities will be those that are intimately connected to their communities, and responsive to society's needs."[105] Surely, to remain relevant to this emergent mission of the institution of higher education, and to remain successful in the 21st century, academic libraries must be likewise connected, responsive, and engaged.

To advocate for the academic library—whether on campus, in the community, or with ones friends and supporters—one must present the full range of the library's riches, and the full scope of what it contributes to the mission of the college or university of which it is a part. Campuses have recognized that public engagement is critical to their success because it is through engagement that institutions of higher education build communities of advocates for their cause beyond the traditional communities of teachers, students, researchers, and scholars. The library, too, may build broader communities of advocates, both on campus, among its alumni, and within its community by making a strategic and sustainable commitment to public engagement as a core feature of its mission.

Notes

1. Macomb County, "About Macomb County"
2. Macomb County Library, "About the Library"
3. Macomb *Macomb County Report*,
4. Selweski, "Library May Reduce Hours"
5. DeRosa, et al., *From Awareness to Funding*, vii
6. Blumenstein and Oder, "Bridgeport Public Library Faces Drastic Cuts,"
7. American Library Association, "Surge in Library Usage" Jackson, "The Library—A Recession Sanctuary,"; Marbut, "Markets Down, Libraries Up"; Enriquez, "Libraries' Many Benefits"
8. DeRosa, at al., 2008, *From Awareness to Funding*,viii; American Library Association, "Visibility @ Your Library"
9. Selweski, "Wayne State to 'Save' Library,"
10. Breivik, Budd, and Woods, "We're Married!" ; Fugate, "Only Connect"; Mount Vernon Public Library, "One-of-a-Kind Library,"
11. McNicol, "Introduction,"; Marie, "One Plus One Equals Three"
12. Bundy, "Joint-Use Libraries"
13. School of Architecture, University of Illinois at Urbana-Champaign, "Public Engagement"
14. Ward, *Faculty Service Roles*, 1
15. Regents of the University of Minnesota, "About the Council on Public Engagement (COPE)"
16. Byrne, "Outreach, Engagement, and the Changing Culture"; Roper and Hirth, "A History of Change in the Third Mission."
17. University of Illinois at Urbana-Champaign, "Public Engagement"
18. Wayne State University, "Community Engagement at Wayne: Mission and Philosophy," Wayne State University, "Community Engagement at Wayne: List of Community Partners,"
19. Lee and Jenda, *The Role of ARL Libraries in Extension/Outreach*; Schneider, "Outreach: Why, How, and Who?".
20. Bok, *Beyond the Ivory Tower*, 238.
21. Roper and Hirth, "A History of Change"
22. Kezar, Chambers, and Burkhardt, *Higher Education for the Public Good*
23. Carnegie Foundation for the Advancement of Teaching, "Community Engagement Elective Classification,"; Wayne State University, "WSU to Apply to Carnegie for Community Engagement Classification,"
24. University Communications Newsdesk, "Hurray for Maryland Day,"; University Libraries, "Maryland Day 2008,"
25. University of California—Irvine Libraries, "About the UC Irvine Libraries' SPIRIT Program," Munoff, "Message from the University Librarian"
26. Youngman, "ACME and the First MILE,"; Youngman, "ACME is Back!,"
27. Westney, "Conspicuous by their Absence"; Herther, "Service Learning and Engagement in the Academic Library"
28. Herther, "Service Learning and Engagement in the Academic Library"; Burhanna, "Instructional Outreach to High Schools"; Love, "Building Bridges"; Walter, "Moving Beyond Collections,"
29. Tancheva, Cook, and Raskin, "Serving the Public"; Reilly and de Verges, "A Dynamic Model of Museum and Academic Library Cooperation"; Allen and Bishoff, "Academic Library/Museum Collaboration"

30. Young, *The ALA Glossary*, 160; Reitz, *Online Dictionary of Library and Information Science*, O

31. Johnson, McCord, and Walter, "Instructional Outreach Across the Curriculum"

32. Rudin, "No Fixed Address"

33. Lynton, *Making the Case for Professional Service* 19.

34. Schneider, "Outreach: Why, How, and Who?"

35. Boff, Singer, and Stearns, "Reaching Out to the Underserved"

36. Rudin, "No Fixed Address."

37. Campus Compact, "Service-Learning Resources."

38. Campus Compact, *2007 Service Statistics*

39. Riddle, "Where's the Library in Service Learning?"

40. Westney, "Conspicuous by their Absence"; Herther, "Service Learning and Engagement in the Academic Library".

41. Becker, "Service Learning in the Curriculum"; Elmborg, et al., "Service Learning in the Library"; Roy, "Diversity in the Classroom"; Peterson, "Using a Homeless Shelter"; Ball and Schilling, "Service Learning, Technology, and LIS Education,"; Roy, Jensen, and Meyers, *Service Learning*

42. Ball, "Practicums and Service Learning."

43. Community Informatics Initiative, "About Us,"

44. Elmborg, "Information Literacy and Writing"; Elmborg and Hook, *Centers for Learning*; Hardesty, *The Role of the Library in the First College Year* .

45. U.S. Department of Agriculture, Cooperative State Research, "About Us: State and National Partners,"

46. U.S. Department of Agriculture, Cooperative State Research, "About Us: Extension.

47. University of Illinois at Urbana-Champaign, "University of Illinois Extension."

48. University of Illinois at Urbana-Champaign, "University of Illinois Extension: What We Do."

49. As an example, University of Illinois Extension programs are delivered by staff housed in 77 unit offices, 12 education centers, and 7 research centers located across the State of Illinois. See: University of Illinois at Urbana-Champaign, "University of Illinois Extension: What We Do" and University of Illinois at Urbana-Champaign, "University of Illinois Extension: Research Centers."

50. Rozum and Brewer, "Identifying, Developing, and Marketing Library Services."Although the Web resource described in the Rozum and Brewer no longer appears to be active, a similar site is available for Wisconsin extension agents at <http://www.uwex.edu/ces/librarymediaservices/> (accessed September 13, 2008).

51. Tancheva, Cook, and Raskin, "Serving the Public." The Web resource described in this essay is now available at <http://www.mannlib.cornell.edu/services/cce/index.cfm> (accessed September 13, 2008).

52. AASL/ACRL Task Force on the Educational Role of Libraries, "Blueprint for Collaboration."

53. O'Hanlon, "Good Intentions Are Not Enough"; Burhanna, "Instructional Outreach to High Schools."

54. Walter, "Professional Education."

55. Jesudason, "Academic Libraries and Outreach Services."

56. For another example of successful library involvement with a campus-wide engagement initiative focused on the recruitment of students from historically

underrepresented groups, see: University of California—Irvine Libraries, 2008, "SPIRIT Program."

57. Nichols, "Building Bridges"; Martorana, et al., "Bridging the Gap"; Shinew and Walter, *Information Literacy Instruction for Educators*

58. Burhanna and Jensen, "Collaborations for Success"; Burhanna, "Instructional Outreach to High Schools."

59. Ward, *Faculty Service Roles and the Scholarship of Engagement*, iv.

60. See, for example: Lelle, Fear, and Sandmann, "A Legacy Rediscovered"; Holland, "Institutional Differences".

61. Washington State University, "Facts About WSU."

62. Washington State University, "WSU Statewide."

63. Washington State University, "WSU Extension—History,"; Washington State University, "The Economic Benefits."

64. Washington State University, "Extension—Community Development" Washington State University, "Extension—Sustainable Development,"; Washington State University, "Extension—Energy."

65. Washington State University, "College of Veterinary Medicine—Veterinary Medicine Extension"; Washington State University, "College of Education—School and Community Collaboration Center"; Washington State University, "WSU Center for Civic Engagement".

66. Washington State University Libraries, "Libraries at WSU".

67. Washington State University Libraries, "WSU Library Instruction—Partner Programs".

68. McCord, "Final Report: Central Washington REACH"; Northwest Regional Primary Care Association, "18th Annual Western Migrant Stream Forum".

69. University of Kansas, "Facts".

70. University of Kansas, "Mission".

71. University of Kansas, "Outreach".

72. University of Kansas Libraries, "Instructional Services".

73. University of Kansas Libraries, "Instructional Services—Lifelong Learning and Community Engagement".

74. Territorial Kansas Online, "About this Project—Project Description".

75. Kansas State Historical Society, "Teachers"; Kansas State Historical Society, "Kids"; Kansas State Historical Society, "Genealogists".

76. Territorial Kansas Online, "Lesson Plans".

77. Williams, personal communication.

78. Williams, personal communication; Territorial Kansas Online, "About This Project".

79. University of Illinois at Urbana-Champaign, "Facts 2008".

80. University of Illinois at Urbana-Champaign, "Public Engagement".

81. University of Illinois, "University of Illinois Extension,"; University of Illinois at Urbana-Champaign, School of Labor and Employment Relations, "Labor Education Programs at LER"; University of Illinois at Urbana-Champaign, College of Fine and Applied Arts, "East St. Louis Action Research Project"; University of Illinois at Urbana-Champaign, Graduate School of Library and Information Science, "Community Informatics Initiative".

82. University of Illinois at Urbana-Champaign, "Public Engagement—Arts and Culture,".

83. University of Illinois at Urbana-Champaign Library, "Library Locations,".

84. University of Illinois at Urbana-Champaign Library, Education and Social Science Library, "Take Us to School"; University of Illinois at Urbana-Champaign Library, "Health Information Portal".

85. University of Illinois at Urbana-Champaign Library, Rare Book and Manuscript Library, "The No, 44 Society,".

86. University of Illinois at Urbana-Champaign, "Preservation Working Group,".

87. Center for Home Movies, "Home Movie Day 2008"; University of Illinois at Urbana-Champaign, "Events—Preservation Working Group".

88. Schwartz, personal communication, June 8, 2008; Schwartz, personal communication, November 3, 2008.

89. University of Illinois at Urbana-Champaign Library, "Gaming Events,".

90. Schwartz, personal communication, January 6, 2009; University of Illinois at Urbana-Champaign Library, Sousa Archive and Center for American Music, "Lincoln and His Music."

91. Schwartz, personal communication, January 6, 2009; Lynn, "U. of I. Granted Affiliate Status".

92. 40 North | 88 West, "4th Annual ACE Awards,"; University of Illinois at Urbana-Champaign, "Public Engagement—Campus Awards."

93. Boyer, *Scholarship Reconsidered.*

94. See, for example: Lynton, *Making the Case for Professional Service*; Glassick, et al., *Scholarship Assessed*; Driscoll and Lynton, *Making Outreach Visible*; Braxton, Luckey, and Helland, *Institutionalizing a Broader View of Scholarship*; and Ward, *Faculty Service and the Scholarship of Engagement.*

95. Ward, *Faculty Service and the Scholarship of Engagement*, iii. See also: Ward, "Rethinking Faculty Roles and Rewards for the Public Good."

96. Holland, "Factors and Strategies that Influence Faculty Involvement in Public Service"; Weerts and Sandmann, "Building a Two-Way Street."

97. University of Illinois at Urbana-Champaign, *Communication 9: Promotion and Tenure.*

98. See, for example: Michigan State University, *Points of Distinction.*

99. Lynton, *Making the Case for Professional Service*; Holland, "Factors and Strategies that Influence Faculty Involvement in Public Services"; Ward, *Faculty Service Roles and the Scholarship of Engagement.*

100. Weerts and Sandmann, "Building a Two-Way Street," 87; Ward, *Faculty Service Roles and the Scholarship of Engagement*, 2.

101. Burhanna and Jensen, "Collaborations for Success"; Holland, "Factors and Strategies that Influence Faculty Involvement in Public Service."

102. See, for example, Weerts and Sandmann, "Building a Two-Way Street," 89-93.

103. Kezar, Chambers, and Burkhardt, *Higher Education for the Public Good*, xiii.

104. Ray, "Outreach, Engagement Will Keep Academic Relevant to Twenty-First Century Societies," 21.

105. Spanier, "The Engaged University: Our Partnership with Society".

Works Cited

40 North | 88 West. *4th Annual ACE Awards.* http://www.40north.org/ace_awards/home.html (accessed January 1, 2009).

AASL/ACRL Task Force on the Educational Role of Libraries. "Blueprint for Collaboration." http://www.ala.org/ala/acrl/acrlpubs/whitepapers/acrlaaslblueprint.cfm

(accessed September 14, 2008).

"About Us: Extension." *U.S. Department of Agriculture, Cooperative State Research, Education, and Extension Service.* 2008. http://www.csrees.usda.gov/qlinks/extension.html (accessed September 13, 2008).

"About Us: State and National Partners." *U.S. Department of Agriculture, Cooperative State Research, Education, and Extension Service.* 2007. http://www.csrees.usda.gov/qlinks/partners/state_partners.html (accessed September 13, 2008).

Allen, Nancy, and Liz Bishoff. "Academic Library/Museum Collaboration: I'm OK, You're OK." Edited by Hugh A Thompson. *Crossing the Divide: Proceedings of the ACRL 10th National Conference, March 15–18, 2001.* Chicago, IL: Association of College and Research Libraries, 2001. 59–61.

American Library Association. *Surge in Library Usage Covered by National, Regional, and Local Media.* December 30, 2008. http://www.ala.org/als/newspresscenter/news/pressrelease2009/january2009/visibilitysurge.cfm (accessed January 8, 2009).

———. *Visibility @ Your Library: News and Information for Librarians and Library Supporters from the ALA Public Information Office and the Campaign for America's Libraries.* http://www.pio.ala.org/visibility/ (accessed January 10, 2009).

Ball, Mary Alice. "Practicums and Service Learning in LIS Education." *Journal of Education for Library and Information Science* 49, no. 1 (2008): 70–82.

Ball, Mary Alice, and Katherine Schilling. "Service Learning, Technology, and LIS Education." *Journal of Education for Library and Information Science* 47, no. 4 (2006): 277–290.

Becker, Nancy J. "Service Learning in the Curriculum: Preparing LIS Students for the Next Millennium." *Journal of Education for Library and Information Science* 41, no. 4 (2000): 285–293.

blumestein, Lynn, and Norman Oder. *Bridgeport Public Library Faces Drastic Cuts.* April 18, 2008. http://www.libraryjourna.com/article/CA6552950.html (accessed September 7, 2008).

Boff, Colleen, Carol Singer, and Beverly Stearns. "Reaching Out to the Underserved: More Than Thirty Years of Outreach Job Ads." *Journal of Academic Librarianship* 32, no. 2 (2006): 137–147.

Bok, Derek. *Beyond the Ivory Tower: Social Responsibilities of the Modern University.* Cambridge, MA: Harvard University Press, 1982.

Boyer, Ernest L. *Scholarship Reconsidered: Priorities of the Professoriate.* Princeton, N.J.: Carnegie Foundation for the Advancement of Teaching, 1990.

Braxton, John M., William Luckey, and Patricia Helland. *Institutionalizing a Broader View of Scholarship through Boyer's Four Domains.* [ASHE-ERIC Higher Education Report, vol. 29, no 2], San Francisco, CA: Jossey-Bass, 2002.

Breivik, Patricia Senn, Luann Budd, and Richard F. Woods. "We're Married!: The Rewards and Challenges of Joint Libraries." *Journal of Academic Librarianship* 31, no. 5 (2005): 401–408.

Bundy, Alan. "Joint-Use Libraries: the Ultimate Form of Cooperation." In *Planning the Modern Public Library Building,* by Gerard B. McCabe and James R. Kennedy, 129–148. Westport, CT: Libraries Unlimited, 2003.

Burhanna, Kenneth J. "Instructional Outreach to High Schools: Should You Be Doing It?" *Communication in Information Literacy* 1, no. 2 (2007).

Burhanna, Kenneth, and Mary Lee Jensen. "Collaborations for Success: High School to College Transitions." *Reference Services Review* 34, no. 4 (2006): 509–519.

Byrne, John V. "Outreach, Engagement, and the Changing Culture of the University." *Journal of Public Service and Outreach* 3, no. 2 (1998).

Campus Compact. *2007 Service Statistics: Highlights and Trends of Campus Compact's Annual Membership Survey.* 2008. http://www.compact.org/about/statistics/2007/service_statistics.pdf (accessed September 12, 2008).

———. *Service—Learning Resources.* 2007. http://www.compact.org/resources/service-learning_resources/ (accessed September 12, 2008).

Carnegie Foundation for the Advancement of Teaching. *2008 Community Engagement Classification.* 2008. http://www.carnegiefoundation.org/files/assets/2008_community_engagement.pdf (accessed January 4, 2009).

———. *Community Engagement Elective Classification.* 2008. http://www.carnegiefoundation.org/classifications/index.asp?key=1213 (accessed September 8, 2008).

Center for Home Movies. *Home Movie Day 2008—Champaign-Urbana, Illinois.* http://www.homemovieday.com/urbana.html (accessed January 8, 2009).

Community Informatics Initiative, Graduate School of Library and Information Science. *About Us.* 2008. http://www.cii.uiuc.edu/about (accessed September 27, 2008).

DeRosa, Cathy, and et. al. "From Awareness to Funding: a Study of Library Support in America." *OCLC.* 2008. http://www.oclc.org/us/en/reports/funding/fullreport.pdf (accessed September 7, 2008).

Driscoll, Amy, and Ernest A. Lynton. *Making Outreach Visible: A Guide to Documenting Professional Service and Outreach.* Washington, D.C.: American Association for Higher Education, 1999.

Elmborg, James K. "Information Literacy and Writing Across the Curriculum: Sharing the Vision." *Reference Services Review* 31, no. 1 (2003): 68–80.

Elmborg, James K., and others. "Service Learning in the Library and Information Science Curriculum: the Perspectives and Experiences of One Multimedia/User Education Class." *Research Strategies* 18, no. 4 (2001): 265–281.

Elmborg, James K., Sheril Hook, and eds. *Centers for Learning: Writing Centers and Libraries in Collaboration.* Chicago, IL: Association of College and Research Libraries, 2005.

Enriquez, Darryl. "Libraries' Many Benefits Rediscovered in Hard Economic Times." *Milwaukee Journal-Sentinel.* January 21, 2009. http://www.jsonline.com/news/38082709.html (accessed January 25, 2009).

Fugate, Cynthia. "Only Connect: the Collocation of the University of Washington, Bothell and Cascadia Community College." *College & Research Libraries News* 62, no. 1 (2001): 9–10.

Glassick, Charles E., and others. *Scholarship Assessed: Evaluation of the Professoriate.* San Francisco, CA: Jossey-Bass, 1997.

Hardesty, Larry L., and ed. *The Role of the Library in the First College Year.* Columbia, SC: National Resource Center for the First-Year Experience and Students in Transition, 2007.

Herther, Nancy K. "Service Learning and Engagement in the Academic Library: Operating out of the Box." *College & Research Libraries News* 69, no. 7 (July/August 2088).

Holland, Barbara A. "Factors and Strategies that Influence Faculty Involvement in Public Service." *Journal of Public Service and Outreach* 4, no. 1 (1999): 37–44.

Holland, Barbara A. "Institutional Differences in Pursuing the Public Good." In

Higher Education for the Public Good: Emerging Voices from a National Movement, by Adrianna J. Kezar, Tony C. Chambers and John C. Burkhardt, 235–259. San Francisco, CA: Jossey-Bass, 2005.

Jackson, Derrick Z. "The Library—A Recession Sanctuary." *Boston Globe*. January 3, 2009. http://www.boston.com/bostonglobe/editorial_opinion/oped/articles/2009/01/03/the_library__a_recession_santuary/ (accessed January 8, 2009).

Jesudason, Melba. "Academic Libraries and Outreach Services through Precollege Programs: a Proactive Collaboration." *Reference Services Review* 21, no. 4 (1993): 29–36+.

Johnson, Corey M., Sarah K. McCord, and Scott Walker. "Instructional Outreach Across the Curriculum: Enhancing the Liaison Role at a Research University." *The Reference Librarians*, no. 82 (2003): 19–37.

Kansas State Historical Society. *Classroom Materials*. http://www.kshs.org/teachers/classrooms/index.htm (accessed January 2, 2009).

———. *Genealogists*. http://www.kshs.org/genealogists/index.html (accessed January 1, 2009).

———. *Kids*. http://www.kshs.org/kids/index.htm (accessed January 1, 2009).

———. *Teachers*. http://www.kshs.org/teachers/index.htm (accessed January 1, 2009).

Kezar, Adrianna J., Tony C. Chambers, and John C. Burkhardt, . *Higher Education for the Public Good: Emerging Voices from a National Movement*. San Francisco, CA: Jossey-Bass, 2005.

Lee, Tamara, and Claudine Jenda. *The Role of ARL Libraries in Extension/Outreach*. ARL SPEC Kit No. 233, Washington, D.C.: Association of Research Libraries, 1998.

Lelle, Mark A., Frank A. Fear, and Lorilee R. Sandmann. "A Legacy Rediscovered: Public Service at Private Colleges." *Journal of Public Service and Outreach* 3, no. 2 (1998): 48–53.

Love, Emily. "Building Bridges: Cultivating Partnerships Between Libraries and Minority Student Services." *Education Libraries* 30, no. 1 (2007): 13–19.

Lynn, Andrea. *U. of I. Granted Affiliate Status by Smithsonian Institution*. 2005. http://news.illinois.edu/news/05/0920smithsonian.html (accessed January 6, 2009).

Lynton, Ernest A. *Making the Case for Professional Service*. Washington, DC: American Association for Higher Education, 1995.

———. *Making the Case for Professional Service*. Washington, D.C.: American Association for Higher Education, 1995.

Macomb County Board of Commissioners. *Macomb County Report*. 2007. http://www.macombcountymi.gov/publicAffairs/pdf/annualreport2007.pdf (accessed September 7, 2008).

Macomb County Library. *About the Library—Library Mission*. 2008. http://www.libcoop.net/mcl/mission.htm (accessed September 7, 2008).

Macomb County, Michigan. *About Macomb County*. 2008. http://www.macombcountymi.gov/aboutcounty.htm (accessed September 7, 2008).

Marbut, Max. "Markets Down, Libraries Up." *Financial News & Daily Record*. January 8, 2009. http://www.jaxdailyrecord.com/showstory.php?Story_id=51575 (accessed January 8, 2009).

Marie, Kirsten L. "One Plus One Equals Three: Joint-Use Libraries in Urban Areas—the Ultimate Form of Library Cooperation." *Library Administration and Management* 21, no. 1 (2007): 23–28.

Martorana, Janet, and others. "Bridging the Gap: Information Literacy Workshops for High School Teachers." *Research Strategies*, 2001: 113–120.

McCord, Sarah. "Final Report: Central Washington REACH (Resources and Education for Achieving Community Health)." http://nnlm.gov/pnr/funding/reports/REACHFinalReport.pdf (accessed January 1, 2009).

McNicol, Sarah. "Introduction." *Library Trends* 54, no. 4 (2006): 485–87.

Michigan State University. "Points of Distinction: A Guidebook for Planning and Evaluating Quality Outreach." 1996/2000. http://www.outreach.msu.edu/documents/pod.pdf (accessed January 1, 2009).

Mount Vernon Public Library. *One-of-a-Kind Library*. http://colelibrary.org/oneofa-kind.shtml (accessed September 27, 2008).

Munoff, Gerald J. *Message from the University Librarian: SPIRIT Program Helps Faculty Meet NSF Funding Goals*. 2008. http://www.lib.uci.edu/libraries/update/fall08/index.html (accessed January 4, 2009).

Nichols, Janet. "Building Bridges: High School and University Partnerships for Information Literacy." *NASSP Bulletin*, 1999: 75–81.

Northwest Regional Primary Care Association. *18th Annual Western Migrant Stream Forum*. http://www.nwrpca.org/education-a-training/conferences/21-conferences/128-18th-annual-western-migrant-stream-forum.html (accessed January 1, 2009).

O'Hanlon, Nancy. "Good Intentions Are Not Enough: Toward Cooperative Teaching of Basic Information Seeking Competencies." *Ohio Media Spectrum* 44, no. 1 (1992): 14–19.

Peterson, Lorna. "Using a Homeless Shelter as a Library Education Learning Laboratory: incorporating Service Learning in a Graduate-Level Information Sources and Services in the Social Sciences Course." *Reference & User Services Quarterly* 42, no. 4 (2003): 307–310.

Ray, Edward J. "Outreach, Engagement Will Keep Academic Revelevant to Twenty-First Century Societies." *Journal of Public Service and Outreach* 4, no. 1 (1999): 21.

Regents of the University of Minnesota. "About the Council on Public Engagement (COPE)." *Council on Public Engagement*. 2006. http://www.engagement.umn.edu/cope/about/index.html (accessed September 11, 2008).

Reilly, Karen, and Jolene de Verges. "A Dynamic Model of Museum and Academic Library Cooperation: Cataloging Image Collections." *College & Undergraduate Libraries* 8, no. 1 (2001): 15–24.

Reitz, Joan M. "Online Dictionary of Library and Information Science." http://lu.com/odlis/odlis_o.cfm (accessed September 12, 2008).

Riddle, John S. "Where's the Library in Service Learning?: Models for Engaged Library Instruction." *Journal of Academic Librarianship* 29, no. 2 (2003): 71–81.

Roper, C., and Marilyn A. Hirth. "A History of Change in the Third Mission of Higher Education: the Evolution of One-Way Service to Interactive Engagement." *Journal of Higher Education Outreach and Engagement* 10, no. 3 (2005): 3–21.

Roy, Lorien. "Diversity in the Classroom: Incorporating Service Learning Experiences in the Library and Information Science Curriculum." *Journal of Library Administration* 33, no. 3/4 (2001): 213–228.

Roy, Loriene, Kelly Jenson, and Alex Hershey Meyers. *Service Learning: Linking Library Education and Practice*. Chicago, IL: American Library Association, 2009.

Rozum, Betty, and Kevin Brewer. "Identifying, Developing, and Marketing Library

Services to Cooperative Extension Personnel." *Reference & User Services Quarterly* 37, no. 2 (1997): 161–169.

Rudin, Phyllis. "No Fixed Address: the Evolution of Outreach Library Services on University Campuses." *The Reference Librarian*, no. 101 (2008): 55–75.

Schneider, Tina. "Outreach: Why, How, and Who?: Academic Libraries and their Involvement in the Community." *The Reference Librarian*, no. 82 (2003): 199–213.

School of Architecture, University of Illinois at Urbana-Champaign. *Public Engagement.* 2007. http://www.arch.uiuc.edu/programs/engagement/ (accessed September 14, 2008).

Schwartz, Scott. "Personal communication to the author, January 6, 2009."

———. "Personal communication to the author, June 8, 2008."

———. "Personal communication to the author, November 3, 2008."

Selweski, Chad. *Library May Reduce Hours After County Slashes Budget.* November 23, 2006. http://www.macombdaily.com/stories/112306/loc_library001.shtml (accessed September 7, 2008).

———. *Wayne State to 'Save' Library* . June 4, 2008. http://www.macombdaily.com/stories/060408/loc_local01.shtml (accessed September 7, 2008).

Shinew, Dawn, Scott Walter, and eds. *Information Literacy Instruction for Educators: Professional Knowledge for an Information Age.* Binghamton, NY: Haworth Press, 2003.

Spanier, Graham B. "The Engaged University: Our Partnership with Society." *Office of the President—Graham B. Spanier.* February 22, 2001. http://president.psu.edu/speeches/articles/engaged.html (accessed September 9, 2008).

Tancheva, Kornelia, Michael Cook, and Howard Raskin. "Serving the Public: the Academic Library and Cooperative Extension." *Journal of Extension* 43, no. 3 (2005).

Territorial Kansas Online. *About this Project—Project Description.* http://www.territorialkansasonline.org/cgiwrap/imlskto/index.php?SCREEN=description (accessed January 1, 2009).

———. *About This Project.* http://www.territorialkansasonline.org/cgiwrap/imlskto/index.php?SCREEN=about_this_project (accessed January 1, 2009).

———. *Lesson Plans.* http://www.territorialkansasonline.org/cgiwrap/imlskto/index.php?SCREEN=lesson_plans (accessed January 1, 2009).

University of California-Irvine Libraries. *About the UC Irvine Libraries' SPIRIT Program.* 2009. http://spirit.lib.uci.edu/ (accessed January 4, 2009).

University of California-Irvine Libraries. *SPIRIT Program.* 2008. http://course.lib.uci.edu/ed/spirit/ (accessed September 14, 2008).

University of Illinois at Urbana-Champaign College of Fine and Applied Arts. *East St. Louis Action Request Project.* http://www.eslarp.uiuc.edu/ (accessed January 1, 2009).

University of Illinois at Urbana-Champaign. "Communication 9: Promotion and Tenure." *Office of the Provost.* 2009. http://provost.illinois.edu/communication/09/index.html (accessed March 7, 2009).

———. *Events—Preservation Working Group.* http://will.illinois.edu/pwg/events/ (accessed January 8, 2009).

———. *Facts 2008: Illinois by the Numbers.* http://illinois.edu/about/overview/facts/facts.html (accessed January 1, 2009).

University of Illinois at Urbana-Champaign Library. *Gaming Events.* http://www.library.uiuc.edu/gaming/events.html (accessed January 2, 2009).

————. *Health Information Portal.* http://www.library.uiuc.edu/health/ (accessed January 1, 2009).

————. *Library Locations.* http://www.library.uiuc.edu/services/find.php (accessed January 1, 2009).

University of Illinois at Urbana-Champaign Library, Education and Social Science Library. *Take Us to School: Resources for Student Teachers.* http://www.library.uiuc.edu/edx/taketoschool/index.htm (accessed January 1, 2009).

University of Illinois at Urbana-Champaign Library, Rare Book and Manuscript Library. *The No. 44 Society.* http://www.library.uiuc.edu/rbx/no44.htm (accessed January 1, 2009).

University of Illinois at Urbana-Champaign Library, Sousa Archive and Center for American Music. *Lincoln and His Music: Melodies that Moved the Man and the Nation: Concerts, Lectures, Master Classes, and Exhibitions.* http://www.library.uiuc.edu/sousa/?p=special (accessed January 1, 2009).

University of Illinois at Urbana-Champaign. *Preservation Working Group.* http://will.illinois.edu/pwg (accessed January 1, 2009).

————. *Public engagement—Arts and Culture.* http://engagement.illinois.edu/arts_and_culture.html (accessed January 1, 2009).

————. *Public Engagement—Campus Awards for Excellence in Public engagement.* http://engagement.illinois.edu/award_recipients.html (accessed January 1, 2009).

————. *Public Engagement.* http://engagement.illinois.edu (accessed September 11, 2008).

————. *Public Engagement.* http://illinois.edu/about/overview/facts/facts.htm (accessed Janury 1, 2009).

————. *University of Illinois Extension.* 2008. http://web.extension.uiuc.edu/state/ (accessed September 13, 2008).

————. *University of Illinois Extension: Research Centers.* 2008. http://web.extension.uiuc.edu/state/research.html (accessed September 13, 2008).

————. *University of Illinois Extension: What We Do.* 2008. http://web.extension.uiuc.edu/state/whatwedo.html (accessed September 13, 2008).

University of Illinois at Urbana-Champaign, Graduate School of Library and Information Science. *Community Informatics Initiative.* http://www.cii.uiuc.edu/ (accessed January 1, 2009).

University of Illinois at Urbana-Champaign, School of Labor and Employment Relations. *Labor Education Programs at LER.* http://www.ler.illinois.edu/labor/index.html (accessed January 1, 2009).

University of Illinois. *University of Illinois Extension.* http://web.extension.uiuc.edu/state/ (accessed January 1, 2009).

University of Kansas. *Facts.* http://www.ku.edu/about/facts.shtml (accessed December 31, 2008).

University of Kansas Libraries. *Instructional Services—Lifelong Learning and Community Engagement.* http://www.lib.ku.edu/instruction/community/ (accessed January 1, 2009).

————. *Instructional Services.* http://www.lib.ku.edu/instruction/ (accessed December 31, 2008).

University of Kansas. *Mission.* http://www.ku.edu/about/mission.shtml (accessed December 31, 2008).

————. *Outreach.* http://www.ku.edu/outreach/ (accessed December 31, 2008).

University of Maryland, University Communications Newsdesk. *Hurray for Maryland Day.* 2008. http://www.newsdesk.umd.edu/uniini/release. cfm?ArticleID=1650 (accessed December 31, 2008).

University of Maryland, University Libraries. *Maryland Day 2008.* 2008. http://www. lib.umd.edu/groups/mdday05/mdday_2008.html (accessed December 31, 2008).

Walter, Scott. "Moving Beyond Collections: Academic Library Outreach to Multicultural Student Centers." *Reference Services Review* 33, no. 4 (2005): 438–458.

Walter, Scott. "Professional Education." In *A Guide to the management of Curriculum Materials Centers for the 21st Century: the Promise and the Challenge,* by Jo Ann Carr and ed, 1–24. Chicago, IL: Association of College & Research Libraries, 2001.

Ward, Kelly. *Faculty Service Roles and the Scholarship of Engagement.* San Francisco, CA: Jossey-Bass, 2003.

Ward, Kelly. "Rethinking Faculty Roles and Rewards for the Public Good." In *Higher Education for the Public Good: Emerging Voices from a National Movement,* by Adrianna J. Kezar, Tony C. Chambers and John C. Burkhardt, 217–234. San Francisco, CA: Jossey-Bass, 2005.

Washington State University. *College of Education—School and Community Collaboration Center.* http://education.wsu.edu/collaboration/ (accessed January 1, 2009).

———. *College of Veterinary Medicine—Veterinary Medicine extension.* http://vetextension.wsu.edu (accessed January 1, 2009).

———. *Extension—Community Development.* http://ext.wsu.edu/economicbenefits/community-development.html (accessed January 1, 2009).

———. *Extension—Energy.* http://ext.wsu.edu/economicbenefits/energy.html (accessed January 2009).

———. *Extension—Sustainable Development.* http://ext.wsu.edu/economicbenefits/sustainable-dev.html (accessed January 1, 2009).

———. *Facts about WSU.* http://futurestudents.wsu.edu/why/profile.aspx (accessed January 1, 2009).

Washington State University Libraries. *Libraries at WSU.* http://www.wsulibs.wsu. edu/index2.htm (accessed January 1, 2009).

———. *WSU Library Instruction—Partner Programs.* http://www.wsulibs.wsu.edu/usered/partners.htm (accessed January 1, 2009).

Washington State University. *The Economic Benefits of Washington State University Extension Programs.* http://ext.wsu.edu/economicbenefits/index.html (accessed January 1, 2009).

———. *WSU Center for Civic Engagement.* http://cce.wsu.edu (accessed January 1, 2009).

———. *WSU Extension—History.* http://ext.wsu.edu/about/history.html (accessed January 1, 2009).

———. *WSU Statewide.* http://www.about.wsu.edu/statewide/ (accessed January 1, 2009).

Wayne State University. *Community Engagement at Wayne: List of Community Partners.* 2008. http://communityengagement.wayne.edu/partners.php (accessed September 7, 2008).

———. *Community Engagement at Wayne: Mission and Philosophy.* 2008. http:// communityengagement.wayne.edu/mission.php (accessed September 7, 2008).

———. *WSU to Apply to Carnegie for Community Engagement Classification.* 2008.

http://communityengagement.wayne.edu/news.php?id=1836 (accessed September 8, 2008).

Weerts, David J., and Lorilee R. Sandmann. "Building a Two-Way Street: Challenges and Opportunities for Community Engagement at Research Universities." *Review of Higher Education* 32, no. 1 (2008): 73–106.

Westney, Lynn C. "Conspicuous by the Absence: Academic Librarians in the Engaged University." *Reference & User Services Quarterly* 45, no. 3 (2006): 200–203.

Williams, Sherry. "Personal communication to the author, October 6, 2008."

Young, Heartsill, ed. *The ALA Glossary of Library and Information Science*. Chicago, IL: American Library Association, 1983.

Youngman, Daryl. *ACME and the First MILE*. October 6, 2005. http://ksulib.typepad.com/bulletin/2005/10/acme_and_the_fi.html (accessed January 4, 2009).

———. *ACME is Back!: Kansas State University Libraries Grants and Collaborations Blog*. March 8, 2007. http://ksulib.typepad.com/grants/2007/03/acme_is_back.html (accessed January 4, 2009).

Appendix 1:
University of Illinois at Urbana-Champaign Library
Public Engagement Working Group

Description
The Public Engagement Working Group is charged by the Advisory Committee to the Associate University Librarian for Services to promote Library activities that support the public engagement mission of the University of Illinois at Urbana-Champaign. The Chair of the Public Engagement Working Group serves as an ex officio member of the Advisory Committee to the Associate University Librarian for Services.

Charge
The charge of the Public Engagement Working Group is to:
- Collaborate with appropriate Library units, committees, working groups, or task forces on the design, delivery, and assessment of public engagement programs
- Collect and disseminate information regarding the public engagement programs of the University Library
- Develop and oversee a "Public Engagement" section of the Library Web site
- Promote the public engagement programs of the University Library through presentation and publication of relevant information in Library publications, University publications, and other venues
- Promote the conduct of the "scholarship of engagement" among Library faculty
- Identify opportunities for Library involvement in public engagement programs at the campus level
- Advocate for the provision of financial and human resources appropriate to the pursuit of public engagement programs as a strategic priority of the University Library

Membership
The membership of the Public Engagement Working Group should be drawn from Library faculty and staff with direct responsibilities for public engagement programs or expertise in the scholarship of engagement. Core public engagement program areas include, but are not limited to: Cultural Engagement, Extension, K–12 Engagement,

Lifelong Learning, Health Information and Services to Health Care Professionals, E-Government, and the Mortenson Center for International Library Programs.

URL

http://www.library.uiuc.edu/committee/public/charge.html

Librarians, Advocacy, and the Research Enterprise

D. Scott Brandt

In what is considered an innovative perspective on advocacy, Julie Todaro notes that it is a tool used to "influence and persuade" entities external to the library to expand opportunities and "critical support for library value, worth and initiatives," and it relates not only to legislative environments, but to areas within the academy itself.[1] Obvious examples may be seen in advocacy involving campus information technology or administrative units not otherwise integrated within reporting relationships, such as physical facilities or development. But one area in which the need for and influence of advocacy may not be so obvious is within the research enterprise itself—identifying and pursuing collaborations to partner and engage in (as opposed to supporting) research. Opportunities are opening up to create and promote new roles for librarians, identifying and building new services, and ultimately increasing funding and visibility for the academic library, especially given the evolving nature of research in a data intensive environment.

The goal of the academic research enterprise is to produce new knowledge, as well as new educators and researchers. Research may be expressed as "pure," or as the "search for solutions to the most complex professional issues to everyday problems," and it may or may not involve collaboration with industry or international partners. But increasingly, delivery is key. As noted recently, even land grant institutions (predicated on a service role) have begun to redefine themselves to become greater collaborators with industry and local economic partners, partly related to solving problems and partly related to selling answers.[2] One thing is certain, academic research is growing—in complexity, time to delivery and interdisciplinarity[3]. And the university looks to everyone to help it grow. Typically, a research university strategic plan is likely to list research (or "discovery") as its first goal. It may even list as a key strategy creating incentives for faculty production in research and related scholarship. For many such universities, the goal is "to take on the biggest challenges and solve the greatest problems."[4] And yet, as is likely evidenced in the institution's metrics, it is extramural funding for research that is critical—annual reports are more likely to list levels of research dollars gained than number of societal problems solved. Research in academia can be a money making enterprise, sometimes referred to as the "business of research."

As research, reflecting the needs of society and economy, has become increasingly knowledge and information based, the importance of data and information have become more central.[5] And understanding how this data and information is organized, navigated and archived becomes critical. McLuhan's assertion that "the medium is the message"[6] may be no more relevant than with research in the new millennium where computation, cyberinfrastructure and data merge and blend into the medium by which new knowledge is found, created, and disseminated. But understanding this medium is not an endeavor that can be done in a vacuum—researchers need to know more about the organization and navigation of information and data to leverage their research, and librarians, who can help them, must know more about their research processes, products and practices to do so.

Supporting vs. Engaging in Research

It is important to emphasize the distinction between supporting research and engaging in research. For some, supporting research (e-Research, e-Science, etc.) means to support the creation of research products, connecting communities and curating data.[7] For others, supporting research means to "integrate discovery/management/creation/sharing tools into the workflow of scientists."[8] And for others, the importance lies in focusing on the development of an infrastructure necessary "to support the processes of research and the full life cycle of research assets."[9] The approach of the Purdue University Libraries evolved from a slightly different course of action, engaging in interdisciplinary research endeavors where investigators who are able to address a piece of the problem are invited to participate as collaborators in discovering a solution.[10] For librarians, such participation can be seen as a natural extension of exploring service needs, in that collaborating on research funded projects could demonstrate how library skills, knowledge and expertise may be applied to solve problems. From participation on several individual small projects information can be collected on what general services might be developed for the campus as a whole.

In institutions with tenure track library faculty, this type of approach suggests that by leveraging an existing pool of library science research skills and knowledge among library staff, this model for research engagement might lead to new avenues of interaction, in addition to developing new library services. This is the point where one opportunity for advocacy becomes apparent—librarians can learn more about the research enterprise and how to leverage interactions by collaborating in research. Interactions could explore new models for determining what tools and resources researchers need and could help to build services based on researcher perspectives. For instance, building a data repository might be overkill if only metadata services are needed.

Issues related to the evolving nature of research and its impact on libraries has been discussed in various settings. Gold's cyberinfrastructure biased overview highlights many pertinent issues: high performance computing, grid science, e-Science, data archiving , preservation, curation, access, interoperability, policies, services, tools, and business models.[11] Lynch's commentary in *Nature* brings home the point with a focus on data as the manifestation of research to which scientist must tend, noting the key role librarians play.[12] The importance of data was identified earlier by the National Science Foundation's (NSF) "Report of the Blue-Ribbon Advisory Panel on Cyberinfrastructure,"[13] which sounded the alarm that research not only involved computing, but the data that came from sensors, instruments, modeling and analysis. The ARL/NSF Workshop "To Stand the Test of Time" proved to be a real turning point for libraries to demonstrate a national level of interest and interaction.[14] And the NSF's Cyberinfrastructure Vision for 21st Century Discovery[15] devoted a chapter to data and virtual organizations, and along with the ARL workshop, set the stage for the NSF's DataNet solicitation, which encapsulates in its call many of the issues noted above, and specifically pointed out that librarians should work with scientists to find answers to these immensely important questions about the role of data in research computing.[16]

Engagement in collaborative research for Purdue University Libraries grew out of the investigation of the needs of interdisciplinary research at the university, based on the Libraries' goal to become a more integral partner in campus research and align with the institution's strategic directions and priorities. For the Purdue Libraries, advocacy in the research enterprise necessarily implied interaction in a predominantly agriculture, engineering and science setting, although it was not meant to exclude other research disciplines and cultures. Through many interactions with leading research faculty, centers and department heads, librarians demonstrated expertise in organization and access to information to contribute to research problems, especially in e-Science areas. Researchers were not sure how or whether to share data, complained they lacked time to organize data sets, said they needed help describing data for discovery, wanted to find new ways to manage data, and needed someone to archive their data sets/collections.[17]

Building Collaborations

Advocating the research enterprise means working with researchers on problems, and often on proposals for grants to pay for the work. But foremost it means making introductions, building rapport, being able to follow up and follow through on communication, developing relationships and forging partnerships.

Researchers' buying in to working with librarians does not seem to be a hard sell. For one thing, they are motivated by tenure, promotion, peer recognition and acclaim—anything that makes their work or proposal better is definitely in their best interest. They are pragmatic, understand the need for funding to do work, and recognize useful help when they see it. They tend to respond well to activities which publicize their work, especially if they are interested in dissemination, or which helps them comply to funding requirements to make their work accessible. Activities planned to increase participation could include exploring new ways to use digital object identifiers (DOI) for persistence or automating OAI-PMH metadata to facilitate harvesting, and thus accomplishing wider discovery.

So it is useful to engage researchers who "get it" that collecting, organizing and providing access to data and information are not only important activities, but critical, and that librarians need to be involved. Researchers are more likely to see that library science expertise can help them understand or solve problems related to data management and similar issues of organization, dissemination and archiving. Librarians can build interest by digging deeply into what researchers are doing—traditional service might also apply, such as reference, collection management, and instruction discussions.

Librarians should be prepared to be problem solvers, addressing that which is at the heart of research—what problem can be solved?—but where appropriate, they should also insist on being a co-investigator. Researchers understand clearly the need to be involved in grants and the need to bring in money to fund research assistance, travel or other resources.

Of course, for libraries to engage with researchers, they need their librarians to buy-in to this model of operation. This is a type of collaboration that can be overlooked. As Judy Stokker, of Queensland University of Technology notes, "There is a difference between cooperation and collaboration." She argues that cooperation means that people are willing to participate, but collaboration means that people are committed to producing results.[18]

Librarians also want to know what is in it for them—including recognition, reward or promotion. Sometimes a top-down strategy is needed, identifying new roles and finding ways to exert gentle pressure on employees to comply. It helps when projects are directly related to work, or an extension of their "everyday role" (e.g., a natural segue from liaison work). It also helps when a project is something new and exciting, something that breaks new ground in the field or represents a change from the day-to-day routine. Sometimes participation can be facilitated through strategic planning in the organization. Librarians will want to know how day-to-day work will get done and may then need help in prioritizing or deciding what and what not to do. They likely will want to increase their knowledge and skills, focusing especially on learning to write grants but also on how to implement and manage projects in order to be successful at these new endeavors.

The involvement of the library administration is critical to paving the way for change. Administrators can promote campus awareness of what librarians are able to do and verify what the library will support. For instance, Purdue Libraries' dean visited all college deans, departments and major center heads to discuss both interdisciplinary research and what librarians could do to assist researchers. In terms of providing incentives and rewards, Purdue created a dean's award to recognize contribution to strategic directions such as interdisciplinary research and provided travel funding for faculty to present on leading edge research projects.

Other roles that administration can play in helping librarians are identifying "hot" research areas; helping to prioritize liaison focus;

determining the percentage of effort that may be dedicated to investigation or research; identifying journal articles which fit with current or future research endeavors and discussing them (i.e., a "journal club" or brown bag sessions); helping with research grant solicitations, by brainstorming ideas and drafting proposal sections; and promoting research updates and achievement.

Helping Scientists Do New Things

Another big difference between supporting research and engaging in it is that the latter attempts to apply the knowledge, principles, expertise and skills inherent in library science to solve a problem in a new or different way, as opposed to helping somebody use or access available resources or services, the more traditional application of library science tools. While for disciplinary problems that could mean applying library science to solve a library problem (e.g., measuring usability of an information resource to design more efficient or effective ways of using that resource); for interdisciplinary problems, it would mean applying library science to other disciplines or domains to solve larger or more complicated problems (e.g., identifying what metadata is generated at creation of a data set and how to enhance the process for wider applications). For many libraries or librarians interdisciplinary research may seem like new ground, but such collaborations simply utilize familiar skills and expertise in new ways.

Users of cyber-enabled sensors and instruments generate research data and need to manage, disseminate and preserve it at some point. It is not clear when researchers will ask for data repository support. For instance, it depends on the culture of the discipline (e.g., geneticists may be more willing to share raw data than chemical engineers). However, if a funding agency requires that a data repository solution should be developed as part of a research solicitation, it is possible that a proposal could include a library science member on the team to help address this issue. This could allow a library to get paid to explore the design of repository services without committing other resources. For instance, a librarian could help design tools to provide standardized metadata to enable interoperability and long term preservation of data sets.

Participating on grant proposals could also allow librarians to explore not only whether a group of researchers would share data, but what various services could help to do so. There may be a difference between so called "large science" (e.g., particle physics, astronomy) needs, and those of small science. In the latter case, it is more likely that research group would not catalog or preserve data or do much in the way of archiving, although they may want to increase accessibility of the datasets they create to share or reuse. Librarians could help create a functional proof-of-concept system for automating the generation of descriptive metadata that could help provide greater discoverability, even if only via Web site spidering.

Other exploratory projects pursued through collaboration on grants might include:

- Constructing a hybrid controlled vocabulary to lower barriers of participation for tagging resources/objects in subject specific portal
- Preserving and increasing the accessibility of "small science" datasets by automating metadata and ingesting them into a repository
- Developing an OAI-PMH interface to expose metadata from a web enabled database to Internet metadata harvesters
- Investigating the use of persistent identifier system (e.g. D.O.I.) for citing resources and preserving linkages that will not break over time

The "Business of Research"

Most academic institutions have an organizational structure to ensure effective communication and policy administration for research which centers on relationships between colleges/schools and university offices for research and sponsored programs activity. This may be coordinated via associate dean for research positions. Such positions serve as liaisons for major research funding (i.e., extramural) activity, ensuring that local and external policies and regulatory compliance are followed. It might be very useful for libraries determine how best to interface with this structure. At Purdue, after discussions between the dean of Libraries and the Provost, it was determined that the solution to assure participation was to mirror the university's organization. The existing library organization of a dean, associate dean for public services, and directors for IT/technical services and administrative services was restructured to create five associate deans with respective areas of responsibilities. The single associate dean position was split to accommodate two areas, learning and information resources and scholarly communications. The director positions were changed to associate deans for IT and administration/planning, and a new position, associate dean for research, was created.[19] (Mullins 2007)

For example, an associate dean for research in an academic library oversees the "business of research" by ensuring library participation in funding opportunities and related collaborations at the university, with other universities, and with funding agencies. This includes interacting with the university's office of research (perhaps the VP or chancellor of research), a unit that oversee sponsored programs (i.e., extramural) services, strategic research initiatives groups if there are any, as well as liaison with program managers, such as at NSF, IMLS, etc. Responsibilities include providing leadership in fostering productive partnerships and sustained relationships between the library and other faculty; working with other associate deans and faculty to increase participation in collaborative research and discovery initiatives; providing linkages between university research and programs within the university and the library; identifying and contributing to the success of opportunities in intramural and extramural research development; and raising and leveraging new resources from multiple sources that the library can strategically apply towards its research agenda.

Those are explicit roles. But it is one thing to learn the "business of research" and another to build the skills and momentum to leverage or take advantage of it for garnering partnerships and increased funding—that is, to strengthen more implicit roles. For instance, one can create opportunities by leveraging advocacy with the research enterprise, but it takes the ability to forge collaborations to get on interdisciplinary grant proposals. It takes listening and proactive involvement to identify, explore, and build partnerships before one can ever leverage the opportunity to test and assess which services, systems and tools are needed by researchers. Implicit business skills are also needed to leverage understanding, which builds support, which leads to funding, which can help achieve strategic directions.

Entrepreneurial Advocacy

So, what can involvement in research get librarians? What is the advantage of advocacy? Can success be measured just in the amount of funds acquired from grants and other fundraising opportunities? After all, there is a familiar, if not common, saying among researchers that "a hundred conversations lead to twenty discussions, lead to five proposals, and lead to one award." If one seeks only to gain new funds, research advocacy may not look like an efficient strategy.

A typical small, single investigator grant in the university setting usually involves one person writing the proposal, putting the budget together, making sure guidelines are followed, and getting appropriate approval/sign-off within the unit. Usually the grant then goes through a central university check to set up accounts and verify commitments before being sent off. In a large interdisciplinary grant several people contribute sections, and each contribution is usually edited by a grant writer; a large business office (within a college or the central administration) puts a budget together based on each contributor's input, and approval/sign-off is required often not only by all the units but by the university as well if large commitments are being made (e.g. for the creation of a center). By participating in these larger efforts, libraries not only learn how to engage at a higher and deeper level, but build relationships within, and gain a greater understanding of, the university as a whole. This requires not only learning more about research activities and priorities, but about the strategic priorities of the university. The library becomes visible as a partner in the university as a whole, and not an individual entity.

And while it is possible that disciplinary (i.e., library science) research by itself can successfully engage the research enterprise (e.g., "win" extramural funds for an Institute for Museum and Library Services grant), it is more likely that through interdisciplinary research librarians will engage a broader spectrum. . This broader spectrum of the research enterprise, supported by increased participation in interdisciplinary research, would ideally include activities that are involved on a deeper level and with more constituents than are currently engaged. Those who have contributed in intense, lengthy interdisciplinary research proposal development meetings know that deep insight can be gained about research areas as well as how scientists interact from contact with individuals outside the library context.

An obvious difference becomes apparent when working with large research grants in the science fields. This provides insight into the university's overhead mechanism, which otherwise libraries might not experience, since many library grants do not allow overhead (i.e., charges associated with the ongoing expense related to operating the buildings, facilities, etc.). Without overhead charges there is little opportunity for libraries to negotiate return of overhead. Whereas with NSF grants, which may allow over 50% extra overhead tacked on, libraries might successfully lobby the university for a return of some of the overhead monies.

This is in addition to the amount of return that comes out of a $10,000 grant versus a $1,000,000 grant—obviously the order of magnitude in large NSF or NIH grant has respectively larger returns in terms of salaries, etc. And there are multiple gains when staff time is paid for by an award. For instance, when a grant pays salary for a librarian, the money that the libraries saves is called "cost savings," and usually can be marked as discretionary funds to be used in variety of ways. Depending on the amount it could be used to pay for a student employee (undergraduate or graduate). Or it could be used for travel to disseminate research and reward the grantee. If it is a large amount, or it there are multiple grants, the funds could be used to pay for part-time or temporary staff, presumably to do work which would be put off to accommodate time for the research.

If as part of an award one agrees to "cost share" ("donate") staff time, as opposed to seeking funds for the staff time used, there may still be advantages. First of all, if cost share is required, the time uses implicit, not explicit, costs, thus there is not direct out-of-pocket expense. Second, by cost sharing a librarian, it may be possible to leverage funds for a graduate student from the grant, and thus there is a gain (as long as the work which is put off does not offset the gain).

It should be worth noting that most of the resources expended are for personnel. There are explicit costs that can be quantified in the budget, but there are implicit costs as well. There are always trade-offs and cost opportunities gained or lost. What does it mean for a project to be "worth it"? For instance, explicit costs are related to how much the library can get other people to pay, based on a certain value of worth (usually salary x time). But implicitly the library must ask what the costs for a specific interaction entail (e.g., what internal work must be shifted?).

At many universities the research enterprise builds increased capability within larger research units, such as a college of engineering or a biomedical center of national stature, and collaborating with them may have advantages. Such capabilities include large business office staffs to ensure that budgets are created (and carried out) correctly, cost sharing capability (possibly funded out of returned overhead), and other dedicated staff, such as grant writers and administrative staff to track down information, schedule meetings, and ensure award packages are complete, etc.

Advocating the research enterprise may not be for everyone. It may be out of scope for libraries that focus in other areas, such as learning or engagement. It may be inappropriate based on academic mores or rules. It may not be doable in libraries that don't have the resources, especially personnel. Or it may be something in which libraries just don't to participate. However, involvement need not be substantial or an "all or none" proposition. It is possible to start by "putting a toe in the water" by doing an environmental scan to see whether it is possible or needed. Involvement could be phased in—first by building deeper liaison relationships, then getting further involved as opportunities arise. Involvement could be limited to discipline or domain, such as medical science or agriculture where a history of such activity exists. But it is likely that as research moves forward, needs and opportunities will arise. Libraries can watch them go by, or they can engage in advocacy to enhance their value and worth.

Notes

1. Todaro, "Power of Persuasion."
2. Tornatzky, "Innovation U."
3. Sadlack and Altbach, *Higher Education Research at the Turn of the New Century.*
4. Purdue University. *Strategic Plan Annual Report 2007.*
5. National Academy of Sciences, *Fateful Choices.*
6. McLuhan, *Understanding Media.*
7. Luce, "A New Value Equation Challenge."
8. Marcus, *Understanding Research Behaviors*
9. E-Science, Joint Task Force on Library Support for, Agenda for, *Agenda for Developing E-Science*
10. Brandt, "Librarians as partners in e-research."
11. Gold, "Cyberinfrastructure, Data, and Libraries."
12. Lynch, "Big Data."
13. Atkins, *Revolutionizing Science and Engineering*
14. Association for Research Libraries, "To Stand the Test of Time."
15. *Cyberstructure Vision for 21st Century Discovery.*
16. *Sustainable Digital Data Preservation and Access Network Partners*
17. Brandt, "Librarians as partners in e-research"
18. Stokker, "eResearch."
19. Mullins, "Enabling International Access to Scientific Data Sets."

Works Cited

Atkins, Daniel, et al. *Revolutionizing Science and Engineering Through Cyberinfra-structure: Report of the National Science Foundation Blue-Ribbon Advisory Panel on Cyberinfrastructure.* January 2003. http://www.nsf.gov/od/oci/reports/

Brandt, D. Scott. "Librarians as partners in e-research." *College & Research Libraries News*, 68, no. 6 (June 2007): 365–367, 396.

Cyberinfrastructure Vision for 21st Century Discovery. NSF Cyberinfrastructure Council. March 2007.

E-Science, Joint Task Force on Library Support for. *Agenda for Developing E-Science* in *Research Libraries: Final Report and Recommendations*. Washington D.C: Association of Research Libraries, November 2007.

Fateful Choices: The Future of the U.S. Academic Research Enterprise. Washington, D.C.: National Academy of Sciences, 1992.

Gold, Anna. "Cyberinfrastructure, Data, and Libraries, Part 1." *D-Lib Magazine*. Volume 13, no. 9/10 (September/October 2007).

Luce, Richard E. "A New Value Equation Challenge: The Emergence of eResearch and Roles for Research Libraries." *No Brief Candle: Reconceiving Research Libraries for the 21ˢᵗ Century*. Washington, D.C., Council on Library and Information Sources, August 2008.

Lynch, Clifford. "Big data: How do your data grow?" *Nature* 455, 28-29 (4 September 2008) http://www.nature.com/nature/journal/v455/n7209/full/455028a.html (last accessed July 21, 2009)

Marcus, Cecily, with Stephanie Ball, Leslie Delserone, Amy Hribar, and Wayne Loftus. *Understanding Research Behaviors, Information Resources, and Service Needs of Scientists and Graduate Students: A Study by the University of Minnesota Libraries*. University of Minnesota Libraries, June 2007. http://www.lib.umn.edu/about/scieval/Sci%20Report%20Final.pdf (last accessed July 21, 2009)

McLuhan, Marshall. *Understanding Media: The Extensions of Man*. Cambridge, MA: MIT Press, 1994.

Mullins, James L. "Enabling International Access to Scientific Data Sets: Creation of the Distributed Data Curation Center (D2C2)." Paper presented at the 28th Annual Conference of the International Association of Technological University Libraries (IATUL) in Stockholm, Sweden. June 2007

Purdue University. *Strategic Plan Annual Report 2007: the Sixth Year*. http://www.purdue.edu/strategic_plan/2001-2006/pages/2007_pdf/2007_strat_plan_report.pdf (last accessed July 21, 2009)

Sadlack, Jan and Philip G. Altbach, eds. *Higher Education Research at the Turn of the New Century: Structures, Issues, and Trends*. New York: Garland Pub, 1997

Stokker, Judy. "eResearch: Access and Support to University Researchers." Purdue University Libraries Seminar, Purdue University, August 1, 2008.

Sustainable Digital Data Preservation and Access Network Partners (DataNet). Program Solicitation (NSF 07-601). 2007. http://www.nsf.gov/pubs/2007/nsf07601/nsf07601.htm

"To Stand the Test of Time: Long-term Stewardship of Digital Data Sets in Science and Engineering." ARL Workshop on New Collaborative Relationships: The Role of Academic Libraries in the Digital Data Universe. Final Report. September 26-27, 2006. http://www.arl.org/bm~doc/digdatarpt.pdf

Todaro, J. "The power of persuasion: Grassroots advocacy in the academic library." *College & Research Libraries News* v. 67 no. 4 (April 2006)

Tornatzky, Louis. "Innovation U: New Practices, Enabling Cultures." *Creating Knowledge, Strengthening Nations: The Changing Role of Higher Education*. Ed. by Glen A. Jones, Patricia Louise McCarney, Michael L. Skolnik. Toronto: University of Toronto Press, 2005

Librarians and Scholarly Communication: Outreach, Advocacy, and Leadership within the Academic Community

3

Beth McNeil

The traditional system for disseminating scholarship, or scholarly communication, continues to undergo a tremendous change and the current models for scholarly publishing are not sustainable. Some consider this a crisis, others an opportunity; for libraries it is, perhaps, both. Lewis suggests that universities and libraries have "danced around this issue for the last decade and it is now time to be frank about what the future holds for scholarly communication and how academic libraries will spend the money they devote to collections", and offers an ambitious and perhaps daring formula for collections budgeting strategy to prepare for future digital content needs.[1] Hahn notes that "scholars and researchers generally remain remarkably naïve and uninformed" about changes in scholarly publishing" and that "[O]nly active engagement by those undertaking research and scholarship can ensure that the advancement of research and scholarship takes priority in the development and adoption of new models."[2] Regardless of one's viewpoint and perspective, librarians at all levels have advocacy and leadership roles to play in helping to reshape scholarly communication.

Advocacy, or "the collective action of individuals working in concert to move forward a specific action or idea", is a role that librarians must play in order to "take that transformative step from passive intellectual support to intelligent action."[3] Todaro has associated advocacy with persuasion and influence, two important concepts within the field of leadership studies. Todaro observed the following,

> "No matter who we are trying to influence, we have so little time with those we are trying to convince and—as in other professions—people in legislative arenas and in our own institutions really know very little about what we do. Realistically speaking, sitting down with a legislator, a legislative aide or, for our initiative

at hand, a department chair, dean, or even classroom faculty for 15 minutes at a time (no matter the educational content we bring) is a matter of getting attention, creating a teachable moment, indicating value and worth of what we do, making an impact, connecting with a promised outcome or a memorable, unique or targeted fact, and seeking follow-up opportunities."[4]

While these and other ACRL leaders have argued that advocacy is important there is little empirical evidence that advocacy has been incorporated into managerial practice within the academic library community.[5] Simmons-Welburn, McNeil, and Welburn studied advocacy as a strategy by library administrators to exert power and influence outside the library to other campus-level decision makers, using the early work of Kipnis and Schmidt (1982) and the *Profiles of Organizational Influence Strategies* (POIS) instrument.[6] Their findings suggest that just two of the POIS measures proved salient, assertiveness and coalition, and that the need to exercise lateral influence is not an insignificant characteristic of library administrators' managerial styles. Lateral influence, or influencing colleagues over whom you have no direct influence, would seem to be important for liaison librarians/subject specialists and other librarians, as well as administrators, but has not been empirically studied.

Current Environment

Much has been written about and presented on the challenges libraries face when trying to support change in the scholarly communication system[7] (English 2003; Ogburn, 2003; and others), and challenges may be summarized as falling into several areas including "engaging faculty and keeping their attention, making scholarly communication a campus issue, not a library issue, reconciling visions of different groups and moving in concert, (and) keeping conversations relevant and fresh".[8] Of particular note are several recent large studies or reports, including the ACRL Scholarly Communication Committee report, *Establishing a Research Agenda for Scholarly Communication: A Call for Community Engagement; Faculty Attitudes and Behaviors regarding scholarly communication: Survey of findings from the University of California;* and the Center for Studies in Higher Education (CSHE)'s *Assessing the Future Landscape of Scholarly Communication: An In-depth study of faculty needs and ways of meeting them.*

In 2007, the ACRL Scholarly Communications Committee released a report, *Establishing a Research Agenda for Scholarly Communication: A Call for Community Engagement,* based on discussions at an invitational meeting in July 2007 with representatives from ACRL, ARL, CLIR, CNI, Ithaka, and Mellon Foundation, and SPARC. The report highlights issues and presents themes to "frame a far reaching research agenda" and encourages readers to post comments to the ACRL Web site.

The Mellon Foundation funded a major study at the Center for Studies in Higher Education (CSHE), led by C. Judson King and Diane Harley, in late 2006 to investigate faculty needs relating to scholarly communication. The study focused on several selective disciplinary areas, including archaeology, astrophysics, life sciences, economics, history, music, and political science; and in addition to providing a descriptive analysis of faculty needs, also predicted future scenarios for the selected disciplines. Findings included the perhaps unsurprising idea that "peer review is the coin of the realm", the conundrum that scholars and researchers use and value electronic forms of print publications but that the promotion and tenure system continues to value "high stature print publications," as well as the conclusion that indirect measures of quality are increasingly valued, that is valued "with the institution differ significantly from those for making one's name within a discipline", and that universities do not yet have systems in place to "support storing, archiving, and sharing data and other significant products of research."[9]

The University of California Office of Scholarly Communication and the California Digital Library eScholarship Program, in association with Greenwood Associates, explored UC faculty members opinions and perspectives on many aspects of scholarly communication, including its role in the promotion and tenure process, copyright, public policy, and scholarly communication-related services that faculty might desire and for which the university may or may not provide. Survey results indicated that faculty are "strongly interested in issues related to scholarly communication," and "generally conform to conventional behavior in scholarly publishing."[10] It also suggests that attitudes are changing but behavioral changes will be slow to appear, that the promotion and tenure system "impedes change in faculty behavior", the "disconnect between attitude and behavior is acute with regard to copyright", and that University-wide mandates are likely to be controversial.[11]

And, finally, Hahn, in the *Journal of Electronic Publishing*, calls for campus dialogue on the topic of new models, and identifies six dangers of the current moment, as well as six topics for wider campus discussion, and concludes that while "librarians play a leadership role in the dialogue needed to develop new and richer perspectives on issues, perspectives that are scholar-centric rather than library-centric" real change in research and scholarship will not happen "without the contributions and actions of their practitioners."[12]

Institution, Consortial, and Association Efforts

Institutions and consortiums have led major efforts in recent years to make changes in the system. The Harvard Faculty of Arts and Sciences Open Access (OA) mandate, announced in early 2008, followed by the Harvard Law School, and soon after Stanford's School of Education's OA mandate were significant events which surprised many in the U.S. academic community. While OA mandates are more common in other parts of the world these efforts at Harvard and Stanford have prompted much discussion on U.S. campuses. The Center for Library Initiatives (CLI) of the Committee on Institutional Cooperation (CIC), or the academic Big 10, worked with Big 10 Provosts to encourage members to pass the CIC Statement on Publishing Agreements, or as it is more commonly referred to, the CIC author rights addendum. The CIC author addendum retains three rights for authors: (1) a non-exclusive right to make and use derivative works, even for future publication, (2) a non-exclusive right to self-archive the published version six months after publication, in any repository, and (3) a non-exclusive right for the author's institution to use and copy the work for any activity at the institution.

Perhaps as a result of the ACRL/ARL Scholarly Communication Institutes and activities on campuses, articles with practical advice about various efforts to work to advance scholarly communication efforts on campuses have been written.[13] A 2007 article on science librarians as advocates for scholarly communication offers a list of practical steps for librarians to practice scholarly communication advocacy, including:

- Become familiar with the issues
- Make it part of your job
- Be a role model
- Hold focus groups
- Question high-cost journals

- Encourage faculty to publish in Open Access journals
- Support new publishing initiatives
- Stay current
- Develop your pitch
- Attend the ARL/ACRL Institute on Scholarly Communication[14]

These recommendations include several which seem to be natural extensions of the traditional liaison librarian role, including becoming familiar with the issues, making it part of your job, and questioning high cost journals: effective liaison librarians endeavor to discover the research interests and curricular needs of their disciplinary faculty and share information about the costs of library resources. Other recommendations may seem to be more of a stretch for a librarian comfortable functioning in a more traditional role in the relationship with academic departments, but in fact are not all that dissimilar from the types of connections librarians have had for decades with faculty, but extensions of the relationships into new areas. Developing effective skills in these areas might include aptitude or experience with some of the influence strategies noted by Kipnis and Schmidt and Yukl and Falbe.[15] For many years, to be an effective liaison librarian has been to know the liaison area disciplines—the key journals, the monograph needs, curriculum, etc. At a most basic level, this role has not changed; what is changing, however, is the scholarship of the disciplines and the strategies necessary for influence and leadership.

The changing scholarly communication landscape offers librarians an opportunity to lead their faculties and campuses, to develop new skills sets, and to work with faculty in new ways. Modern research is increasingly interdisciplinary and collaborative, and research output is being disseminated and preserved in new ways, as new technologies develop. The explosive growth of the Internet and migration from analog to digital is changing scholarly communication, causing libraries to consider new roles for liaison librarian/ subject specialists. These roles include applying the principles of library science to interdisciplinary research, embedding librarians into the curriculum, and collaborative projects with teaching faculty that teach laboratory concepts and at the same time contribute to the research endeavor. Whether through smaller efforts to educate faculty on increased costs of journals, large campaigns to radically change funding patterns, such as Lewis suggest, or librarians collaborating with faculty in major grants, librarians can be leaders and advocates for needed change. In the field of leadership studies, three types of leadership, transformational, charismatic, and servant leadership, may have implications for this new leadership role for librarians.

Defining Leadership Roles

But, first, what does it mean to say that librarians are or should or could be advocating for and leading changes on campuses relating to scholarly communication? Some might argue that leadership is easy to identify, e.g. "you know it when you see it". However, leadership can be difficult to define, both for practitioner/library administrator hoping to help librarians to learn to lead, as well as for the leadership studies scholars and researchers trying to study it. Because librarians have no formal authority over the faculty they hope to influence, they must develop the skills necessary to influence.[16] Kipnis and Schmidt's *Profiles of Organizational Influence Strategies* (POIS) includes the following dimensions of influence:

- *Friendliness*, attempting to influence by getting people to "think well of you."
- *Bargaining*, an attempt to influence by "negotiation and the exchange of benefits or favors"
- *Reason*, or influencing through data and information as support
- *Assertiveness*, or influence in a "forceful manner"
- *Higher authority*, or influence that "relies on the chain of command"
- *Coalition*, or influence that relies on "mobilizing other people in the organization to assist you."[17]

While it seems likely that librarians have been using some of these dimensions quite effectively in their work with faculty and students, no formal studies exist to confirm this, with the exception of the exploratory study by Simmons-Welburn et al. Because the POIS measures solely from the perspective of the influencing agent, a future study, using the *Influence Behavior Questionnaire* (IBQ), might be a worthwhile follow-up study. Yukl and Falbe found that the direction of influence—downward, lateral and upward influence—had a stronger effect on influence objectives than on influence tactics.[18] Future work on lateral influence of liaison librarians might add valuable information to both the literature and the practice of advocacy relating to scholarly communication.

Leadership Theories and Librarians as Leaders

Leadership studies as a discipline rests on over 100 years of leadership research and yet there is still no one accepted definition of leadership.[19] Nearly 35 years ago, Stogdill stated that, there are almost as many different definitions of leadership as there are persons who have attempted to define the concept.[20] While there are some variances in various scholars' definitions, Antonakis, Cianciolo, and Sternberg state that "[m]ost leadership scholars would probably agree, in principle, that leadership can be defined as the nature of the influencing process—and its resultant outcomes—that occurs between a leader and followers and how this influencing process is explained by the leader's dispositional characteristics and behaviors, follower perceptions and attributions of the leader, and the context in which the influencing process occurs."[21]

Certainly, the actions of library directors and library deans, as with many managers, fit within this general definition of leadership, and in these roles, library leaders regularly exhibit leadership characteristics of various leadership theories. Librarians "in the trenches," such as liaison librarians and subject specialists, also may regularly display characteristics of both leaders and "followers," a concept discussed within the leadership research. Effective followers demonstrate "enthusiastic, intelligent, and self-reliant participation—without star billing—in the pursuit of an organizational goal."[22] In the mid 1980s, a new area surfaced, sometimes called the New Leadership School, by Bass and others, which promoted visionary and charismatic leadership theories.

Transformational Leadership

Transformational leadership involves "follower outcomes being centered on a sense of purpose and an idealized mission"[23] and results from a leader working toward acceptance by all of those participating in the mission.[24] Transformational leaders encourage followers to think independently, meeting challenges to gain both personal and professional development. Transformational leadership moves individuals from idolizing the leader to directing energies to commitment to organizational goals instead of own self-interest. Transformational leadership is one of the most researched theories of leadership, and is characterized by intellectual stimulation (thinking outside the box), individualized consideration (compassionate leader), inspirational motivation, and idealized influence.[25]

For librarians working with researchers and scholars on scholarly communication issues aspects of all four areas of transformational leadership may apply: empathizing with individual needs and making interpersonal connections (individualized consideration); challenging the old ways of doing things, looking for better ways to do things, willingness to take risks for potential gains (intellectual stimulation); inspiring others, creating a strong sense of purpose, and aligning individual and organizational needs (inspirational motivation); as well as walking the walk, exhibiting commitment and persistence in pursuing objectives, developing trust and confidence, and demonstrating that the course of action is the right one (idealized influence).[26]

Servant Leadership

Greenleaf first defined servant leadership in 1970, and stated it "begins with the natural feeling that one wants to serve, to serve first. Then conscious choice brings one to aspire to lead. That person is sharply different from one who is leader first, perhaps because of the need to assuage an unusual power drive or to acquire material possessions."[27] Servant leadership has been the subject of programs at library association conferences, appears in library-related training, and was a theme for the 2006/2007 LITA President. Herb Kelleher, former Chairman of Southwest Airlines notes that Southwest looks for "people who, on their own initiative, want to be doing what they are doing because they consider it a worthy objective."[28] Librarians who are working to educate campus constituents about the changing nature of scholarly communication likely have many motives, and for those who consider this role a worthy objective, something to attempt for the greater good of the larger organization and to fill an organizational purpose or initiative, this could be described as servant leadership.

Leader-Member-Exchange Theory or LMX

Leader-member-exchange (LMX) theory is also referred to as Vertical Dyad Linkage Theory, and involves the tacit exchange agreements between leaders and the groups within which they work. LMX is similar to servant leadership, particularly in the context of high quality exchanges (Barbuto, Wheeler, 2006).[29] Servant leaders develop strong supportive relationships,[30] while relationships developed by high LMX leaders are "trusting and mutually beneficial,"[31] similar to the strong supportive relationships that servant leaders develop with others.[32]

Barbuto and Wheeler describe the role of the leader, role of the follower, outcomes expected, and compare five levels (individual, interpersonal, group, organizational, and societal) and report that the role of leader varies in the theories, from serving in servant leadership, to inspiring in transformational leadership, and in LMX to a position of developing positive relationships with followers. The followers' roles include becoming wiser, freer, and more autonomous (servant leadership), pursuing organizational goals (transformational leadership) and developing positive relationships with leaders (LMX). Outcomes expected include follower satisfaction, development, and commitment to service, societal good (servant leadership); goal congruence, increased effort, satisfaction, and productivity, and organizational gain (transformational leadership); and high satisfaction, mutual trust, and increased effort (LMX).[33] Further study, comparing librarians' leadership and the leadership theories could have interesting implications for future research.

Some researchers believe that both servant leadership and transformational are inspirational and moral methods.[34] In contrast, others believe that charismatic leadership and transformational leadership, with an organizational focus, may override follower's moral misgivings to behave in a way that would not suggest servant leadership.[35] Both transformational and servant leadership focus on the "others" in the leader-follower model. Based on the work of Avolio and Bass, and Spears, Smith and others found several behaviors common to both transformational and servant leadership, including modeling appropriate behavior, strong interpersonal relationships, envisioning the future, goal clarification, facilitating a shared vision, providing opportunities to grow and learn, collaboration, share power and release control, and share status and promote others. Much of servant leadership matches well with the transformational leadership model, with the exception of intellectual stimulation dimension, according to Smith.[36] Overall, some similarities can be drawn between aspects of transformational leadership, charismatic leadership, and servant leadership, although without empirical examination of servant leadership it is not possible to say definitively.[37]

Barbuto and Wheeler chart a comparison of servant leadership and transformational leadership in the following areas: nature of theory, role of leader, moral component, the outcomes expected at the individual level, interpersonal level, group level, organizational level, and societal level.[38] Of these, nine show at least minor distinctions between servant leadership and transformational leadership. At the societal level, slight differences exist for transformational and servant leadership. Transformational leadership leads to an empowered, dynamic culture within an organization, while servant leadership leads to spiritual, generative culture.[39] At the organizational level, the differences are greater. Charismatic leaders gain a high level of organizational commitment to their followers, transformational leaders inspire followers to pursue organization goals, and servant leaders prepare followers to serve the organization or community.[40]

As mentioned previously, Graham believes that both transformational leadership and servant leadership are forms of charismatic leadership. She extends this to describe servant leadership as exceeding transformational leadership in the areas of a leader's responsibilities to serve those marginalized and in dedication to follower's needs as opposed to their own (leader's) needs.[41] Although Barbuto and Wheeler do not suggest servant leadership is an extension of or exceeds transformational leadership their comparisons of servant leadership and transformational leadership in the areas of interpersonal level, group level, and societal level seem to support this difference between servant leadership and transformational leadership.

Empirical studies exist for both charismatic leadership and transformational leadership, although not specifically relating to academic librarians in subject specialist or liaison librarian roles. Servant leadership, which has been the topic of conference programs at American Library Association annual conferences, does not yet have this same empirical basis, but may soon with more testing of the Servant Leadership Questionnaire. The biggest difference between these theories seems to be the motivation of the leader to serve.[42] Motivation for librarians, working as leaders and advocates, to influence changes in the scholarly communication arena likely varies, running the gamut from the altruistic desire to do the right thing (for example, through education about open access, being good models for authors' rights, etc.) to the very practical and pragmatic situation of high subscriptions costs and limits to library budgets, and would be an interesting focus for future studies in leadership.

Charismatic, transformational, and servant leadership theories, while different and distinct modes of leadership, may have, in fact, evolved from each other: charismatic leadership to transformational leadership to servant leadership. Regardless of their origins, these theories, along with LMX theory, may have implications for the advocacy role that librarians play or could play in scholarly communication process. Until very recently, the literature on servant leadership has been largely anecdotal or based on ideas and conclusions drawn from careful study of Robert Greenleaf's writings. A more precise clarification of the servant leadership construct is necessary, as noted by Barbuto and Wheeler. Once this is clarified, more will be known about servant leadership, and possibly, a more complete answer to the larger question of whether charismatic leadership, transformational leadership, and servant leadership are different theories. As noted earlier, librarians are and should be taking leadership roles on campus relating to scholarly communication and the changing nature of research and publication. What leadership theory or style is most effective or applicable to librarians as leaders in the scholarly communication arena, however, is not yet known.

Notes

1. Lewis, Scholarly Communication, 271.
2. Hahn, "Scholarly Communication.
3. Linke, "The Purposeful Advocate", 464.
4. Todaro, "The Power of Persuasion: Grassroots Advocacy", 228-229.
5. Todaro, "The Power of Persuasion: advancing the academic library agenda; Alire, "Advocating to advance academic libraries" 590-591; Linke, "The Purposeful Advocate" 464-465.
6. Simmons-Welburn, "Perceptions of Campus Level Advocacy"; Kipnis, "Profile".
7. English, "Scholarly Communication and the Academy,"337-340; Ogburn, "SPARC forum."
8. Ogburn, "SPARC forum."
9. King, "Assessing the Future", 2.
10. "Faculty Attitudes and Behaviors", 1.
11. Ibid.
12. Hahn, "Talking about Talking ", p 12.
13. Fishel, "Learning Advocacy"; Turtle, "Scholarly Communication. "
14. Turtle, "Scholarly Communication."
15. Kipnis, "Profiles"; Yukl, "Influence Tactics".
16. Enns, "When Executives Successfully Influence," 257-278; Simmons-Welburn, "Perceptions of Campus Level Advocacy."
17. Kipnis, "Profile of Organizational Influence Strategies".
18. Yukl, "Influence Tactics," 132-140.
19. Antonakis, "The Nature of Leadership", 4-5.
20. Stogdill, "Handbook of Leadership", 7.
21. Antonakis, "The Nature of Leadership," 5.
22. Kelley, "In Praise of Followers", 195.
23. Antonakis, "The Nature of Leadership," 9.
24. Deluga, "Relationship of Transformational and Transactional Leadership," 457.
25. Bass, "The Future of Leadership," 18-40.
26. Barbuto, "Full Range Leadership."
27. Greenleaf, "The Servant as Leader," 4.
28. http://www.amca.com/sl/index.html

29. Barbuto, "Scale Development," 304.
30. Greenleaf, "The Servant Leader."
31. Barbuto, "Scale Development", 303.
32. Danserau, "Vertical Dyad Linkage Approach."
33. Barbuto, "Scale Development."
34. Graham, "Servant leadership in organizations", 105-119.
35. Smith, "Transformational and Servant Leadership."
36. Smith, "Transformational and Servant Leadership."
37. Conger, "Toward a Behavior Theory"; House, "A Path Goal Theory of Leader Effectiveness"; Gardner, " The Charismatic Relationships"; Smith, "Transformational and Servant Leadership"; Barbuto, "Scale Development."
38. Barbuto, "Scale Development."
39. Smith, "Transformational and Servant Leadership"; Barbuto, Scale Development."
40. Barbuto, "Scale Development"; Conger, "Charismatic Leadership."
41. Graham, "Servant Leadership in Organizations."
42. Barbuto, "Scale Development"; Smith, "Transformational and Servant Leadership."

Works Cited

ACRL Scholarly Communications Committee. Establishing a research agenda for scholarly communication: a call for community engagement. 2007.

Alire, C. A. (2005) Advocating to advance academic libraries: the 2005–06 ACRL President's focus, *C&RL News*, 66(8), 590–591.

Antonakis, J., Cianciolo, A.T., and Sternberg, R. J. 2004. *The Nature of Leadership*. Thousand Oaks, CA: Sage Publications Inc.

Barbuto, J.E. (1997). Taking the charisma out of transformational leadership. *Journal of Social Behavior and Personality*, 12(3), 689–697.

Barbuto, J. E. and Brown, L. L. Full Range Leadership. University of Nebraska-Lincoln NebGuide. Accessed from http://ianrpubs.unl.edu/consumered/g1406.htm

Barbuto, Jr., J. E., Fritz, S. M., and Marx, D. (2002) A Field examination of two measures of work motivation as predictors of leaders' influence tactics. *Journal of Social Psychology*, 142(5), 601–616.

Barbuto, J.E. and Wheeler, D. W. (2006). Scale development and construct clarification of servant leadership. *Group and Organizational Management*, Vol. 31, No. 3, 300–326.

Bass, B.M (1985). Performance beyond expectations. New York: Free Press.

Bass, B. M. (2000). The future of leadership in learning organizations. *The Journal of Leadership Studies*, 7, 18–40.

Conger, J.A. and Kanungo, R.N. (1987). Toward a behavior theory of charismatic leadership in organizational settings. *Academy of Management Review*, 12, 637–647.

Conger, J.A. and Kanungo, R.N. (1998). Charismatic Leadership. San Francisco: Jossey-Bass.

Danserau, F., Graen, G. and Haga, W.J. (1975). Vertical dyad linkage approach to leadership within formal organizations: A longitudinal investigation of the role making process. *Organizational Behavior and Human Performance*, 13, p. 46–78.

Deluga, R. J. (1988). Relationship of transformational and transactional leadership with employee influencing strategies. *Group and Organization Studies.* 13, 4. P456–467.

English, R. Scholarly communication and the academy: The importance of the ACRL initiative. portal: *Libraries and the Academy,* 3, 2, pp.337–340.

Enns, H.G. and McFarlin, D.B. (2005) When executives successfully influence peers: the Role of target assessment, preparation, and tactics. *Human Resource Management,* 44(3), 257–278.

Faculty Attitudes and Behaviors regarding scholarly communication: Survey of findings from the University of California. University of California, Office of Scholarly Communication. (July 2007).

Gardner, W. L. and Avolio, B. J. (1998). The Charismatic Relationship: A Dramaturgical Perspective. *The Academy of Management Review* 23:11, 32–58.

Graham, J. W. (1991). Servant leadership in organizations: Inspirational and moral. *Leadership Quarterly,* 2(2), 105–119.

Greenleaf, R.K. (1970). The servant as leader. Indianapolis: The Greenleaf Center.

Hahn, K. Talk About Talking About New Models of Scholarly Communication. *Journal of Electronic Publishing,* Vol. 11, No. 1. (Winter 2008) http://hdl.handle.net/2027/spo.3336451.0011.108

House R. J. (1971). A path goal theory of leader effectiveness. *Administrative Science Quarterly,* 16, 321–328.

Kelley, R. E. (1995). In praise of followers. In The Leader's Companion: Insights on leadership through the ages. J. Thomas Wren, editor. New York: The Free Press.

King, J. and Harley, D. Assessing the future landscape of scholarly communication: an in-depth study of faculty needs and ways of meeting them: Summary of proposal to A. W. Mellon Foundation, September 7, 2006. Accessed fromhttp://cshe.berkeley.edu/research/scholarlycommunication.edu

Kipnis, D. and Schmidt, S.M. (1982). Profile of organizational influence strategies. San Diego: University Associates.

Lewis, D. Library Budgets, Open Access, and the Future of Scholarly Communication: Transformations in Academic Publishing. *C&RL News.* May 2008. 271–273.

Linke, E. C. (2008) The purposeful advocate: The 2008–09 ACRL President's focus. Speaking out, speaking up column. *C&RL News.* September p. 464–465.

Ogburn, J. L. 2003. SPARC Forum—Scholarly communication advocacy on campus. ALA Annual meeting. Toronto.

Price, T. L. (2003). The ethics of authentic transformational leadership. *Leadership Quarterly,* 14, 67–81.

Simmons-Welburn, J., McNeil, B., and Welburn, W. (2007). Perceptions of Campus-Level Advocacy and Influence Strategies among Senior Administrators in College and University Libraries. *Proceedings of the 13th ACRL National Conference.*

Smith, B.N., Montagno, R.V., and Kuzmendo, T.N. (2004). Transformational and servant leadership: Content and contextual comparisons. *Journal of Leadership and Organizational Studies,* 10, 80–91.

Spears, L.C. (1995). Servant-Leadership and The Greenleaf Legacy. In Reflections on Leadership. New York: John Wiley and Sons. P. 1–14.

Stemper, J. and Williams, K. 2006. Scholarly Communication: Turning Crisis into Opportunity. *C&RL News* 67 (11): 692–696.

Todaro, J. (2006). The Power of Personal Persuasion: Advancing the Academic Library Agenda from the Front Lines. Chicago: Association of College and

Research Libraries

Todaro, J. (2006). The Power of persuasion: Grassroots advocacy in the academic library. *C&RL News*, 67(4), 228–229.

Turtle, E. C. and Courtois, M.P. 2007. Scholarly Communication: Science Librarians as Advocates for Change. Issues in Science and Technology Librarianship. Summer 2007, http://www.istl.org/07-summer/article2.html

Yukl, G. and Falbe, C.M. (1990). Influence tactics and objectives in upward, downward, and lateral influence attempts. *Journal of Applied Psychology*, 75, 2, 132–140.

The NIH Public Access Policy: Advocating for Open Access to Federally Funded Research

Heather Joseph and Ray English

Introduction

The National Institutes of Health (NIH) has become the first United States federal agency that is legally required to make the results of its funded research openly accessible to the public. A provision in the Consolidated Appropriations Act of 2008 directs the NIH to require that its funded investigators submit their final peer-reviewed manuscripts to PubMed Central, the National Library of Medicine's online archive of biomedical literature. Manuscripts must be deposited upon acceptance in a peer-reviewed journal and made publicly available online within twelve months of publication.

The passage of this law came after several years of intense advocacy efforts on the part of the American library community and a broad coalition of allied organizations. This paper summarizes those advocacy efforts and the major developments that led to the law's enactment in the context of the broader national and international move toward public access to government-funded research.

Open Access: Background

The continued escalation of journal subscription prices in recent decades has placed increasing pressure on academic and research libraries to examine new ways of providing access to the resources and information their patrons need in order to conduct scholarly research. In the mid- to late-1990s, libraries began experimenting with a variety of new approaches designed to foster positive change, including alternative publishing models, the creation of new journals to compete with expensive commercial titles, encouraging editorial boards to examine journal business practices, new licensing arrangements, and consortial purchasing of electronic journals. Many of these experiments were spearheaded by the Scholarly Publishing and Academic Resources Coalition (SPARC), which formed in 1997.[1]

While some of those early efforts provided some measure of relief, they had only limited potential for creating transformative change in the system of scholarly communication.

The concept of "Open Access"—defined as the free, immediate, online availability of peer-reviewed journal literature, with few restrictions on subsequent use—emerged in early 2002 with the Budapest Open Access Initiative.[2] Open Access is characterized by two broad, complementary strategies: open-access journals and author self-archiving (or open archiving) of scholarly articles. The Open Access movement has gained traction as the most promising avenue to bring down barriers to the wide distribution of research results, and to introduce a measure of cost control into the scholarly publishing marketplace.

International Context

Advocacy for public access to federally funded research in the U.S. has taken place within a much broader worldwide context. Private and public funding agencies around the world have shown strong interest in Open Access, particularly in open archiving, as a means of ensuring access to their funded research. Funding agency discussions have focused on the expectation that their investment in research will result in improvements to the public good. They have increasingly recognized that wide dissemination of the results of an experiment is an essential component of the research process. Since this process is cumulative, advancing through shared results and successive experimentation, agencies have come to understand that the value of their investment in research can only be maximized through greater access to and use of research findings.

At the same time, public and private funding agencies have also recognized that the results of the research they fund have not been widely available to potential users, whether researcher or the general public . Results are published as articles in costly scientific journals with prices that make them inaccessible for many libraries. Members of the public can gain access to that research only with the investment of considerable effort and personal expense.

The lack of access to scientific research information became even more apparent as new information technologies developed. The Internet provided new opportunities to distribute information to worldwide audiences at marginal cost, allowing researchers to use previous findings in new and innovative ways. The lack of access through the journal subscription model and the potential of Open Access through the Internet meant that the status quo became simply unacceptable to many research funders.

Such considerations led funding agencies worldwide to consider a new policy framework designed to allow research results to be more easily accessed and used. Important early developments in that regard were the October 2003 decision of The Wellcome Trust (Britain's largest private biomedical funder) to endorse Open Access, and the United Kingdom House of Commons' inquiry into scientific publishing, which recommended in July 2004 that research funded by the United Kingdom Research Councils be made publicly accessible. Several funding agencies worldwide, both public and private, have since adopted policies that require, or strongly encourage, access to their funded research, and many others are considering similar measures. Agencies that have adopted requirements include the Wellcome Trust (2005); six of the seven of the United Kingdom Research Councils (2005–2007), the European Research Council (2007), the Australian Research Council (2006), the Canadian Institutes of Health Research (2007), and the Howard Hughes Medical Institute (2007).[3]

Early Developments at NIH

In 1999 the Director of the National Institutes of Health, Dr. Harold Varmus, introduced the idea of making all of the NIH-funded research outputs publicly accessible. His proposal, "E-Biomed," called for an NIH-wide policy that would have required all manuscripts resulting from research funded by the agency to be deposited into an electronic repository, where they would then be made freely available for anyone to access. Dr. Varmus' idea was quite novel and it generated significant discussion. While no policy was implemented at the time, the NIH did establish a robust digital repository called PubMed Central, which began posting articles submitted to it voluntarily by a number of journals in the biomedical disciplines. As PubMed Central became an established, trusted repository for journal articles, the NIH began talking with stakeholders about new opportunities for sharing results more broadly.

These efforts caught the attention of Congressman Ernest Ishtook (R-OK), who in 2003 included language in the report accompanying the FY04 Labor, Health and Human Services (LHHS) Appropriations Bill. His report language expressed concerns about the lack of access to research data and the corresponding sharp increases in journal subscription prices. The language encouraged the National Library of Medicine "to examine how the consolidation of for-profit biomedical research publishers, with their increased subscription charges, has restricted access to vital research information to not-for-profit libraries."[4] The library community took the inclusion of this language in a key legislative instrument as a cue to begin a coordinated campaign to raise as a public policy concern the issue of limited access to research that is publicly funded.

Library Community Creates Mechanisms to Respond to New Opportunity

As these developments progressed the American library community, led by SPARC, worked to organize a new, collaborative mechanism to respond to opportunities presented by these emerging trends. The Open Access Working Group (OAWG) was created in 2003 with a mission to build broad-based recognition that the economic and societal benefits of scientific and scholarly research investments could be maximized through Open Access to the results of the research. The OAWG reflected the growing recognition that the library community should undertake collaborative action where its collective voice could achieve greater persuasive force than the individual voice of any single member. Original membership in the OAWG included the seven major U.S. library organizations.[5] Additional members joined over time, including the Open Society Institute, Public Library of Science, and Science Commons.

The initial strategy developed by OAWG centered on building recognition of the benefits of Open Access among various stakeholder groups, including the general public, advocacy groups, scholars, scientists, physicians, lawyers, research funders, and federal policy makers. Through the use of this strategy, the OAWG was able to leverage its member organizations' resources to seek crucial professional guidance in helping to develop a comprehensive strategy to build momentum surrounding Open Access and "public access." The group consulted a professional firm for specific advice on creating a strategy to approach key policy makers, and consulted another professional firm to help build and sharpen its communications efforts.

As the OAWG worked to raise awareness of the issues and opportunities inherent in expanding access to research results, and as Congressional interest in a NIH Public Access Policy grew, it became clear that other stakeholders outside the library's traditional community partners shared a desire for expanded access to research results—particularly those funded by public dollars. In August 2004, SPARC and the OAWG convened the Alliance for Taxpayer Access (ATA), a larger umbrella group dedicated to educating policy makers on the benefits of Open Access. In addition to library organizations and individual libraries, ATA members include patient advocacy groups, universities and colleges, publishers sympathetic to public access, public interest groups, and health advocacy organizations. These members were organized around four strongly held general principles:

1. Taxpayers are entitled to open access on the Internet to the peer-reviewed scientific articles on research funded by the U.S. Government.

2. Widespread access to the information contained in these articles is an essential, inseparable component of our nation's investment in science.

3. This information should be shared in cost-effective ways that take advantage of the Internet, stimulate further discovery and innovation, and advance the translation of this knowledge into public benefits.

4. Enhanced access to and expanded sharing of information will lead to usage by millions of scientists, professionals, and individuals, and will deliver an accelerated return on the taxpayers' investment.[6]

The Alliance worked to advance these principles through a very active advocacy, education and communication program specifically in support of government-wide public access and other policies that support the sharing of science made possible by the Internet and taxpayer investment.

The First (Voluntary) NIH Public Access Policy

In 2004 much of the library community's advocacy work centered around efforts to support NIH adoption of a strong public access policy. In July of that year, the House Appropriations Committee passed the FY05 Labor, Health, and Human Services Appropriations Bill, which included report language explicitly calling for NIH to implement a public access policy requiring researchers to submit an electronic copy of their final, peer-reviewed manuscript to PubMed Central to be released six months after the article's publication.

The Congressional language prompted NIH to move forward with a process of drafting a policy that would ensure greater access to the results of the research it funded. Under the draft policy, which was announced in September 2004, NIH would have requested all recipients of NIH-funding to deposit final, peer-reviewed manuscripts of articles resulting from their research into PubMed Central, to be made freely and publicly available no later than six months after publication in a journal. The NIH draft was weaker than the House bill language in that it was not a requirement, but it did retain the six-month embargo period.

Once the policy was proposed, the agency held an extensive public consultation process, which included three large stakeholder meetings attended by publishers, librarians, researchers, and members of the general public. The consultation process also included publication of the proposed policy in Federal Register and a further solicitation of public comments. This process was notable, as more than 6,000 comments were received, compiled and made public by the NIH. The vast majority of the comments were highly favorable to the proposed policy.

During this process, the library community submitted comments to NIH strongly supporting a mandatory, six-month policy. Comments were submitted by individuals, institutions, membership organizations, and larger coalitions like the ATA. Additionally, OAWG and ATA members undertook an active communications campaign, calling on NIH Director Zerhouni both in writing and in face-to-face meetings to adopt the public access policy.

The library community also worked to educate members of Congress as to the importance of enacting a strong NIH public access policy. The community leveraged many channels, such as Congressional visits and letter-writing campaigns, to promote the importance of supporting this groundbreaking new policy within Congress. It was crucial for the community to identify and support Congressional champions of the policy who were emerging.

The appropriations bill moved through Congress and was eventually signed into law in December 2004, with compromise report language endorsing the draft NIH plan. While the full House of Representatives had adopted the stronger recommendation of the House Appropriations Committee to require deposit with a six month embargo, the Senate version of the bill was silent on the issue. Because of that, the House-Senate conference committee adopted the compromise language reflecting the NIH draft policy.

In addition to its intense advocacy with Congress, the library-led advocacy campaign also involved a strong external media effort, taking care to inform a range of media contacts in the popular and trade presses. Dateline NBC was one venue that highlighted public access and the benefits for patient care. It was also critical that academic and library communities be kept up to date on progress and opportunities surrounding the policy. Coalition members engaged in an active schedule of public presentations to ensure that this was accomplished.

Despite the positive public comments and strong support from Congress, the NIH appeared to bow to well-funded special interest publishers in crafting and issuing its final policy. Unveiled in February 2005, the final policy was considerably weaker than the House report language in two major areas:

1. It "requested and strongly encouraged" rather than requiring taxpayer-funded authors to post their articles.
2. It extended the embargo period from six months to one year.

This voluntary policy was implemented by NIH on May 1, 2005. Subsequent compliance with the policy by NIH-funded researchers proved to be exceedingly low.

Supporters of public access in the library community and supporting coalitions were understandably disappointed by the weakened policy. Members of Congress were also concerned about these changes. Both the House and Senate subsequently included strong report language demanding accountability from NIH in their respective versions of the FY 06 LHHS appropriations legislation. They requested that formal reports from NIH evaluating participation levels and the average embargo period chosen by funding recipients be delivered to Congress in short order.

Congressional Interest in Public Access Expands

While the drama of the NIH Public Access Policy continued to unfold, the library community stepped up its efforts to promote the broader principle of public access to federally funded research. In one six month period, two additional pieces of legislation were introduced in the U.S. Congress calling for expanded access to the results of publicly funded research.

In December of 2005, the "American Center for CURES Act" (The CURES Bill) was introduced in the U.S. Senate. While the bill's focus was on creating a new research complex dedicated to speeding the evolution of basic research into treatments and cures, a crucial component of the bill was language requiring that recipients of funding from all Health and Human Services agencies make the results of their HHS-funded, published research publicly available within six months of publication in peer-reviewed journals.

Shortly thereafter, on May 2, 2006, with active support from the library community, the "Federal Research Public Access Act" (FRPAA) was introduced into the U.S. Senate. The bill, sponsored by Sen. John Cornyn (R-TX), was purposely introduced on the first anniversary of the disappointing voluntary NIH Public Access Policy. This sweeping proposed bill called for six-month, mandatory public access to articles resulting from the research funded by eleven federal agencies with annual extramural research budgets of $100 million or more.

The public access provisions in both the CURES Bill and FRPAA had the full endorsement the library community. These two highly visible pieces of legislation, combined with the simmering NIH policy, combined to create an important window of opportunity for the library-led coalition to step up its advocacy and education efforts. The resulting campaigns on campuses, which called on constituents to contact their members of Congress in support of these pieces of legislation, significantly raised the level of awareness and interest in the issue of public access in new and important arenas.

A growing number of university provosts, understanding the profound potential benefits of unlocking the public's investment in scientific research for higher education institutions, galvanized behind FRPAA. As one group of provosts eloquently noted in an open letter to the higher education community in 2006:

> "The broad dissemination of the results of scholarly inquiry and discourse is essential for higher educa-tion to fulfill its long-standing commitment to the advancement and conveyance of knowledge. Indeed, it is mission critical."[7]

This group was joined in short order not only by additional university provosts, but also by a number of university and college presidents who publicly voiced their support.[8] Support from these critical strata of the academy provided important new momentum for library community's efforts.

The proposed policies also served as a catalyst to engage students. On some campuses (such as the University of Florida), student leaders not only publicized the proposed public access policies, but they engineered and passed student senate resolutions in support of the movement. Ultimately a number of student organizations signed on for membership in the ATA and forged strong working relationships with the library community around these advocacy efforts.

In order to determine the extent of general support for public access to federally funded research and build further political support for the principle, the library coalition also worked with professional advisers who had contacts with polling organizations, and encouraged them to conduct a public poll on the issue. On May 31, 2006 *The Wall Street Journal* published Harris poll data indicating that an overwhelming majority—82%—of Americans support public access.[9] The poll results added exciting new momentum to the library community's advocacy efforts.

One significant, unexpected effect of the community's advocacy was the explosion of interest and coverage of public access to federally funded research in both the mainstream and trade media—and in the blogosphere. Some of the most extensive coverage and in-depth discussion and debate of the merits of these policies began to take place on a variety of blogs, bringing the issue to an entirely new constituency in a new and far-reaching manner. As the library community and the ATA waged a sustained campaign of education and support for FRPAA in Senate, strong collaborative alliances were established with these new and critical groups.

Momentum behind the push for public access continued to roll as consideration of the NIH policy resumed in Congress. For the first time, in 2006, the House Appropriations Committee moved the NIH public access language from the report accompanying the LHHS appropriations bill into the actual text of the bill itself—a significant move that signaled increased interest in the policy.

Congress' heightened concern was well-placed. As indicated in testimony by NIH Director Elias Zerhouni before both the U.S. House and Senate over the course of 2006, less than 5% of eligible NIH investigators were complying with the voluntary policy. Misgivings from Congress and the library community over the viability of a voluntary policy were given substance.

As a result, the full House of Representatives passed the appropriations bill with language indicating the NIH should strengthen the policy by making it mandatory for researchers to participate. The OAWG and ATA waged a strong campaign of education and advocacy in Congress support of the House bill language. Ultimately, however, the appropriations bill was not passed in 2006. Mid-term elections saw control of Congress change hands and the appropriations process was abandoned to a stalemate in favor of a continuing resolution.

Communications Challenges—from Pit Bull to PRISM

The library community soon faced another major challenge in its advocacy efforts. While public access had strong support from many stakeholders and the general public, one very vocal group actively and aggressively opposed the idea. From the time the NIH announced its proposed policy, a subset of the publishing community led mainly by commercial players staged their own efforts to influence the debate over public access. These publishers waged an extensive, vocal, and very expensive campaign to discredit the notion of public access and derail the progress of the proposed policies.

As in any advocacy effort, a significant portion of the proponents' time and resources must be devoted to understanding the nature and scope of the opposing groups' objections, and providing reasoned, measured, and data-driven responses to the concerns raised. Responses to the ever-changing range of objections introduced by opponents of public access took on an entirely different timbre in January of 2007 when it became widely reported (first in *Nature*,[10] and subsequently in the *Washington Post*[11] and other media outlets) that the Association of American Publishers had retained a public relations firm notorious for its aggressive tactics to stage a campaign against public access. Elements of the tactics recommended by Dezenhall Associates, the so-called "Pit Bull of PR," were made public when memos outlining proposed strategy were leaked to the media.

Dezenhall recommended a campaign to confuse the issue and keep public access advocates on the defensive. Conceding that "the message of public access is almost bullet-proof," he suggested aggressive slogans (rather than evidence or argument) designed to combat the issue and delay consideration. Elements of the campaign included "imagine a world without peer review," "public access equals government censorship," and other similar threads.

The revelation of this strategy was met with a large negative outcry from almost all quarters of the academy as well as from many segments of the publishing industry. It also received extensive coverage in the press and especially in the blogosphere.[12] While the full impact of this strategy was largely diffused by its exposure to the public, the opponents of public access appeared to adhere to it nonetheless.

Just a few months after this engagement was revealed, the Association of American Publishers unveiled a Web site called "PRISM" (the Partnership for Research Integrity in Science and Medicine). Text on the site initially noted that its explicit charge was to educate policymakers on dangers of public access policies. Strikingly, the text of the Web site closely mirrored the arguments suggested in the leaked "Pit Bull" memos.

While it required a great deal of time and resources for the library community to effectively respond to the initial "Pit Bull" story, by the time PRISM was introduced, the academic community and most policy makers were aware of the issues being raised by some publishers. The extremely negative outcry, once again, from almost all quarters was extremely helpful in reducing the time and resources that the library community and its allies had to invest in responding to the charges made by the Pit Bull and PRISM campaigns.

A Watershed Year: 2007

2007 proved to be a breakthrough year, despite the aggressive counter-efforts of public access opponents. Language calling for the NIH policy to be made mandatory was included for the first time in the text of the Appropriations Bill passed by both houses of Congress. The revised policy recommendation faced many challenges in the course of the Congressional legislative cycle; it was debated in appropriations subcommittee and full committee hearings in both the House and the Senate, and faced the possibility of amendment or exclusion in both chambers during debate and voting on final bills.

Throughout this six-stage, year-long process, the library community's main advocacy challenge was to keep high-level attention focused on the opportunities presented by this new policy and to underscore the extremely broad base of support for it. It was also necessary for the coalition to remain constantly aware of the activities and communications of opponents of the policy, in order to craft and deploy targeted, timely educational campaigns to dispel misconceptions and misleading claims.

In addition to the earlier message derived from the Pit Bull campaign, opponents of the policy raised new issues that had not been part of the previous three years of debate. Most of these new concerns centered on how the policy might or might not impact copyright and intellectual property rights enforcement mechanisms. The well-funded opposition was (and remains) relentless in raising objections to public access in virtually every conceivable venue of the federal government. The coalition worked to meet these challenges by stepping up communication and education efforts within Congress, with other interested outside agencies, and with several departments in the Executive Branch.

Current Status and Future Plans

The new, mandatory NIH Public Access Policy was signed into law on December 26, 2007 by President Bush as part of the Consolidated Appropriations Act of 2008. There was little time to celebrate the occasion however, as within two weeks opponents of the policy announced their intention to delay the policy by demanding that NIH undergo another lengthy, formal rule-making procedure. The advocacy coalition strongly opposed such a move, given the extensive original comment period and the nearly three years during which the voluntary policy had been in place. Once again, the coalition found itself deeply engaged in outreach and education to key policy makers, as it worked to convey these messages.

Regardless of these ongoing attempts to stall the policy, on January 11, 2008 NIH made public a set of implementation guidelines and announced its intention to set April 7, 2008 as the first date for compliance with the policy. With this announcement the coalition's advocacy work took on another dimension altogether—raising awareness of the implementation guidelines and helping the academic community effectively prepare to facilitate implementation.

This new phase underscored the critical nature of the library community's expanding partnerships with other campus constituencies. In considering the four steps needed for NIH grantees to comply with the policy—ensuring they had the rights necessary to comply, physically depositing and approving their manuscripts, setting the embargo period, and properly citing their works—it became clear that libraries had new opportunities to leverage campus collaborations with NIH-funded researchers, research administrators, and legal counsels.

The coalition worked quickly to provide a new layer of educational and support activities on the local, institutional level as well as continuing the robust outreach campaign to policymakers at all levels. Several meetings were held within weeks of the publication of the NIH implementation guidelines and strategies for designing "best practices" to facilitate campus compliance began to emerge. The coalition supported these emerging efforts with an active schedule of campus visits and Web casts. It also published a white paper specifically outlining a series of strategies for ensuring compliance with both the policy and copyright law.

While these efforts to support implementation of the NIH Public Access Policy proved quite successful, it remains apparent that the publishing lobby will continue to vigorously oppose such policies, and to support legislative efforts to overturn or supplant them. For example, in September of 2008, Representative John Conyers, Chairman of the House Judiciary Committee, introduced the "Fair Copyright in Research Works Act (FCRWA)," a bill that would alter U.S. copyright law in a manner that would prohibit federal agencies from requiring their funded researchers to make articles resulting from their research publicly accessible. This bill would have the effect of overturning the mandatory NIH Public Access Policy and it would make similar policies by other federal agencies impossible to enact.

The introduction of the FCRWA bill made it necessary for the advocacy coalition to develop and deploy an additional Congressional strategy focused on opposition to a specific bill. Grass roots advocacy from librarians, students, and patient advocacy groups combined with grass tops advocacy from prominent individuals in key Congressional districts as well as in Washington helped to keep the bill from gaining initial traction. The coalition was also successful in securing a witness slot to provide testimony in opposition to the bill at a key House Judiciary Committee hearing, which further slowed its momentum. While the bill was reintroduced early in 2009 in the 111th Congress, it appears at this time to have little chance of advancing due to strong continued grass roots opposition.

In June of 2009, Senators Lieberman and Cornyn reintroduced the Federal Research Public Access Act (FRPAA). Citing the successful implementation of the NIH Public Access Policy, the sponsors of FRPAA indicated that the time was ripe for all other federal science agencies to follow suit. Combined with the strong emphasis that the Obama administration has placed on openness and transparency for all activities of the federal government, the reintroduction of this bill provides a new opportunity to build on the success of the NIH policy and extend public access to federally funded research across all major research-funding agencies.

Lessons Learned

The creation and deployment of an advocacy effort on this scale required the development of new collaborative structures and creative leveraging of resources among a broad pool of contributing organizations. Several key lessons were learned that may help provide guidance as future programs are considered and deployed. They include:

- The importance of first building a solid commitment from the library community to play a leading role in advocating for the issue. Without the initial resolve of the original OAWG members, the advocacy campaign would not have had sufficient traction or resources to get off the ground.

- It is crucial to establish active, agile, broad-ranging coalition(s) to support national advocacy efforts. A shared commitment to the goals of the advocacy effort by multiple stakeholder groups is keenly important. This helps in establishing a grassroots advocacy network with a reach that one community alone could simply not produce and it also makes a higher-level advocacy network possible.

- The creation of a succinct, targeted message is at the heart of ensuring a successful campaign. The use of professional counsel is essential in helping to establish a clear message and to identify potentially receptive audiences.

- The coalition needed to be prepared to communicate its message widely and regularly, and to be completely consistent in message and strategy. It was particularly difficult, but absolutely necessary to keep to the course and not get sidetracked into responding or playing defense when negative messaging surfaced.

- The identification and support of allies and champions within key organizations—agencies, Congress, and other highly visible entities—plays a critical role in ensuring the advocacy programs effectiveness.

- In this particular campaign, it was important for the coalition to have access to legal expertise. As much discussion centered on authors rights, copyright law, and other legal issues, the support of knowledgeable attorneys is a key component.

- Finally, be prepared to go to the wall for such an effort. Building and maintaining support for an issue that meets with well-funded and well-organized opposition is nothing short of a 24/7 proposition.

Notes

1. SPARC has grown into an international alliance of academic and research libraries. For a description of the organization, see: http://www.arl.org/sparc/about/index.shtml
2. See: http://www.soros.org/openaccess/
3. For a complete and current list of funding agency and other institutional open access mandates, see: ROARMAP (Registry of Open Access Repository Material Archiving Policies): http://www.eprints.org/openaccess/policysignup/
4. House Report 108–188, Departments of Labor, Health and Human Services, and Education, and Related Agencies Appropriation Bill, 2004: http://www.congress.gov/cgi-bin/cpquery/?&dbname=cp108&&r_n=hr188.108&sel=TOC_288266&
5. Initial OAWG members were the American Association of Law Libraries, American Library Association, Association of Academic Health Science Libraries, Association of College and Research Libraries, Association of Research Libraries, Medical Library Association, Special Libraries Association, and SPARC.
6. Alliance for Taxpayer Access website: http://www.taxpayeraccess.org/
7. Open Letter to the Higher Education Community, July 28, 2006: http://www.taxpayeraccess.org/frpaa/Provosts_openletter_06-JUL.pdf.
8. See, for example, the letter signed by 56 presidents of colleges in the Oberlin Group: http://www.oberlingroup.org
9. Americans support free access to research, May 31, 2006: http://www.taxpayeraccess.org/media/Release06-0531.html
10. PR's 'pit bull' takes on open access, Nature, January 25, 2007: http://www.nature.com/nature/journal/v445/n7126/full/445347a.html
11. Publishing Group Hires 'Pit Bull of PR'—Association Turns to Dezenhall to Fight Patient Advocacy Groups, The Washington Post, January 26, 2007: http://www.washingtonpost.com/wp-dyn/content/article/2007/01/25/AR2007012501705.html?nav=emailpage
12. See http://www.taxpayeraccess.org/media/blogs.html for some blogger comments.

Works Cited

SPARC: The Scholarly Publishing and Academic Resources Coalition. What is SPARC? http://www.arl.org/sparc/about/index.shtml (last accessed July 21, 2009).

Budapest Open Access Initiative. http://www.soros.org/openaccess/ (last accessed July 21, 2009)

ROARMAP (Registry of Open Access Repository Material Archiving Policies). Open Access and Institutional Repositories with EPrints. http://www.eprints.org/openaccess/policysignup/ (last accessed July 21, 2009)

U.S. Congress. House of Representatives. Committee Reports for the 108th Congress. Partial Report. House Report 108–188, Departments of Labor, Health and Human Services, and Education, and Related Agencies Appropriation Bill, 2004. http://www.congress.gov/cgi-bin/cpquery/?&dbname=cp108&&r_n=hr188.108&sel=TOC_288266& (last accessed July 21, 2009)

Alliance for Taxpayer Access. http://www.taxpayeraccess.org/ (last accessed July 21, 2009)

Alliance for Taxpayer Access. Open Letter to the Higher Education Community, July

28, 2006: http://www.taxpayeraccess.org/frpaa/Provosts_openletter_06-JUL.pdf. (last accessed July 21, 2009)

Alliance for Taxpayer Access. Americans support free access to research, May 31, 2006: http://www.taxpayeraccess.org/media/Release06-0531.html (last accessed July 21, 2009)

The Oberlin Group. Open letter on the FRPAA. http://www.oberlingroup.org (last accessed July 21, 2009)

Giles, Jim. "PR's 'pit bull' takes on open access." *Nature* 445, no. 347 (January 25, 2007) http://www.nature.com/nature/journal/v445/n7126/full/445347a.html (last accessed July 21, 2009)

Weiss, Rick. "Publishing Group Hires 'Pit Bull of PR'—Association Turns to Dezenhall to Fight Patient Advocacy Groups." *The Washington Post*, January 26, 2007. http://www.washingtonpost.com/wp-dyn/content/article/2007/01/25/AR2007012501705.html?nav=emailpage (last accessed July 21, 2009

http://www.taxpayeraccess.org/media/blogs.html (last accessed July 21, 2009)

II. Advocacy and the Campus Milieu

Frontline Academic Library Advocacy: Whose Job Is It Anyway?

5

Camila Alire

Introduction: Frontline Advocacy and the Academic Library

How *frontline* are advocacy efforts within our library profession and particularly in academic libraries? Library advocacy as we know it today usually involved academic library administrators, campus faculty and students. Why shouldn't we enlist another level of advocates within our libraries' organizational charts? In library advocacy, it makes sense that the more trained voices we have to advocate for the value of libraries and library personnel, the better. For the author, academic libraries can't have enough advocates; and it should be everyone's job to do it.

This chapter encompasses definitions of advocacy and frontline advocacy. It ties educational concepts and social work topology to frontline advocacy efforts as well as explains why frontline librarians and other library workers would excel as library advocates. It also addresses the need for training of frontline academic librarians and other library workers.

Advocacy, in general, has different connotations. The best place to start is to define what academic advocacy really is. William Harris and Aubrey Taggard provided a more comprehensive, non-library related definition of academic advocacy which refers more to enlisting campus faculty in legislative action. However, they concentrate on the concept of *grassroots* advocacy. They stated that advocacy includes the concept of citizen-initiated (grassroots) action to improve the quality of life in their environment; and they defined advocates as people who should promote the interests of their client group. They supported grassroots advocacy stating that university administrators must also empower their faculty to be advocates.[1] Although this type of advocacy is legitimate in an academic environment, it is not quite what the author intends when promoting academic library frontline advocacy.

The best way to differentiate between advocacy and frontline advocacy would be to describe advocacy as the role of paid lobbyists and university administrators, and frontline advocacy as the role of university employees—faculty and staff. These are people who work daily on the frontlines in the university. At the academic level, colleges and universities usually enlist paid lobbyists (government relations staff or individuals on contract) to assist their administrators in advocating for their issues, particularly with legislators at the state and federal levels. Frontline advocacy is the next level down where academic faculty and university staff also participate in advocacy for the university.

Within academic libraries, the usual advocates are the academic library administrators who advocate internally (campus level) and externally (state and federal levels). However, real frontline library advocacy should include academic librarians and other library staff. Their more-developed relationship with campus faculty and students has the potential to make both groups (librarians/staff and library administrators) more effective advocates in an academic setting. When both library groups work on library advocacy, it enhances the academic library's chances for receiving its fair share of the campus' resources and helps to maintain their credibility throughout the academy and beyond. The library employees are the frontline advocates, and the students and faculty become the grassroots advocates for the academic library.

The concept of establishing strong relationship with campus faculty is supported by the American Counseling Association which stated that counselors should build a rapport with their faculty. This relationship enhances their effectiveness in advocacy because it gives them access for presenting their case and allows them to enlist faculty as grassroots advocates for counseling services.[2] This same model would be very effective for the academic library on most college and university campuses.

Who better to advocate for the academic library than those people working in the library who have an already established relationship with faculty and students on campus? Library administrators cannot even begin to have the kind of rapport that their librarians and staff have with faculty on campus. Rank and file, front line librarians have established relationships with campus faculty because they work with faculty through providing reference and other information services and through coordinating information literacy efforts for the faculty. Many librarians also work alongside campus faculty on university governance as members of the campus governing body.

Another reason for involving frontline librarians in academic library advocacy relates to Sandra Kaplan's scaffolding principle of learning. This principle maintains that learning increases when students take new learning and connect it to previously acquired knowledge making the learning experience more relevant and stronger. She held that advocacy is stronger when teachers, as advocates, can build their advocacy message from their background knowledge base.[3]

"Action...is best implemented by individuals who have a frame of reference on which to build advocacy."[4] In the case of academic librarians as frontline advocates, their frame of reference is more relative to building a stronger case for academic library advocacy. They can share real-life, library service experience that most library administrators cannot. They have almost daily exposure to teaching/research faculty and students that library administrators do not.

Kaplan also took to two other educational concepts—metacognition and transfer—and applied them to advocacy. Metacognition encompasses the importance of assisting students in the development of insight into their own learning. Applying that concept to academic library frontline advocacy means that librarians need to reflect on their own behavior as they advocate for the academic library so that they are respected and successful when advocating among faculty and students on campus.

Kaplan's transfer concept, where one applies learning by explaining the conditions where learning can be used, is very applicable to frontline library advocacy. The advocate should be able to "make the information clear and provocative enough so it inspires the user to transfer it to other situations." In the case of academic librarians as frontline advocates, they can demonstrate the many ways in which information shared during the process of advocacy can be transferred. By doing this, they are more effective in involving teaching/research faculty and students in the frontline library advocacy process on campus.[5]

In the field of social work, Michael So sin and Susan Coolum wrote about the topology of advocacy in the academic environment. This advocacy topology includes three situations—alliance, neutral, and adversarial. The situation that is most applicable to academic library frontline advocacy is alliance. According to the authors, the alliance situation is where the advocate is viewed as someone with whom the person(s) being approached is in basic agreement. That is, the advocacy role is perceived legitimate.[6]

Applying the alliance situation to academic library frontline advocacy means that many academic librarians already have developed good and strong relationships with their teaching and research faculty such that their role as advocates would be considered by those faculty members as legitimate. Both faculty and librarians are already in basic agreement that the academic library's role is to support the teaching and research mission of the university and to serve/support the faculty and students on their campuses. It would take a much longer time and effort for academic library administrators to develop the same level of effectiveness with the campus faculty. Again, their advocacy is important but is most effective at another level working with campus administrators, board of regents, and state/federal legislators.

Most recently, there is a stronger push for involving more academic library advocacy at the frontline level. However, it is important to note that those involved should receive training on how to be more skilled and successful in academic library advocacy.

The Trained Frontline Academic Library Advocate

"Advocacy must become a central element in an academic library's everyday existence.... Advocacy is not just an action; it is a skill that people learn over time."[7] An important realization is that effective library advocacy requires great skill. Academic librarians as frontline advocates need training to prepare them for library advocacy. When the librarians' campus relationships with faculty and students are coupled with their trained ability to advocate and engage those faculty and students to support library advocacy efforts, academic librarians can become valuable advocates at a different level than academic library administrators.

Julie Todaro uses the techniques of power and personal persuasion to advance the academic library agenda. These techniques prepare frontline academic librarians and other library workers to be more helpful in academic library advocacy. When these techniques are coupled with advocacy skills developed through systematic training, librarians become essential to effective campus advocacy. The academic library administrator must ensure that the frontline librarians and others involved in frontline advocacy are adequately trained.[8]

Conclusion

So, whose job is it anyway? There can never be too many effective advocates to advance the academic library's agenda on any campus.

With the funding pie becoming smaller and smaller in our colleges and universities, effective library advocacy at the frontline level becomes more important. Preparing librarians and other library workers to work hand-in-hand with library administrators in developing and executing the library's advocacy agenda only strengthens the effort. There is an untapped group of potential advocates who have developed solid campus relationships that library administrator don't have. Taking the time to tap into and train those frontline individuals only increases the quantity and quality of advocacy efforts. It should be the job of every adequately trained staff member and librarian, to do frontline academic library advocacy.

Notes

1. Harris and Taggard, "University-based Planning," 190.
2. American Counseling Association, *Effective Counseling*
3. Kaplan, "Advocacy as Teaching," 45
4. Kaplan, "Advocacy as Teaching," 44
5. Kaplan, "Advocacy as Teaching," 45.
6. Sosin and Caulum, "Advocacy," 13.
7. Kirchner, "Advocacy 101," 3.
8. Todaro, *Power of Personal Persuasion*

Works Cited

American Counseling Association. *Effective advocacy and communication with legislators.* Alexandria, VA: Office of Public Policy and Information, 1998.

Harris, William M. and Aubrey Thagard. "University-based planning: faculty advocacy roles." *The Western Journal of Black Studies* 25 (2001): 189–93.

Kaplan, Sandra. 2003. "Advocacy as teaching; the teacher as advocate." *Gifted Child Today* 26, no. 3 (Summer 2003): 44–45.

Kirchner, Terry. "Advocacy 101 for academic librarians: Tips to help your institution prosper." *College and Research Libraries News* 60, no. 10 (November, 1999): 844–6.

Sosin, Michael and Sharon Caulum, "Advocacy: A conceptualization for practice." *Social Work* January-February 28, no. 1 (January—February, 1983): 12–17.

Todaro, Julie. *The power of personal persuasion: Advancing the academic library agenda from the front lines.* Chicago, IL: Association of College and Research Libraries, 2006.

Library Advocacy in the Campus Environment

6

Jean Zanoni and Scott Mandernack

It is often assumed that faculty, students, staff, administrators, and others associated with institutions of higher education understand the inherent value of the academic library's services and resources, yet recent trends of diminishing reference transactions, declining gate counts, and the competition from the web for ubiquitous access to information may suggest otherwise. Surrounded by growing numbers of alternative information service providers, libraries increasingly find themselves in what Hughes refers to as "competitive space," and the role of the library as "primary aggregator and purveyor of content to its community is less and less unique."[1] Furthermore, in higher education, "the value of a library to the university's mission and its priority in the university's allocation of funds can no longer be assumed…. As institutions make difficult decisions about where to allocate precious resources, libraries are faced with effectively defending their worth to campus administrators."[2]

The academic library's vision is informed by the institution it serves. If the library cannot fulfill its role of optimizing access to information in support of the institutional mission of fostering research & discovery, teaching & learning, and service & engagement, or if that information is more readily available elsewhere, the library risks losing its relevancy. In the face of these developments it becomes essential for college and university libraries to actively promote their place in the academy and to communicate the value and benefits of the library to the campus and its diverse audiences.

> "If librarians are committed to sustaining their role as providers of an important common good in the emerging turbulent competitive space of higher education… it will take energy, an in-depth knowledge of our users' preferences and the changes they face, and a willingness to grapple with ambiguity

and complexity on a daily basis… [It] may behoove librarians to experiment more, get out of the library building and talk to people who don't use the library, and get involved with the issues that are shaping higher education in general."[3]

With the advent of new and emerging information and communication technologies, and the evolving role of libraries in the scholarly communication process, college and university libraries have the opportunity and the obligation to position themselves as central to the intellectual and educational mission and goals of the campus.

Successfully advocating for libraries in their new roles within the higher education landscape will be predicated on understanding the needs and behaviors of current and potential users and thoroughly educating our constituencies of the value of libraries to the mission of the institution. Libraries must constantly demonstrate how they can enhance, facilitate, and promote the education and scholarly production of the faculty, students, staff, administration, alumnae, and other stakeholders. In order for libraries to thrive amidst the competition from multiple information providers, as well as from other campus departments and units, a multifaceted marketing campaign addressing each unique audience with a consistent yet targeted message must become a strategic initiative in order to actively and effectively communicate to the campus community the value and benefits of the library's services and resources.

Advocacy through Strategic Planning

For libraries that have adopted the practice of strategic planning, communicating the library's message and establishing its brand to the wider campus community can begin with the strategic planning process itself. Strategic planning can provide "wonderful public relations opportunities and can serve as the vehicle for moving the library more dynamically into the university environment."[4] However, it should be noted that strategic planning for academic libraries will likely have greater impact when library administrators and staff understand the political nature of the decentralized academic system within which they operate and how decisions are made in their institutions. The pluralistic character of the university environment, in which different campus groups use various forms of political power to pursue their own self-interests and those they view as best for the institution, cannot be ignored. Strategic planning based on political decision-making rather than rational decision-making is often more effective in the academic environment.[5] The political decision-making planning model begins with issues, "which by definition involve conflict, not consensus.... As efforts proceed to resolve these issues, policies and programs emerge to address them that are politically rational; that is, they are politically acceptable to involved or affected parties.... The various policies and programs are, in effect, treaties among the various stakeholders."[6] Certainly, the inclusion of representatives from multiple campus constituencies in the strategic planning process—as members of a steering committee, working groups, or focus groups, for example—ensures that additional perspectives on library services and resources are given due consideration in assessing and planning for the future. However, it also serves to inform and educate those stakeholders about the issues facing the library and its vision for the future. Such a collaborative and inclusive visioning process can "set the stage for engaging university officials, faculty, and other major stakeholders in discussions about institutional policies and priorities for library resources and services,"[7] ultimately leading to the goal of generating alliances, coalitions, and advocacy from a broad base of current and potential user groups.

A critical component of any library's strategic planning process is communicating the library's message to the campus community. The most effective strategic plans have a clear sense of their potential readerships, and the strategic directions should be clearly aligned with both the institutional goals and particular interests of key stakeholders.[8] An organizational commitment to telling the "library story" can facilitate strategic planning and the achievement of organizational goals, and can be effectively articulated through a strategic marketing planning process. The strategic marketing planning process is a cyclical, data-driven, comprehensive, decision-making process that is based on market research of the target audiences. It includes four essential steps: customer and market research, strategic planning, promotion, and the provision of products and services. This continuous process is framed by user needs—those that are being met and those that are unmet. "Strategic marketing provides libraries a process through which audience research can be conducted and its results used to deliver the most relevant product or message in the most audience-appropriate way to capture the attention and understanding of the audience."[9] The American Library Association's @ *your library Toolkit for Academic and Research Libraries: Messages, Ideas, and Strategies for Promoting the Value of Our Libraries and Librarians in the 21ˢᵗ Century* identifies the following elements of a strategic marketing plan:

- the context of current and future challenges and opportunities facing the library;
- goals and objectives to be accomplished;
- a positioning statement, defining the desired image of the library as perceived by others;
- the key messages to be delivered;
- prioritized target audiences;
- implementation strategies for delivering the key messages;
- evaluation measures[10]

When considering the audiences of the academic library, it is important to differentiate among them because each brings different expectations and perceptions of needs for library services and resources. As articulated by Conley and Tucker[11], there are many ways of identifying and labeling targeted markets. Markets may be divided into primary and secondary markets, where the primary audience is comprised of on-campus groups, such as students, faculty and staff, and the secondary audience includes those outside the campus community. Similar, but with a slightly different perspective, markets may be divided into internal and external, where internal audiences are directly associated with the university (students, faculty, staff, administrators, alumnae, friends groups, etc.) and external audiences are not (media outlets, community leaders, community organizations, schools, companies, etc.). There are a few other possibilities for identifying markets, including distinguishing audiences by their relationship to the organization or by specifying geographic, demographic, behavioral, psychographic, and lifestyle groups. Relationship marketing emphasizes customer retention and establishing long-term relationships between the customer and the organization. In the context of academic libraries, the relationships may be customer markets (students, faculty, university staff and administrators), internal markets (employees and departments of the library), supplier and alliance markets (publishers, vendors, etc.), referral markets (satisfied patrons or early adopters of library services), recruitment markets (venues for attracting and training qualified employees), and influence markets (boards of directors/trustees, friends groups, legislators, etc.). Whichever market segmentation strategy is employed, the distinct audience groups must satisfy certain criteria in order to be targeted successfully: each must be homogenous, accessible, and measurable.

Effective promotional and advocacy implementation strategies will approach each group with different messages, using different media, directed at addressing the unique needs and perceptions of each. Additionally, consideration should be given to the frequency and timing of the communication to each group. This strategic approach to marketing, promotion, and advocacy should lead to more effective services, greater visibility, and ultimately improved funding.[12]

In addition to the obvious distribution of the strategic plan document to key administrators and other major stakeholders on campus, other proven methods of message distribution include:

- Word of mouth. This type of distribution is thought by some to be more credible than other marketing techniques because it originates from people who have no vested interest in persuading another to use the product or service, and therefore are not inclined to distort the truth. "The power of word-of-mouth marketing lies in its honesty."[13] Alire further outlines several approaches to word of mouth marketing, including the use of experts (e.g. advisory groups of students, faculty, or donors; early adopters of library services or resources, etc.); participation (by librarians or other advocates) in seminars, workshops, or programs; canned word of mouth, i.e. preparing presentations that may be used by others; referral selling (testimonials); and, networking and increasing visibility at campus events and meetings.
- Banners, posters, or displays highlighting library-related events, or library and information resources associated with campus issues and/or events.
- Handouts/giveaways (i.e. bookmarks, mugs, pens, etc.) at orientation and other campus events.
- Campus and community media outlets (newspapers, radio, TV) to raise awareness of library issues, events, or changes, or the connection of the library/information to campus initiatives, etc.
- Print materials, such as a newsletter, flyers, table tents, annual reports, etc.
- Web sites.
- E-mail lists.

- Online course management systems, integrating library resources and services with course assignments or general assistance.
- Collaborations with other campus and community departments, units, or organizations.

Strategically utilizing these various approaches with the key campus constituencies, as determined by careful and deliberate audience analysis, will optimize campus partnerships and offer the greatest potential for successful integration of the library's goals into institution-wide planning efforts.

Advocacy with University Administration and Administrative Units

It is critically important for libraries to understand the organizational climate, culture, and structures of the local campus environment in order to strategically position themselves in the planning and decision-making processes that occur throughout campus. The institutional culture itself will be defined, in part, by the nature and type of the institution, whether community college, liberal arts college, comprehensive college/university, doctoral granting or research institution. Among these institutions, there is a continuum of value and degree of emphasis placed on undergraduate teaching and learning, graduate education, research and discovery, and service and engagement. The generalization typically holds that, as we move from two-year colleges to research universities the emphasis changes from a local to a more global perspective. Another factor that contributes to the institutional culture is the institution's base of support, whether publicly or privately funded.[14] The library's role and mission in each of these environments will necessarily conform to the institutional culture, which will have an impact on the library mission, message, communication channels, and opportunities for collaboration and partnerships. Furthermore, each segment of the academic community (college, school, department, administrative unit, etc.) comprises a distinct culture, often with subcultures within it. Understanding the unique aspects of each of those subcultures will contribute significantly to the library's ability to successfully articulate and promote its brand message and advocate for support and resources among its diverse constituencies and stakeholders.

Equally essential in the strategic positioning of the library is for the library to become familiar with the institution's strategic plan. It must be understood intimately and the library's mission and goals directly related to it. Demonstrating how library initiatives will benefit the campus and advance the strategic plan ensures a broader understanding of the value of the library to the institutional mission and, therefore, a broader base of support. "The greatest potential for alliances occurs when library goals become a prominent part of the institution's priorities."[15]

Communicating to the component departments or units of the institution with messages or initiatives that emphasize how the library can enhance, facilitate, support and promote what they value will help them recognize their interdependence on the library, thereby leading to stronger campus partnerships and greater support. Academic libraries forge campus partnerships for a number of reasons: furthering the institutional goals; building relationships with key user groups and constituencies; and/or obtaining additional funding.[16] Other campus concerns which may benefit from creative use of library resources and services include promoting more effective and productive campus operations, enhancing fundraising efforts, fostering campus/high school relations, recruiting and retaining students, contributing to faculty development, and addressing globalization concerns.[17]

Campus librarians can assist campus administrators in academic decision-making by collecting and organizing relevant information, instructing administrative staff in accessing and evaluating information, and participating directly in campus planning groups. Supporting the institution's mission to be more engaged with the community may be effectively accomplished through partnerships with the library and the educational opportunity office, student recruitment and retention programs, and/or campus multicultural centers. Fostering information and communication technology literacy among the students may be best addressed in collaboration with the campus information technology (IT) division, instructional support services, the writing center, departmental faculty, and/or the faculty governance organization. Providing library services and access to resources for alumnae may require the cooperation of IT, the alumnae association, and/or the advancement office. Accreditation reviews may be strengthened with evidence of levels of access to information resources and/or student learning outcomes of information literacy, compiled through joint efforts of the library and the campus assessment office or institutional research office. Campus librarians can assist campus administrators in academic decision-making by collecting and organizing relevant information, instructing administrative staff in accessing and evaluating information, and participating directly in campus planning groups.

The relationship of libraries to campus computing centers or IT departments continues to be an issue of great concern on college and university campuses. Technological advances have driven some of the most dramatic changes in libraries in recent years, yet few campus units outside the libraries truly understand the depth of the impact, causing a gap between expectations and reality and an underutilization of library resources and services. Successful integration of new and emerging information technology into the university mission requires tremendous cooperation between libraries and IT. The very different backgrounds and perspectives of library and IT personnel have been characterized as involving organizational culture, social distinctions, compensation differentiation, subcultural patterns, and dissimilar professional backgrounds. These differences may pose very real challenges to meaningful collaboration, but thoughtful planning, investment in staff development, and clearly articulated service goals can lead to very promising results in providing seamless support to scholars and students.[18]

Understanding the mission and goals of other campus offices, and demonstrating their interrelatedness to the library's mission and goals, can build on already established programs, thereby advancing the library's contributions to the campus while also furthering the goals and objectives of the other offices. Bunnell[19] quotes Larry A. Braskamp and John F. Wergin, stating that "collaboration does not occur without the partners spending time together to foster mutual trust." The best partnerships are those in which the participants understand each other from their own individual perspectives and work with the strengths of the partners and capitalize on their skills. The key is to continue the dialog with these units and to maintain an interest in the common issues and initiatives that have been established.

Advocacy with Faculty

Services to faculty must meet both their own teaching and research needs and support the needs of their students. Reaching faculty in either arena will lead to greater awareness of available services in the other. While all faculty share the common goal of promotion and tenure, they are a unique and diverse group of individuals. Faculty operate independently from their departmental colleagues and other faculty on campus. The insular nature of faculty work, differences in research needs among disciplines, and the split between junior and senior faculty regarding differences in expectations and compensation and how disciplinary changes in scholarship are viewed[20] mean that serving faculty cannot be a one-size-fits-all approach. In a study that involved interviewing 300 faculty members from eight different institutions, a number of factors that impeded faculty collaboration were identified: Fragmented communication patterns that are the result of research specialization and the tendency for faculty to work in isolation[21]; limited resources which promote competition among faculty for funding; and lack of time due to the pressures of teaching, research, and administrative duties to interact with faculty colleagues. Also, the methods of evaluation and reward can put faculty at odds with each other. For example, the overemphasis on research and ineffective methods of assessing teaching can create resentment not to mention salary differentials that are perceived as unfair.[22] Therefore, libraries must develop strategies to work with members of the campus faculty while simultaneously taking a broader perspective and looking at service to faculty as a whole in terms of support for teaching and research.

While faculty individual identity and self interest are important, how faculty members view academic libraries and librarians is a key component in defining the relationship between the two groups. According to the Ithaka report, *2006 Studies of Key Stakeholders in the Digital Transformation in Higher Education,* faculty are becoming less dependent on the library to meet their research and teaching needs, yet faculty continue to view the library's role as important.[23] Faculty most value the library's role as purchaser of the journals, books and databases necessary to support their teaching and research. They also value the library's role as repository and preserver of those resources. While librarians still consider the library a vital starting point for research, faculty members are beginning to view this gateway role as less important to their needs.[24] Librarians also place a high priority on providing service in support of faculty research, but the faculty often undervalues the consulting role of the librarian.[25] Academic libraries must bridge the gap between the faculty's belief that they will be less dependent on the library and the librarian's view that their role will continue to be important in the future. This provides a useful framework for academic library advocacy to faculty.

So what can the academic library do to provide support to faculty now and in the future? The library can serve in the role of "intellectual ombudsman" and remove any obstacles to learning and the creation of new knowledge[26] through the provision of core services of instruction and access to resources. Since the library serves all academic departments, it is "uniquely situated to work at the nexus of disciplines,"[27] and the library can provide both space and resources in support of interdisciplinary research. The library is just one source for information, but librarians can serve as navigational guides to finding information that is either freely available on the Internet or that has been licensed by the library.[28] Academic libraries can position themselves as a key player in the transformation of scholarly communication if they seize the opportunity. The creation of digital repositories to collect, preserve and showcase institutional scholarship and educating faculty on the benefits of open access and authors' rights should be on the library's agenda.[29] The library can also provide institutional support for issues related to copyright, intellectual property and information policy. There are collaboration opportunities between faculty, librarians and educational technologists for data curation which encompasses archiving, organization and preservation of digital data sets being created by faculty and graduate student researchers.[30] Academic libraries can maintain their role as purchasers and repositories and enhance their gateway and consultative functions.

The role of the academic library in support of the faculty and their teaching and research endeavors can expand in a positive and fruitful manner yet librarians must be mindful of what roles the faculty want them to play or risk alienating them. Most tenure processes prefer traditional forms of publication, i.e., monographs and journal articles. Faculty who are seeking tenure still look to the library to provide the resources they need and could be unsupportive of any new initiative that may divert attention or resources from the library's traditional services. For example, many do not think of academic libraries in alternative roles such as data curation or a more direct involvement in student learning. The latter may have the unintended effect of allowing faculty to focus exclusively on their own research and thereby shortchanging their students.[31] Therefore, it is essential that librarians and faculty collaborate on how best to serve the faculties' teaching and research needs.

Jason Kramer, Executive Director for the New York State Higher Education Initiative and recently hired as a legislative advocate for academic libraries in the state of New York, points out that "while academic libraries have no passionate enemies, too many libraries have cultivated no passionate allies."[32] Often the library's most vocal faculty supporters tend to be those who champion the library's traditional roles. A balance between ensuring that traditional needs are continually met and engaging with faculty on new initiatives must be maintained.[33] Faculty who support the library in turn can be the library's most influential advocates to faculty colleagues, administration and students. Greater engagement with faculty on issues both current and new, will ultimately lead to improved communication and more opportunities for collaboration.

Relationship building opportunities abound. Membership on university committees, attendance at campus events, involvement in campus activities are all avenues to promote the library. These activities serve as a method for the academic library to promote what it has to offer and provide opportunities for librarians to learn about campus initiatives in which the library can play a part. Keeping in mind the independent nature of the faculty, advocacy must also be pursued by interacting with faculty individually either formally or informally. Attention should be given to meeting the needs of and addressing the unique character of the institution the library supports, and the ways the larger institutional mission frames and influences the mission of the library itself.

Advocacy with Students

Identifying "students" as a single user group may be a gross over-simplification of this target audience, as today's student body is in fact tremendously diverse. Students at today's universities represent a heretofore unseen level of diversity in their racial and ethnic backgrounds, cultural heritages, socio-economic status, life experiences, and even their ages span a much larger divide than in the past. Nonetheless, some broad generalizations may be helpful in understanding how to develop effective messages to this segment of the campus population. Cox[34] offers what he feels are the primary characteristics of the millennial generation of students (those born between 1982 and 2002, representing the largest generation in history): they are ethnically and racially diverse; they are nontraditional; they expect choices and instant gratification; they are digital natives; they enjoy gaming and media; and, they learn best experientially and collaboratively. ACRL's *Power of Personal Persuasion: Advancing the Academic Library Agenda from the Front Lines*[35] identifies additional characteristics of contemporary students as: practical, immediate problem solvers; autonomous and relevancy-oriented; prefer doing to knowing; motivated by accessibility, connectedness, advancement, and external expectations; are accustomed to change and fast-paced activities; have shorter attention spans; and blur lines between work, recreation, and "life." All of these characteristics significantly impact students' expectations and use of library services and resources, which in turn, have implications for how the library develops services and most effectively communicates with them.

Of interest when considering library marketing strategies to college students is the OCLC report, *College Students' Perceptions of Libraries and Information Resources: A Report to the OCLC Membership,*[36] which found that 70% of college students associate "library" first and foremost with "books."[37] The report further states that even though college students may be more aware of and familiar with library electronic resources than the general population, many are not sure what libraries offer.[38] In light of this evidence, the challenge facing the academic library today is to clearly define and market its services and resources and demonstrate its relevance to today's students. As the OCLC report concludes, "Rejuvenating the [library] brand depends on reconstructing the experience of using the library."[39]

As previously stated, the most successful marketing and promotional strategies will clearly articulate the specific message, tailored for the target audience, utilizing the most effective medium. The wide variety of subgroups that may be differentiated within the student population—freshmen; undergraduate researchers; honors students; graduate students; nontraditional students; on-campus residents; commuters; distance learners; multicultural student groups; international students; fraternities/sororities; student organizations; student government; student advisory boards, and more—provides for countless opportunities to engage with students and inform them of library services and resources. Heeding the experiential, collaborative, "doing-versus-knowing" nature of college students, more active and programmatic marketing strategies that actively engage the students in an experience with the library may be more effective with this segment of the campus population. Building a sense of community between the students and the library will establish a relationship that encourages continuing interest and involvement, leading to additional partnerships and future advocates.

Some examples:

- Participate in freshmen orientation events, distributing give-aways and literature/information packets, offering presentations or tours, holding an open house, or developing fun activities that acquaint the students with aspects of the library.
- Sponsor research/multimedia project awards, incorporating use of information sources as criteria.
- Encourage submission of student research projects to the institutional repository, highlighting its promotional value to the student, emphasizing their role as a contributor rather than just a consumer of the literature, and providing an opportunity to underscore the ethical use of information (i.e., their work).
- Embed reference and instructional services and resources in the campus online course management system, providing ready access to resources and assistance, especially useful for distance or remote learners.
- Provide office hours, research consultations, or seminars to graduate students on effective research practices in their fields of study.
- Become a member/advisor/instructor of a learning community, promoting the library as a resource for both academic and social/recreational purposes.
- Host lectures, poetry readings, book discussions, or film viewings as tie-ins to other campus events or initiatives.
- Collaborate with students on class projects that analyze a library-related issue or problem and make recommendations for change and improvement.
- Collaborate with student organizations to archive and/or digitize their records, educating them about the value of record storage and management.
- Provide refreshments during late night hours of finals week.
- Sponsor gaming events as a means of promoting the "library as place" concept.
- Invite student participation in the library's strategic planning process, web site redesign projects, facilities remodeling projects, etc.
- Develop informational materials in various languages, with translation assistance by international students, to help those from other countries more easily acclimate to the library environment.

- Promote library events, resources, and services via Web 2.0 and social networking applications—the mediums that students use—such as Facebook, Twitter, Flickr, blogs, wikis, etc.
- Establish a student advisory board to elicit ongoing feedback and suggestions for continuous improvement of library services.

As Karle states, demonstrating the resourcefulness, versatility, and value of the library and its staff in creative and dynamic ways is crucial to leveraging the library's brand as useful and relevant to college and university students. "Rather than competing with technological advances in an adversarial manner, libraries and librarians need to position themselves as offering complementary, attractive, and relevant resources that supplement their students' media-filled lives… Academic libraries can create experiences that shape the perceptions and heighten the enthusiasm of their students in order to make the overall library experience more appealing."[40]

Advocacy with Friends/Donors

Academic libraries look to external funding to supplement stagnant or decreased budgets, and therefore must extend advocacy efforts to potential and current donors. However, just as colleges and universities must justify to donors that they are worthy of their support, academic libraries must convince their administrations that they are essential and integral to the mission of the university and therefore worthy recipients of donor funds.

Standard arguments against soliciting donor support for the academic library are that it will divert donors' attention away from other university priorities and since no one graduated from the academic library, it does not have its own alumni donor constituency. Libraries can be hard to sell because most alumni have used the library, but no one owns it. Furthermore, donors may not know why the library needs money.[41] Whether the library is involved directly in raising its own funds or supports the university's fundraising efforts, advocating to current and potential donors is essential.

In terms of defining an overall fundraising philosophy, Robert Wedgeworth urges academic libraries to put fundraising within the context of public relations and as part of the overall management of the library.[42] Donor constituencies can have significant influence on the library, and therefore, their support must be consistent with the present and future plans and operations of the library. Librarians must connect the strategic mission of the library to the public relations campaign and relate the interests and financial resources of the donor community to the library. However, as dollars become scarcer, librarians will need to articulate the societal importance of their work to those grant agencies and donors who do not traditionally support higher education and academic libraries.[43]

Reaching out to potential donors requires an understanding of why people give and why they give to libraries. Donors' reasons for giving are based on what the library will do for the donor not what the donor will do for the library. Charitable giving can supply a sense of belonging and fulfill the esteem needs of approval and recognition. Some donors feel a moral obligation; some feel that if they give, they will receive.[44] When choosing what to support, donors need to believe in the cause or the institution. They give to visionary leaders and successful organizations. The library dean or director must be the key figure in fundraising and connecting with donors as he or she provides the vision, purpose and sense of mission to motivate donors.[45] Most importantly, donors need to be asked to give.[46] Few will make a donation without being asked.

OCLC recently issued a report outlining the attitudes and perceptions regarding public library funding. Even though the study focuses on public libraries, its findings can inform donor advocacy within the academic library. Library supporters do not equate the library's value with specific services or materials. It is the impact on and value of the library to the lives of individuals and to the community that really matter.[47] Shared values of probable and "super" supporters include involvement in their communities, recognition of the value of librarians, and belief that the library is relevant to the community. Interestingly, probable and "super" supporters are not necessarily heavy users of the library.[48] For the library to remain relevant, it cannot be just viewed as a historical institution or one that only provides information. It must be recognized as a transformational force and a necessity that will yield a return on investment for the individuals and community it serves.[49] (6–12). In light of these findings, messages to academic library donors should stress the value of the academic library to the institution and to society, and its role in learning, the transformation of students and support of faculty research.

Academic library donor advocacy can take several forms. Library friends groups can serve to advocate to members about the value of the library and the friends can act as library advocates to others. Friends groups can promote the library within the community, sponsor fundraising events such as book sales, and make financial gifts to the library for collections and services. The provision of an alumni portal to select library resources provides both a service and a connection to the library which may encourage support. Reaching out to alumni and donors through an article on the library in the institution's alumni magazine is another strategy. This could serve to educate those who have graduated several years ago on the essential role that the library plays on campus. Parents of graduates can buy a book in their son's or daughter's name for the library. The library can also be the recipient of money from a senior class gift. Library sponsorship of alumni events, exhibitions, and concerts also contributes to increased awareness by getting people into the library building. These initiatives involve donors and potential donors in library-related activities, educate them on what the library has to offer and illustrate the value of the academic library.

The academic library has long been at the heart of the college campus, but its relevance and continued support cannot be taken for granted. Budget cuts and dwindling support from state governments for public institutions put academic libraries in direct competition with other academic departments, the very people they serve, and with other libraries for resources and external funding. Furthermore, the availability of freely accessible resources on the Web has challenged the assumption that the library is essential or even necessary. The colliding economic and technological forces may be considered a perfect storm. Academic libraries need to respond to changes in higher education, scholarly publishing and the information landscape and turn that perfect storm into the ultimate opportunity to redefine its role. Advocacy for academic libraries is paramount to their success now and as the library redefines its role within higher education.

Notes

1. Hughes, "Information Services for Higher Education"
2. Spalding and Wang, "The Challenges and Opportunities of Marketing"
3. Hughes, "Information Services for Higher Education"
4. Birdsall, "Strategic Planning in Academic Libraries"
5. Ibid; McClamroch, Byrd, and Sowell, "Strategic Planning"
6. McClamroch, Byrd, and Sowell, "Strategic Planning"
7. Birdsall, "Strategic Planning in Academic Libraries"
8. Ibid.
9. Spalding and Wang, "The Challenges and Opportunities of Marketing"
10. Academic and Research Library Campaign, "@ Your Library Toolkit"

11. Conley and Tucker, "Matching Media to Audience"
12. Spalding and Wang, "The Challenges and Opportunities of Marketing"
13. Alire, "Word-of-Mouth Marketing"
14. Budd, *The Academic Library*
15 Birdsall, "Strategic Planning in Academic Libraries"
16. Hernas and Karas, "Campus Partnership in Small Academic Libraries"
17. Breivik and Gee, *Higher Education in the Internet Age*
18. Ibid, 167–171
19. Bunnell, "Collaboration in Small and Medium-Sized Academic Libraries," 148
20. Massey, Wilger, and Colbeck, "Overcoming 'Hollowed' Collegiality," 12
21. Ibid, 11
22. Ibid, 13
23. Housewright and Schonfeld, *Ithaka's 2006 Studies*
24. Ibid, 6
25. Schonfeld and Guthrie, "The Changing Information Service Needs of Faculty"
26. *The Academic Library in 2010*
27. Council on Libraries and Information Resources, "No Brief Candle," 5
28. *Changing Roles of Academic and Research Libraries*
29. Council on Libraries and Information Resources, "No Brief Candle," 10–11
30. Ibid
31. Ibid
32. Ibid, 3
33. Ibid
34. Cox, "Changing Demographics"
35. *Power of Personal Persuasion*
36. *College Students' Perceptions of Libraries*
37. Ibid.
38. Ibid.
39. Ibid.
40. Karle, "Invigorating the Academic Library Experience,"
41. Herring, *Raising Funds with Friends Groups*
42. Wedgeworth, "Donor Relations as Public Relations"
43. Brower and Streit, "Mutually Assured Survival"
44. Steele and Elder, *Becoming a Fundraiser*, 33
45. Ibid, 13
46. Ibid, 33–34.
47. DeRosa and Johnson, *From Awareness to Funding*, 6–8
48. Ibid.
49. Ibid.

Works Cited

@ your library Toolkit for Academic and Research Libraries: Messages, ideas, and strategies for promoting the value of our libraries and librarians in the 21st century. In Academic and Research Library Campaign, 2007 http://www.acrl.org/ala/issuesadvocacy/advocacy/publicawareness/campaign@yourlibrary/prtools/toolkitfinaltext2.pdf. (last accessed April 3, 2009)

The Academic Library in 2010: a Vision: Report of Symposium 2010. Washington, D.C.: American University Library, 2005. http://www.library.american.edu/

Symposium_2010.pdf

Alire, Camila A. Word-of-mouth marketing: Abandoning the academic library ivory tower. New Library World, 108 (11/12): 545. (last accessed April 9, 2009).

Birdsall, Douglas G. Strategic planning in academic libraries: A political perspective. In Schwartz, Charles A. (Ed.), *Restructuring Academic Libraries: Organizational Development in the Wake of Technological Change, Publications in Librarianship No. 49*. Chicago: Association of College and Research Libraries, 1997. http://www.ala.org/ala/mgrps/divs/acrl/publications/booksmonographs/pil/pil49/birdsall.cfm. (last accessed April 3, 2009)

Breivik, Patricia Senn and Gee, E. Gordon. *Higher Education in the Internet Age: Libraries Creating a Strategic Edge*. Westport, CN: American Council on Education / Praeger, 2006.

Browar, Lisa and Streit, Samuel A. "Mutually Assured Survival: Library Fund-raising Strategies in a Changing Economy." *Library Trends* 52, no. 1: (Summer 2003): 69–86.

Budd, John M. *The Academic Library: It's Context, Its Purpose, and It's Operation*. Englewood, CO: Libraries Unlimited, 1998.

Bunnell, David P. (2008). Collaboration in Small and Medium-Sized Academic Libraries. In Hulbert, Janet McNeil (Ed.) *Defining Relevancy: Managing the New Academic Library* Westport, CN: Libraries Unlimited, 2008, 146–160.

Changing Roles of Academic and Research Libraries. Association of College and Research Libraries, 2007. http://www.ala.org/ala/mgrps/divs/acrl/issues/future/changingroles.cfm (last accessed, July 31, 2009)

College Students' Perceptions of Libraries and Information Resources: A Report to the OCLC Membership. Dublin, OH: OCLC Online Computer Library Center, 2006

Conley, Kathleen and Tucker, Toni. Matching media to audience equals marketing success. In Petruzzelli, Barbara Whitney (Ed.) *Real-Life Marketing and Promotion Strategies in College Libraries: Connecting with Campus and Community*. New York: Haworth, 2005, 47–64.

Council on Libraries and Information Resources. *No Brief Candle: Reconceiving Research Libraries for the 21st Century*. Washington, D.C.: CLIR, 2008. http://www.clir.org/pubs/reports/pub142/pub142.pdf (last accessed July 31, 2009)

Cox, Christopher. Changing demographics: Meet the students and faculty of the future. In Hulbert, Janet McNeil (Ed.) *Defining Relevancy: Managing the New Academic Library* Westport, CT: Libraries Unlimited, 2008, 3–15.

De Rosa, Cathy and Johnson, Jenny. *From Awareness to Funding: a Study of Library Support in America*. Dublin, Ohio: OCLC, 2008. http://www.oclc.org/reports/funding/default.htm (last accessed July 31, 2009)

Hernas, Patricia and Karas, Timothy. Campus partnership in small academic libraries: Challenges and rewards. In Hurlbert, Janet McNeil (Ed.) *Defining Relevancy: Managing the New Academic Library*. Westport, CN: Libraries Unlimited, 2008, 131–145.

Herring, Mark Y. *Raising Funds with Friends Groups: a How-To-Do-It Manual for Librarians*. New York: Neal-Schuman, 2004.

Housewright, Ross and Schonfeld, Roger. *Ithaka's 2006 Studies of Key Stakeholders in the Digital Transformation in Higher Education*. New York: Ithaka, 2008. http://www.ithaka.org/research/Ithakas%202006--%20Studies%20of%20Key%20Stakeholders%20in%20the%20Digital%20Transformation%20in%20Higher%20Education.pdf (last accessed July 31, 2009)

Hughes, Carol Ann. "Information services for higher education: A new competitive space." *D-Lib Magazine*, 6, no 12 (2000). http://www.dlib.org/dlib/december00/hughes/12hughes.html. (last accessed April 7, 2009)

Karle, Elizabeth M. (2008). Invigorating the academic library experience: Creative programming ideas. *College & Research Libraries News*, 69 (3): 141–4. http://vn-web.hwwilsonweb.com/hww/results/results_single_fulltext.jhtml;hwwilsonid=T UZ0E0WBPJ15BQA3DIMSFGGADUNGIIV0. (last accessed April 9, 2009)

Lowe, Chrysanne. "Talking with a Library Lobbyist about Selling the Library." *Elsevier Library Connect*. 6, 3: (July 2008). http://libraryconnect.elsevier.com/lcn/0603/LCN0603.pdf (Last accessed July 31, 2009)

Massey, William F., Wilger, Andrea K., Colbeck, Carol. "Overcoming 'Hollowed' Collegiality." *Change*. (July/August, 1994):11–20.

McClamroch, Jo, Byrd, Jacqueline J., and Sowell, Steven L. "Strategic planning: politics, leadership, and learning." *Journal of Academic Librarianship*, 27, no 5 (2001): 372–378.

Power of Personal Persuasion: Advancing the Academic Library Agenda from the Front Line. In *Marketing @ your library*. 2006 http://www.ala.org/ala/mgrps/divs/acrl/issues/marketing/advocacy_toolkit.pdf. (last accessed March 5, 2009)

Schonfeld, Roger C. and Guthrie, Kevin M. "The Changing Information Service Needs of Faculty." *EDUCAUSE Review*: 42:4 (July/August 2007).

Spalding, Helen H., and Wang, Jian. "The challenges and opportunities of marketing academic libraries in the USA." *Library Management*, 27, no. 6/7 (2006): 494–504.

Steele, Victoria and Elder, Stephen D. *Becoming a Fundraiser: the Principles and Practice of Library Development*. 2nd Ed. Chicago: American Library Association, 2000.

Wedgeworth, Robert. "Donor Relations as Public Relations: Toward a Philosophy of Fundraising." *Library Trends* 48. No. 3 (Winter 2000): 530–539.

Outreach Issues for Information Technology in Libraries

Paul J. Bracke

Introduction

Over the years, librarians have been enthusiastic adopters of new technologies, including information technologies (IT). To say that the IT is central to the future of libraries has become such an obvious statement that it hardly bears repeating. What is less obvious, however, is the extent to which librarians will be able to exploit the potentialities and affordances of new technologies effectively. Nor is it clear whether they will be able to find ways to deliver their resources and services to their constituents in ways that make sense in the context of webscale information discovery. There have been many within the profession, in fact, who have expressed grave concerns over the current state of information technology within libraries. For example, the components of library IT infrastructures that are essential to delivering library resources in a web environment are often seen as limited by past design decisions (both of technology and of metadata), by the closed systems provided by many library automation vendors, and by restrictions on the reuse of their own bibliographic data.[1] These issues are not strictly infrastructural, however, and also have an impact on the creation of new services and other IT-related activities in which librarians may wish to engage.

Although there has been some progress in moving toward more open models for library technology, remedying this situation is difficult for a number of reasons.[2] These reasons include entrenched professional cultures and practices, difficulties in attracting and retaining needed technical staff, and the reliance of libraries on commercial entities that may not share their interests in open access to information resources. But the most pressing challenge is the need for library IT departments to form cooperative partnerships with other libraries and with individuals and organizations outside of the library community. Even in areas that have seen the successful deployment of IT in libraries, information commons and other public computing spaces, there are many evolving issues that will have a large impact on the future of learning and collaborative spaces for campuses or communities.

In this chapter I will address advocacy and outreach opportunities related to information technology in libraries. I will present a sociotechnical framework for understanding the issues libraries are facing with regard to IT-related initiatives, as well as some suggestions for putting the framework into practice. The framework will focus on: (1) the ways in which technologies are developed, defined, and understood; (2) the implications of these issues for developing common understandings of library-related IT; and (3) the development of social networks for innovation and diffusion of ideas.

The Social Construction of Technology and Technological Frames

One of the most fundamental issues when communicating about and partnering in technology are the conflicting ways in which technologies are understood, and the ways in which the problems being addressed are understood. Thinking about technology, including technologies used outside libraries, it is not difficult to develop a range of examples of the importance of social context to the technology's development and success. Many fail because they do not offer a reasonable solution to a society's need within the social context of their intended use. Some, like Betamax, were supplanted by rivals, even technically inferior rivals, because of differences in developing social relationships with other firms or with consumers.[3] Others, like bicycles, found substantially different applications than intended once released to the user community.[4]

Developing shared understanding of technologies and their potential applications can be difficult within and among libraries, let alone between libraries and other units on campuses or in the larger information market. This is not only a problem with regard to library technology, but for libraries generally. For example, the struggles many libraries have had in marketing their services on campus may stem from differing understandings of what the purpose/role of the Library is. While few libraries would market themselves solely as places where one can find books, the OCLC Perceptions of Library and Information Resources Report points out that the library "brand" is still books to many users.[5] The basic issue is that communicating the IT-related role of library runs counter to cultural definitions of libraries. The Social Construction of Technology (SCOT), a theoretical framework from the field of Science-Technology Studies, provides several important concepts from this theory that are helpful in understanding the issues libraries have in communicating their interests in, and role with regard to, technology.

The Social Construction of Technology framework emerged in response to technologically deterministic ways of understanding the social impacts of technologies. It argues that technologies must be understood through the social context in which they are developed and adopted. Material properties are only part of the way in which technologies are defined—they are also defined by the social relationships of users and creators[6] and may offer a basis to understanding how this misperception of the library "brand" may cause issues for the public perception of the library's role on campus.

The "technological frame" is a fundamental construct in SCOT that is a good starting point. According to Bijker, a technological frame "structures the interactions among the actors of a relevant social group in solving a problem."[7] At its most basic level, a technological frame is a window through which individuals attempting to solve a technological problem see the world. The boundaries of the frame define what is and is not knowable to the person looking through it, and thus define the range of possible solutions.

A technological frame consists of several elements: goals, key problems, problem-solving strategies, perceived substitution, and artifacts. In aggregate, these elements bound the ways in which individuals approach their task, set goals, and are able to perceive options. Solutions will only be considered if they are knowable and feasible within the problem solver's frame of reference. Table 1 provides a simplified view of how librarians and non-librarians might view the issue of data curation. Although it has been streamlined, perhaps grossly so, the table provides some insight into how two groups interested in the same problem might develop different approaches to solving it based upon their specific professional perspectives.

One of the issues that arise when individuals or groups of individuals use a technology from different perspectives concerns the diverse ways that a technology may be understood. According to the SCOT theory, this is known as interpretive flexibility. But interpretive flexibility is not merely a static characteristic of a technology. It is one part in a large scale social process. Technologies are more than the aggregate of their intrinsic, material characteristics. They are

Table 1. Technological Frame of Data Curation

Problem: Data curation

	Librarians	Computing Professionals
Goals	• Develop collections of research data • Preserve research data	• Develop effective and efficient storage of research data
Key Problems	1. Appropriate representation of content (i.e., metadata schema, controlled vocabulary, etc.) 2. Selection of data to form coherent collections 3. Securing the broadest access mechanisms possible 4. Long-term preservation of critical research data	1. Large-scale storage, including cost models 2. Integration with research computing infrastructure 3. Integration with sensors and other data collection devices 4. Data security
Problem-Solving Strategies	1. Interviews with stakeholder scientists to determine use requirements 2. Small-scale pilots to test description methods 3. Simulations of preservation methods	1. Interviews with stakeholder scientists to determine technical requirements 2. Investigation of new and emerging storage technologies 3. Investigation of best practices in data security and identity management
Requirements to be met by problem solutions	Set by the needs of practicing scientists, and mandates by campuses and funding bodies	Set by the needs of practicing scientists, and mandates by campuses and funding bodies
Current Theories and Tacit Knowledge	Research knowledge of metadata and preservation based upon research in textually-oriented digital libraries and digitization activities. Practical experience in managing large collections of research materials, including born-digital content.	Deep experience with research computing infrastructure, often including the instruments used to conduct research. Experience implementing large-scale systems to support campus communities.
Perceived Substitution	None. There are no existing libraries of scientific research data sets managed by libraries.	Small scale storage based in individual labs or departments
Artifacts	A repository of research data, and associated services.	A large-scale storage infrastructure in the campus research computing unit.

artifacts that are ascribed meaning(s) by social groups.[8] Over time, technologies lose interpretive flexibility and come to have a dominant meaning through a process of closure.[9] The process through which a technology comes to closure is dependent on the various social relationships of inventors, producers, consumers, and more. This process often reflects the characteristics of these relationships: power relationships among groups, degree of connectedness of various social actors, and so forth. So, although there may be a multitude of interpretations of a technology when it is new, it eventually comes to have a single meaning that reflects its social context. This is of fundamental importance for libraries as they attempt to engage in IT-related activities at a number of levels.

Implications of SCOT for Library IT Outreach

At a basic level, the interpretive flexibility of libraries is an issue for their engagement in collaborative IT activities. If one were to think of a library as a technology, it achieved closure in its interpretive flexibility some time ago as an institution that manages collections of books, and book-like, objects. Therefore, most people outside of the library associate the library brand with books. This brand identity provides an immediate, although not the sole, barrier in seeking to become a core participant in the development of information infrastructure, at least in the development of digital information infrastructure.

If libraries are perceived to be engaged primarily with books, how is it that they will come to be active participants in IT initiatives on campus or beyond? Advocacy and outreach efforts are certainly important in helping individual partners better understand the role of libraries, but this is also a level at which cultural assumptions about libraries are so deeply ingrained that this situation will not be effectively addressed through time-limited outreach efforts. The need to communicate the value of libraries in a digital environment needs to be a frequent topic of conversation with potential partners and stakeholders on an ongoing basis. The importance of this communication must not be underestimated. Academic library users are increasingly accustomed to highly aggregated content that is integrated into environments that facilitate personal workflow.[10] These content aggregations, as well as portals or other tools for personal information workflow will often be controlled by entities external to libraries. The scale of digital collection and service development is often such that it is too expensive, either in human or material terms, for any given library to address entirely internally. Developing information commons, or other IT-enabled collaborative spaces, will often require collaboration with other campus units. In other words, libraries must develop partnerships revolving around digital content and IT infrastructure going forward to be effective at delivering content to users in meaningful ways.

The issue of developing better understandings of librarian roles in a digital environment is not a one-sided issue, however. There are important issues that librarians need to grapple with, in concert with professionals from other areas of practice, to develop strategies for integrating themselves fully into the emerging information environment. Although libraries have existing content, services, and technical infrastructure that could play a significant role in broader contexts, there are many challenges related to the core of library practice that must be better addressed to facilitate meaningful IT partnerships. What are the implications of emerging forms of scholarly communication on collection development and management? What does it mean for libraries when collections are less dependent on institutional subscriptions or institutionally-defined collections than in the past? What does it mean for libraries when distribution of content is as concentrated among faculty as much as it is among formal publishers? What does it mean for libraries when users do not need to come to the library, physically or virtually, to access collections? These are but a few of the questions libraries must be able to better answer to engage in effective IT-related partnerships. Unless librarians can better articulate their value proposition in a digital environment for themselves, it will be difficult to convince other providers of digital content and services of that value. It will also be difficult for librarians to understand where external entities might be able to add value to their activities, what sorts of partnerships might be valuable, and how those partnerships might allow a library to be strategically repositioned.

So, there is a significant amount of advocacy that is required for libraries to communicate that they have a role in the digital information environment. These advocacy efforts are particularly challenging because they involve questioning and changing deeply held cultural beliefs about the role of libraries. They are also challenging because they require the individual libraries and the library community at a broader level to question professional values and beliefs in developing a rearticulation of what it is to be a library in a digital environment.

Even if, after a long process of working with individuals from many sectors of information activity, there is progress in this regard, there are many other issues related to professional culture that must be addressed for libraries to be effective in IT-related activities.

Professional Cultures and IT Outreach

Although it may seem like something of an oxymoron, outreach within the library is one of the foremost challenges for moving libraries fully into their digital future. One way of interpreting the social structure of libraries, or any organization, is as a culture, or set of cultures. Although libraries as organizations are usually associated with the profession of librarianship, they are actually quite diverse in terms of professional cultures and values. Even limiting one's focus to librarianship, there is wider range of professional cultures than is apparent on the surface. Viewed sociologically, librarianship may be considered to be a federated profession comprised of a number of affiliated sub-specialties with evolving social relations.[11] While there may be some common principles shared by all, the overall focus of professionals within a federated profession is dictated by the type of organization for which they work and the individual's functional specialization. For example, librarians engaged in technical services may be seen as having a different set of professional values and practices than those providing reference services. These specializations, although different, have contributed to the evolution of a set of coherent and cooperative relationships through a long history of managing academic library collections and services.

But relationships are continually developing, and may change as the position of a profession within a broader sociotechnical context change. If, for example, there are opportunities for librarians to make a claim for professional jurisdiction over the production and management of digital scholarly information that is significantly different than past practice, there will be a need to renegotiate the social relationships among sub-specialties of the profession in order to fulfill the altered mission.[12] Although libraries have been engaged in IT-enabled activities for decades, it is safe to say that the nature and scope of these activities has changed significantly over this time. A set of established roles surrounding library technology, generally focused on the management of integrated library systems but also branching into digitization, are generally well accepted within the library community. This set of roles, however, continues to evolve and requires ongoing outreach among specialties to develop an appropriate balance and understanding of them. This has created a situation in which there is a professional culture employed within libraries, and critical to their future, which is perhaps not fully integrated into their organizational and professional culture.

Where things become particularly complex for libraries is their dependence on external professional knowledge. This can be seen both at the institutional level and within the community as a whole. Most libraries, for example, depend on professionals with backgrounds in IT, Computer Science, Management Information Systems, and other related disciplines to not only provide strategic technology-based services, but also to provide leadership in the application of technologies. Within the library community, many leaders and innovators have backgrounds in disciplines other than library and information science. There are computer scientists, for example, who are valued members of the library community and who are very prominent in providing directions and innovations to libraries. Recent innovations by historians engaged in digital research have provided library users and librarians with important new tools in managing the research process.[13] Evolving practices in the sciences are resulting in new types of information-centric research infrastructure that provides significant new opportunities for libraries and librarians. In short, individuals from professions other than librarianship are hugely important to libraries, and particularly so to digital initiatives within the library setting.

These professionals have different sets of values and needs for professional practice that may conflict with those of librarians. They have been acculturated in a different profession, with different professional values and practices. This will have an impact on how issues will be framed and approached. Professionals from different backgrounds may identify issues in different ways, or even identify different issues altogether. They may ascribe very different values to the material and philosophical aspects of library practices, or potential library practices. They may have very different approaches to problem solving. Different sets of responsibilities may also lead to methods of prioritizing work that are not well understood by others in the library.[14]

There are numerous case studies that demonstrate the issues that can arise when important professional viewpoints are excluded from, or marginalized within, projects. Forsythe, for example, describes how the design and implementation of a clinical information system designed for migraine sufferers was botched because the perspectives of physicians and programmers were privileged over the perspectives of migraine sufferers as well as nurses and other types of health care providers.[15] Novek describes the ways in which the design and implementation of a pharmaceutical automaton system in a hospital excluded non-pharmacists from having control over workflows related to the dispensing of drugs, and the issues that arose as a result.[16]

These different perspectives may cause considerable tension in the workplace. Reconciliation of these differences is critical, as it is not only the various practices of librarians that are important to the success of a library, but also the practices of non-librarians. Failure to develop an inclusive environment along professional lines may very well result in strategic directions and projects that are deeply flawed and do not truly address the needs of library users. Library administrators need to foster an environment where the perspectives of all professional groups are valued. Professionals of all stripes must take every opportunity to communicate their values. It is particularly important that others in their organization understand what they identify as the most important challenges for libraries, how they prioritize work, and the sorts of workloads and practices they must deal with on a daily basis. Conversely, it is important that professionals of diverse fields be willing to listen and be open-minded about the values and practices of others. It is as important that librarians appreciate and embrace web-centric models of developing services and distributing content as it is for IT professionals to develop and understanding of the tradition and heritage of libraries. Developing a better understanding of what IT and library professionals might contribute to the furthering of the library enterprise is critical to transforming library practices in effective ways, but will require ongoing dialogue and the willingness to be open-minded about one's own professional culture.

The situation in resolving professional differences within a library can be seen, at least to a degree, as a microcosm of the challenges that present themselves when libraries partner with external IT organizations. If the issues of role, value, and mission identified earlier can be overcome and opportunities for collaboration or partnership become apparent, there will still be issues of professional culture that must be overcome. These issues overlap almost completely with the situation with libraries, although they may be more difficult to resolve since any resolution cannot rely on shared goals, performance expectations. They must be resolved because both sides see value in doing so.

Professional Networks

A final point of importance is the role of professional networks, both as agents of change and as barriers to change. Although academic libraries ultimately operate and develop strategic directions on a library-by-library basis, it is striking how many similarities there are in the practices of individual libraries and in their responses to change. These isomorphic tendencies are commonplace not only among libraries, but also among other types of organizations as well. DiMaggio and Powell describe three modes of isomorphic behavior through which organizations come to adopt common practices.[17] In the case of academic libraries, normative isomorphism is especially relevant.

Normative isomorphic behaviors are common in organizational fields that rely heavily upon professional labor, and are exhibited as professional education, professional associations, and professional networks facilitate the diffusion of professional norms. In turn, these common professional norms result in common organizational practices. For example, it is not uncommon in many libraries for a librarian to return from a conference with an idea for a new program discovered through a conference presentation. It is also not uncommon for librarians to survey peers at other institutions to learn about their approach to a particular issue. This sort of diffusion to ideas, coupled with professional mobility, lead to a professional environment in which new ideas for practice are readily diffused throughout the profession, and in which the practices of individual libraries come to resemble one another.

Professional networks can certainly play important roles for libraries with regard to IT. One-on-one discussions with peers, discussions at professional meetings, or professional publications, among others, can play an important role in shaping and diffusing new understandings and articulations of the role of IT in libraries, or of the role of libraries in a networked environment. This is true not only of library-focused organizations and conferences, but perhaps more importantly at conferences attracting a broader audience such as EDUCAUSE. Professional networks, for example, could explain the rapid adoption of VUFind, a tool for providing a more web-centric approach to discovering information in library catalogs than most vendor-supplied OPACs. Professional networks, however, can also serve as barriers to change. The development of strong communities based on particular cultural or professional assumptions, or around particular technologies (e.g., MARC) can lead to a situation where possible avenues to change are unexplorable, at least in full, due to the hegemonic power of the entrenched community.[18]

Conclusion

While there are many areas of outreach in which libraries must engage, outreach surrounding IT issues is at the forefront of issues that must be addressed to insure the continued vitality of libraries. Unfortunately, engaging in such issues is a very complex undertaking—complex because of the social relations of librarians and situatedness of libraries more so than the technical issues that must be resolved. Major actors within the sociotechnical environment of information access and management, including libraries, must be able to successfully partner with others in order to be successful and relevant.

Successful partnership, however, requires a shared understanding about the roles and contributions of libraries in a digital world, an understanding that will be difficult to develop given deep-seated cultural assumptions about libraries. Working with external entities is only part of the challenge, however. Incorporating the perspectives of multiple professions within libraries is an equally important challenge. Developing a clear articulation of how libraries can make strategic use of IT is first required to facilitate more effective partnerships with other units on campus or beyond. The significance of overcoming differences in professional cultures and values within libraries, and recognizing the affordances and limitations of professional networks and practice within librarianship cannot be overstated. If we cannot communicate effectively amongst ourselves, it should come as no surprise that communication with external organizations is problematic.

Notes

1. Maloney and Bracke, "Beyond Information Architecture," Ockerbloom, "Open records, open possibilities," Digital Library Federation, "DLF ILS Interface Task Group,"
2. Breeding, "Open Source Integrated Library Systems," Morgan, "Possibilities for open source software" in libraries."
3. Liebowitz and Margolis, "Market processes and the selection"
4. Bijker, *Of Bicycles, Bakelites, and Bulbs*
5. OCLC, *Perceptions of Libraries and Information Resources*, 3–1

6. Bijker, Hughes, and Pinch, The Social Construction of Technological Systems
7. Bijker, *Of Bicycles, Bakelites, and Bulbs,* 123–127.
8. Ibid, 73–77
9. Ibid, 88
10. Johnson, and Smith, *The 2009 Horizon Report*
11. Abbott, "Professionalism and the Future of Librarianship"
12. Abbott, *The System of Professions*
13. Cohen, "Zotero"
14. Bloor and Dawson, "Understanding Professional Culture"
15. Forsythe, "New Bottles, Old Wine"
16. Novek, "Hospital pharmacy automation"
17. DiMaggio and Powell, "The iron cage revisited"
18. Lukes, *Power: a Radical View*

Works Cited

Abbott, Andrew. "Professionalism and the Future of Librarianship." *Library Trends* 46, no. 3 (1998): 430–443.

———. *The System of Professions: an Essay on the Division of Expert Labor.* Chicago, IL: University of Chicago Press, 1988.

Bijker, Wiebe E. *Of Bycicles, Bakelites, and Bulbs: Toward a Theory of Sociotechnical Change.* Cambridge, MA: MIT Press, 1995.

Bijker, Wiebe E., Thomas P. Hughes, and Trevor J. Pinch, . *The Social Construction of Technological Systems: New Directions in the Sociology and History of Technology.* Cambridge, MA: MIT Press, 1987.

Bloor, Geoffery, and Patrick Dawson. "Understanding Professional Culture in Organizational Context." *Organization Studies* 15, no. 2 (1994): 275–295.

Breeding, Marshall. "Open Source Integrated Library Systems." *Library Technology Reports* 44, no. 8 (2008).

Cohen, Daniel J. "Zotero: Social and Semantic Computing for Historical Scholarship." *AHA Perspectives* 45, no. 5 (2007).

DiMaggio, Paul J., and Walter W. Powell. ""The Iron Cage Revisited": Institutional Isomorphism and Collective Rationality in Organizational Fields." *American Sociological Review* 48 (1983): 147–60.

"DLF ILS Interface Task Group Technical Recommendation: an API for the effective interoperation between integrated library systems and external discovery applications." *Digital Library Federation. ILS Discovery Task Group.* 2008. http://www.diglib.org/architectures/ilsdi/DLF_ILS_Discovery_1.0.pdf.

Forsythe, Diana E. "New Bottles, Old Wine: Hidden Cultural Assumptions in a Computerized Explanation System for Migraine Sufferers." *Medical Anthropology* 10, no. 4 (1996): 1996.

Johnson, L, A Levine, and R. Smith. *The 2009 Horizon Report.* Austin, TX: The New Media Consortium, 2009.

Liebowitz, S.J., and Stephen E. Margolis. "Market Processes and the Selection of Standards." *Harvard Journal of Law and Technology* 9 (1996): 283–318.

Lukes, Stephen. *Power: a Radical View.* London: Macmillan, 1974.

Maloney, Krisellen, and Paul J. Bracke. "Beyond Information Architecture: a system-integration approach to web-site design." *Information Technology and Libraries* 23, no. 4 (2004): 145–152.

Morgan, Eric Lease. "Possibilities for Open Source Software in Libraries." *Information Technology and Libraries* 21, no. 1 (2002): 12–15.

Novek, Joel. "Hospital Pharmacy Automation: Collective Mobility or Collective Control?" *Social Science and Medicine* 51, no. 4 (2000): 491–503.

Ockerbloom, John Mark. "Open Records, Open Possibilities." *Paper presented at American Library Association Midwinter Meeting, Denver, CO.* January 2009. http://works.bepress.com/john_mark_okerbloom/10.

OCLC. *Perceptions of Libraries and Information Resources: A Report to the OCLC Membership.* Dublin, OH: OCLC, 2005.

Digital Advocacy: Using Interactive Technologies to Reassert Library Value

Kim Leeder and Memo Cordova

Advocacy Goes Digital

There is a refrain that winds throughout the recent literature of library advocacy related to the question of why libraries need advocacy and why they need it now more than ever. In *The Visible Librarian*, Judith A. Siess observes, "Information at the desktop is no longer necessarily connected to a library or librarian in the user's mind. We are becoming more and more 'invisible'".[1] In an article in *Knowledge Quest*, Ann Martin asserts, "As America entered the information age, libraries were no longer being pictured as a vital part of family life. Instead, technology became the critical resource for a middle-class family."[2] The American Library Association's *Library Advocate's Handbook* comments, "Technology has greatly enhanced library and information services. It has also raised disturbing questions".[3] The refrain, of course, is tied to the concern among librarians that the majority of the American population prefers to get their information from the internet, and that they no longer see value in libraries because they don't see libraries in the places where they're searching for information.

The first and perhaps most obvious response to that concern is what one finds in most books and articles about advocacy: a rolling-up of the sleeves as the author describes the need to put shyness aside and jump into the noisy, messy world of advocacy, marketing, and public relations. Clearly librarians need to get their hands dirty and fight for attention and funding in a world where both are getting scarcer. However, there is also a second-tier response to the concern about libraries' "invisibility" that has not yet received much attention: the felt need to become more active in the very forum that has overshadowed the value of libraries. Almost all libraries have Web sites, many have created profiles on social networking sites, and professional library organizations continue to build and expand their Web presences, but those silos of Web content are merely a fraction of what is needed to make libraries a compelling digital force. In this chapter we will discuss the wide array of additional strategies to engage current and potential library stakeholders through the use of interactive technologies.

Like it or not, this is now a Web 2.0 world where information has become a two-way street. Web 1.0 tactics, those that focus on delivering or publishing information, are no longer enough. Consider for example the sentiment expressed in the single paragraph from the 2006 *Library Advocate's Handbook* that touches on internet advocacy: "The electronic media offer many new opportunities for delivering the library message to a wider audience."[4] While the handbook is a valuable resource, it is also a prime example of the 1.0 perspective. The key word there is "delivering," a verb that connotes an informational one-way street. A mere four years later it has become clear that information goes both ways, and if libraries want to be visible on that busy thoroughfare, they'll need to give and take as well. That means more than just offering up librarian expertise on a silver platter in a static forum; it means taking part in the dialogue and participating in a world that doesn't necessarily consider librarians to be authorities. If librarians want to maintain—or regain—their status as information experts, they'll need to get out there and become part of the virtual conversation without expecting anything in return.

Types of Digital Advocacy

Digital advocacy can take place anywhere there is a computer and an internet connection. Librarians can become advocates on Web sites, email, social networking platforms, media sharing forums, and other online forums. The key to digital advocacy in the current environment can be summed up in one word: interactivity. Whenever possible, librarians should be creating options for conversation about, feedback from, and personalization of any content they post. It's important to allow users full freedom to make a library *their* library by providing them with the tools to personalize library Web sites, edit or rate catalog entries, and comment on blogs. The librarian's role as gatekeeper is no more; today the gateway is always open and the librarian serves as a guide, not an authority. "Engaging with the groundswell means admitting that customers are taking power and that [we] are not in control. It's a scary and difficult first step to take," note Bernoff and Li.[5] Yet "long-term, engaging with the groundswell is the best possible way to promote customer centric thinking within companies."[6] Librarians have to be willing to *earn* people's respect as an essential information resource by taking on their challenging questions, criticisms, and demands publicly and responding creatively in ways that will surpass their expectations. The following media provide a wide array of possibilities for librarians to become more digitally effective in advocating their value.

Library Web Sites

Overall, libraries are doing a good job of using the basic 1.0 features of the internet to advocate their worth. As libraries are accustomed to being information providers, adapting to the one-way Web environment was not difficult. The average library in 2010 has a multi-page Web site including announcements of events, exhibits, services, and collections. Like other forms of digital advocacy these virtual signboards are generally focused on promoting library services and collections, and this has been effective to a limited extent. However, the emergence of social software within the last several years has exploded the possibilities for creating library Web sites that provide dynamic content without

---

Figure 1. LibraryThing for Libraries featured in Kansas State University Libraries' catalog, http://catalog.lib.ksu.edu/cgi-bin/Pwebrecon. cgi?DB=local&BBID=188474

⊙ brief view   ○ full view   ○ staff view

The sun also rises / Ernest Hemingway.

Author: Hemingway, Ernest, 1899-1961.
Title: The sun also rises / Ernest Hemingway.
Published: New York : Scribner, 1954.
Description: 247 p. ; 18 cm.

Location: Hale Library Stacks
Call number: PS3515.E37 S9 1954 → ⓢ Text me this call number
Status: Not Checked Out
If item is missing, at the bindery, or checked out, click to request
Copy no. (s) at this location: 1-2
ISBN: 0684174723 (pbk.)
Tag this item ✒: del.icio.us
Link to this item: permalink, right click to copy
report errors in this record
Related editions:
Similar books:
Moveable feast by Hemingway, Ernest, 1899-1961.
Great Gatsby : a facsimile of the manuscript by Fitzgerald, F. Scott (Francis Scott), 1896-1940.

Tag browser: 1920s **20th century American** American fiction **American literature** bullfighting Ernest Hemingway Europe France **Hemingway** lost generation modernism Nobel Paris **Spain**

Record Options
Select download format: Full Record ▾ [Format for Print/Save]
Enter your email address [   ] [Send]

incurring greater financial and personnel costs. Think big: consider the staid services libraries currently provide and imagine strategies to make them as interactive and customizable as possible. Take the library OPAC, for instance. "The classification schemes used to organize library collections rely on the expertise of a small group of specialists... Although this system works well as far as it goes, a Library 2.0 catalog that could generate additional metadata from the wisdom of library patrons would enhance the value of the OPAC."[7] LibraryThing for Libraries is on the right track here by providing an application that can be added to library OPACs that offers tagging, book recommendations, ratings and reviews, and other social features.

Such a system enables library users to take control of their information searching, add their own knowledge, and create a feeling of stronger personal connection to the library. As of January 2010, LibraryThing for Libraries had been incorporated into the catalogs of over fifteen hundred libraries around the world.[8] By adding such interactive features to a largely static library service, libraries enrich the user experience and add value to the catalog by tapping the collective wisdom of users. Furthermore, they provide a platform that users will

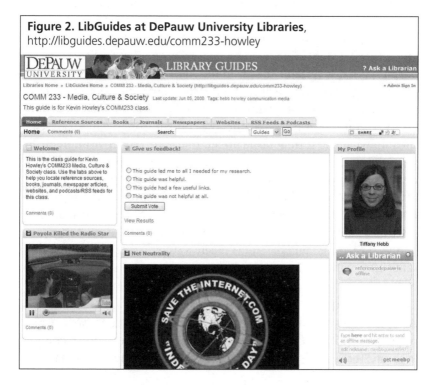

Figure 2. LibGuides at DePauw University Libraries, http://libguides.depauw.edu/comm233-howley

find more valuable and will be more likely to visit again for social as well as informational purposes.

Another interactive offering that can be found on a growing number of library Web sites is the next-generation research guide. LibGuides, for instance. "LibGuides' flexibility and ease of use empowers librarians of any technical skill level to quickly and effortlessly create content-rich, Web 2.0 multimedia guides and share useful information with patrons."[9] This software is one of the most successful of its kind because it encompasses a variety of features common to social networks and harnesses them to allow the librarian to build dynamic subject-specific research guides. Not only can a librarian build in RSS feeds of new books, video tutorials, and Meebo chat widgets, but patrons can subscribe via RSS to be notified of any future changes to the page. Moreover, because LibGuides allows users to comment on specific features within the guide, it constantly invites feedback and suggestions for changes or improvements that the librarian can then incorporate.

LibGuides also has a Facebook application that users can choose to add to their profile, which provides a direct bridge from Facebook into the user's library guides. The availability of new tools such as LibraryThing and LibGuides means that the former static online research guide has suddenly morphed into a vibrant new tool with renewed value. LibGuides is not necessarily a perfect tool for this purpose but it is certainly a step in the right direction.

Adding interactive new content is one step in creating an effective library Web site. To complement and build on this initiative, it is necessary to consider ways to channel the content from the library Web site into whatever format users prefer. In the current environment, "if we are to succeed in providing quality information in a convenient, timely, and efficient manner to our users, we must appear in their information space and not wait for them to discover us as a separate resource, disintegrated, and disengaged from their information discovery sources."[10] The addition of email alerts and—more importantly—RSS feeds can take the Web site a step further by pushing the same information out to users' desktops.

Library Blogs

As both readers and creators of content, internet users are well aware of the possibilities of blogs. Dave Sifry, founder of the blog-tracking Web site Technorati, surveyed blogs in early 2007 and found that there were over 70 million of these self-published online journals worldwide, with over 120,000 new blogs created every day.[11] Technorati has not published a new estimate in the past four years, which may suggest that the number has grown so large they have ceased trying to quantify it. In the U.S. alone, the Pew Internet & American Life Project reported in 2005 that "16% of all U.S. adults (or one in six people) are blog readers."[12] That number has undoubtedly grown in the subsequent years.

What accounts for this tremendous ongoing growth of blogging is the ease with which individuals can publish their ideas on user-friendly platforms like Blogger and WordPress. Blogging services package powerful, customizable, and intuitive "drag and drop" publishing features, allowing an individual to set up a blog, choose customizable features, and begin posting content immediately. When it comes to creating a blog, there are both free and fee-based blogging platforms. Most have scores of colorful design templates, and many come loaded with small applications such as calendars, photograph slideshows, maps, weather, and similar services that can be customized to an individual's own specifications. These are in addition to whatever photographs, videos, and other media the blogger chooses to embed within their posts. Consider, then, coupling these dynamic and helpful features with a library's focused pursuit of advocacy and community engagement and it becomes have a powerful, interactive vehicle to reach users.

A look at the Blogging Libraries Wiki[13] offers an indication of the large number of libraries that have embraced blogging as a successful and inexpensive means to disseminate content. Of course, not all of these libraries are using blogs to their full potential as interactive advocacy tools, as such requires a substantial commitment of time and energy by more than one individual within the library. It is also necessary to have complete buy-in on the administrative level for a blog to reach its full potential. The most effective blogs typically reflect the unbound personality of the blogger(s), while many library administrators shy away from allowing an individual's voice to shine through on an institutional blog. "Ultimately, the only limits on what your blog covers are those imposed by law and your bloggers' imaginations,"[14] explains Stephanie Brookover, author of the article "Why We Blog."

The libraries that use blogs as a venue for advocacy may reap a greater benefit and reach a larger number of internet users than libraries using traditional print-based media. Indeed, given the

Figure 3. Virginia Commonwealth University Library Suggestion Blog, http://blog.vcu.edu/libsuggest/

growing number of blogging platforms and their relative ease of use, libraries can exploit this medium to channel and disseminate library-rich content on the Web.

Chat and Text Messaging Services

For those who are fully immersed in social networks and interactive Web services, online chat (or instant messaging) has become today's telephone. In terms of usage, chat services continue to grow. In 2004 the Pew Internet & American Life Project reported that over 53 million adults were using instant messaging services, while in early 2010 instant messaging aggregator Meebo alone boasted over eight million unique logins per day.[15]

It is only logical that libraries should be available for interaction on such relatively inexpensive and highly trafficked platforms. "Does putting the *library* at the point of your users' needs via a simple, seamless interface sound like it should cost thousands of dollars and require IT support? Guess what? With just some staff time for setup and training, this is another virtually free way to reach out where your users are."[16] Of course, like any additional service features, online chat

Figure 4. Meebo widget on Ithaca College Library Web site,
http://www.ithaca.edu/library/services/refchat.php

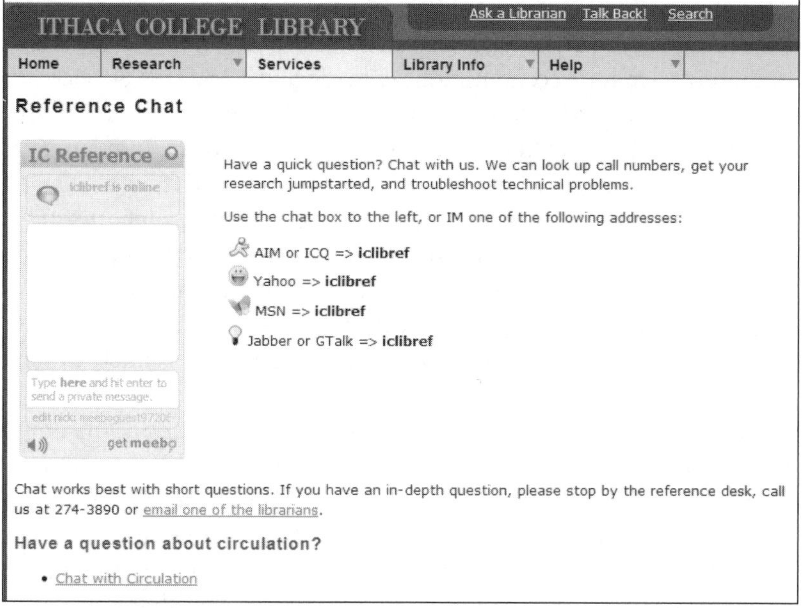

and text messaging (or SMS) reference require staff time to monitor the service and respond to questions, but they can often be folded into existing commitments such as reference desk or other duties.

Chat and SMS have enabled libraries to once again extend beyond their brick and mortar boundaries by using emergent, free technologies to engage users in their own virtual spaces. Meebo is a unique instant messaging aggregator that combines services from America Online (AOL), Google, Yahoo!, MSN, and others on a Web-based platform to make it possible for users of all instant messaging services to chat with each other without installing software. An added bonus for libraries that use Meebo is the ease with which chat widgets—or small embeddable chat windows—can be built and customized for any Webpage. As with RSS feeds, synchronous chat widgets enhance library services by pushing the library outward into the virtual world, a world where users already spend much of their time. What better way to enhance libraries' relationships with their communities than by providing multiple, convenient ways for users to get information at the point of need? By providing this kind of service, libraries are making people aware of the different access points libraries can offer their users and reasserting themselves as a dynamic resource.

Meebo is one example of the kind of synchronous aggregate service points libraries can use to enhance services, but it is by no means the only one. If chat communication has been seen as an effective way libraries can provide another area of service, then developments in mobile telephone computing have made Short Message Service (SMS), or texting via cellular phones, a vital link for communication. According to the Pew Internet & American Life Project, "On a typical day, now more than half of cell users (52%) have used it for a non-voice data activity, such as texting, emailing, snapping a picture, or any one of the other seven activities about which they were asked."[17] The simplicity of SMS appeals to the highly mobile and savvy user. The report continues, "[s]ending text messages remains the mainstay activity for cell phone users; they are more than twice as likely to send a text on the average day as do anything else."

Libraries have begun capitalizing on this effective mode of communication by adopting SMS channels that facilitate this interaction, whether used for reference services, advocacy, or outreach. However, there are challenges for libraries that adopt SMS technology. Texting typically requires a telephone carrier and as such incurs additional costs. While libraries that provide SMS access are few, there are a growing number who are taking advantage of alternative SMS tools such as Google Voice (GV). GV is not yet widely available to the public—at the time of this writing, it requires an invitation by someone who holds an account—but it shows a great deal of promise. It features several free and low-cost functions, such as providing a single telephone number that combines multiple telephone numbers, allowing users to send and receive SMS at no cost, transcribing and playing messages, and sending email notifications of incoming text messages and voice mail, all via the Web. The Library Success Wiki lists several academic libraries making use of GV for all their text messaging needs.[18] For libraries looking to capitalize on a growing mobile Internet market via outreach, advocacy, or services, Google Voice provides yet another venue for adding value in a highly technological environment.

Overall, a service such as Meebo or Google Voice is implicitly valuable for advocacy because it expands the online visibility of libraries and increases their perceived value. In most libraries that offer online chat or SMS, the service is available to everyone whether student, staff, faculty, or community member. Students use online chat to get answers to reference and campus questions, while faculty often ask about policies and procedural topics. Even potential donors may initiate a chat to inquire about resident borrowing privileges or events, and will be pleased to find a responsive, helpful voice on the other end of the line.

Social Networking

If blogging gave the masses instant access to one-click publishing, then social networks exploded the capability of joining disparate participatory audiences in a common ground. The brilliance of social networks lies in the ease with which individuals and organizations can create an online presence and share interests and news with others. This gives everyone a platform to exchange information and engage in ongoing dialogues. Social networks are as varied as the people who use them. Giants like MySpace, Facebook, Bebo, Ning, and others command legions of users from many social demographics. According to the Facebook Press Room, the site hosted over 350

Figure 5. Cal Poly Pomona University Library's Facebook page, http://www.facebook.com/pages/Pomona-CA/Cal-Poly-Pomona-University-Library/13632547215

million active users as of January 2010, half of whom log on daily.[19] Facebook is also notable as the second most popular Web site in the United States, as of January 2010, with only Google showing a greater following.[20] Social networks are having a profound impact on the way people share information with each other.

In a study of Facebook use on college and university campuses, Charnigo and Barnett-Ellis found that "online social networks are dynamically documenting the here and now of campus life and shaping the future of how we communicate."[21] Many libraries are already individually exploring ways to take advantage of these networks to promote events, advance educational initiatives, and connect with users. A search of Facebook, MySpace, or Ning, for instance, will yield a long list of library profiles, pages, groups, and networks.

Thus far, there has been no formal assessment of libraries' success in these endeavors, but based solely on their numbers of "fans" or "friends," it appears that libraries who have the best name recognition (such as major university libraries) and those who are most aggressive in promoting their online forays are the ones with the most vibrant pages and groups.

> User participation is not easy to achieve, it needs a dedicated effort and especially an open and flexible approach that encourages contributions... No rigid ex-ante planning is possible, but rather an effort should be made to let user participation emerge in often unpredictable ways... It is necessary to invest in trial and error, beta testing and continuous improvement listening to users' feedback. One of the great advantages of Web 2.0 is that it lowers the cost of errors, as very little investment is needed to launch a collaboration. However, simply adopting the technologies, without embracing the value, will have little or negative impact.[22]

All of the technologies that we describe in this chapter require regular cultivation; they must be monitored, promoted, and reviewed regularly to ensure both that potential users know about them and that the give-and-take exchange remains active and vibrant. This does take effort, but it is a worthwhile investment when such an initiative succeeds in reasserting the value of libraries for Web users.

Whatever its level of success, building a virtual social presence has the potential to create rich advocacy opportunities for libraries. Many libraries use their Facebook and MySpace pages to promote events and new purchases, as well as to provide an open forum where their communities can offer feedback and ideas about new activities and collections. "One of the interesting side effects of starting to use social tools within our libraries and with our patrons is that all of a sudden we have a closer, deeper-seeming relationship with patrons whom we may otherwise barely know."[23] Once they are "friends," library users' academic majors, study habits, interests, and opinions suddenly become open information. While libraries will always put user privacy at the forefront of their concerns, they can take advantage of this new knowledge in order to better target services and events to their campus community. For instance, if several students complain on Facebook about having nowhere to study late at night during finals, the savvy library would expand hours to meet that expressed need.

While creating individual library presences on social networks is worthwhile in terms of targeting services, there are also opportunities to use these new media communication channels for more direct library advocacy. Many of these possibilities are thus far untested. Taking a cue from the business world, libraries should look at how major international corporations use their Facebook pages. Instead of launching those pages and waiting for clients to become "fans," corporations are advertising and developing ways to match products and services to user interests. Facebook excels at targeted advertising, using the personal information users provide (including age, geographical location, and interests) to determine which ads show up in the site's sidebar for each individual.

Libraries, on the whole, are not taking advantage of this because of the cost to each individual institution. While some libraries are posting fliers, the real impact of such activities will only be tapped when libraries come together nationally to advocate as a single, recognizable force. For instance, the potential impact of a centralized advocacy initiative aimed at the general public on social networking Web sites, sponsored by The American Library Association (ALA) or The Association of College and Research Libraries (ACRL), could rival efforts of some major corporations that are already building new customer bases within those networks. Although ALA and many of its divisions and sections are already using Facebook, Twitter, and the like, their activities in those networks are essentially internal; they speaking to the choir. An effective advocacy campaign would require targeted advertising within the social media sites that is designed to speak to library users and potential users, not librarians and those who are already library supporters. The possibilities of digital advocacy on social networking platforms for a united, national collective of academic—or all—libraries are expansive.

Media Sharing: Audio & Video

The internet does not stop at the boundaries of text, nor does digital advocacy. Media sharing is a rapidly growing online industry, and provides a variety of media that an increasing number of libraries are beginning to exploit for the purposes of outreach and education. As perhaps the simplest (or most familiar) for libraries, Flickr has quickly become a place for libraries to share photos of events and collections. YouTube is the omnipresent vehicle for video sharing, while iTunes U offers hosting for educational podcasts and vodcasts (video podcasts). Each of these applications offers unique opportunities for libraries to assert their value by contributing to the larger conversation.

As of May 2008, there were over 2,200 members in Flickr's "Libraries and Librarians" group, with more than 17,000 images in the group's photo pool; meanwhile, photo hits on the word "library" was creeping up on 900,000. An area of Flickr's site called "The Commons" hosts a pilot of over 3,000 photos from the archives at the Library of Congress, as well as additional photos from the Brooklyn Museum and the Powerhouse Museum (and is open to new institutional partners).

Michael Stephens, author of *Web 2.0 and Libraries* and blogger for the ALA TechSource blog, says that when library photos are tagged with their name and location, "it gets you found in the great pool of all of the photos in Flickr. Maybe someone is searching Flickr for his or her hometown and discovers images of the local library and learns of services or programs he or she didn't know about… Participating in this type of social software community is relatively inexpensive, can offer presence, and it's fun!"[24] For academic libraries, this may involve posting valuable digital images from Special Collections or Archives that would otherwise be buried in digital collection software platforms where users are unlikely to find it. Putting library photos out on an active forum like Flickr is an exceptional way to

Figure 6. Library of Congress Flickr site,
http://www.flickr.com/photos/library_of_congress/

show the value of libraries to a large segment of the campus users and the public by making themselves more visible in a popular forum.

As an example of powerful the exposure this forum can provide, the Library of Congress (LOC) reported that between January 3, 2008 (when their first photos were uploaded), and January 18, 2008, there had been approximately 1.1 million total views on their account, including photos, set, and collection page views.[25] That is 1.1 million views in *fifteen* days. In addition to mere views there had been about four hundred comments on photos in their collection, and the list of tags already added by Flickr users to describe the LOC photos was seemingly endless. LOC blogger Matt Raymond commented, "The response to the Library's pilot project with Flickr has been nothing short of astounding. You always hope for a positive reaction to something like this, but it has been utterly off the charts—from the Flickr community, from the blogosphere, from the news media—it is nothing short of amazing." With a testimony like this, there's little question about Flickr's potential value as a medium for library advocacy through engaging constituents as participants in the provision of information.

Once libraries begin sharing photos, it's only a small jump to the world of video. In *Social Software in Libraries,* Meredith Farkas observed, "Video can be used in libraries to market the library, and to educate and connect with patrons... Libraries could record speakers, events, and classes using a digital video camera and make those videos available online."[26] The possibility of creating library video content opens up a wide array of instructional and promotional opportunities—opportunities that no longer require special funding outside of the purchase of an adequate camera and video editing software. 2008 saw the second annual InfoTubey awards presented by Information Today, Inc., at the Computers in Libraries conference. According to the conference Web site, awards are given to the "top five productions that demonstrate creativity and innovation in marketing a library or library services or enhancing the library's value."[27] Combined, the five winners in 2008 had logged over 35,000 views from YouTube users.

Educational podcasting online, most notably on iTunes U, is another media sharing medium where libraries have the opportunity to make a splash. "[T]he portable media player now is transforming higher education like few distance education initiatives before it. Fueled by the development of iTunes U — a section of Apple's iTunes music store...podcasting is fast becoming an essential educational tool for colleges and universities."[28] Since 2001 when Apple first launched the iPod, Bradley notes, they have sold more than 100 million devices worldwide.

Despite the name, iTunes U is open to all educational content, and even public libraries—such as the New York Public Library—are jumping on board alongside academic institutions. Of course, unlike other types of media sharing outlets, iTunes U is built into Apple's iTunes software, and cannot be accessed unless iTunes is installed on an individual's computer. On the upside, iTunes U podcasts, once downloaded, can be accessed by and transferred to non-iPod music players. Podcasting offers libraries the opportunity to provide recordings of unique events, special interviews, or other notable activities that can then be enjoyed by their community and beyond. Having a library's names in iTunes U, alongside major museums and other media outlets, is an important way to assert their continued relevance in the digital universe.

All of these media sharing opportunities serve the purpose of advocacy by reasserting the value of the library on platforms popular with the mainstream population. By adding content—and therefore, value—to sites like Flickr, YouTube, and iTunes, libraries expand their virtual presence in ways that can reap great benefits. Individuals who formerly thought of libraries as book storage facilities inevitably change their tunes when confronted with high-quality information in the places they already search for information.

Web-based Answer Boards

One of the most exciting grassroots movements in digital library advocacy is the "Slam the Boards" project that began in September 2007. The project was created by reference librarians who decided to reach out and show their value by answering as many questions as possible on Web site answer boards such as Yahoo! Answers.[29] The project's originator, Bill Pardue of Arlington Heights Memorial Library, described his impetus for starting "Slam the Boards" as follows:

> A lot of people who use these [answer board] services probably don't know that libraries also do this. So the idea was…to go out and answer questions on these services, and then also promote the fact that this question was answered by a librarian. So we're not just answering the question but we're also promoting libraries.[30]

Because "Slam the Boards" is a grassroots effort without any required sign-up for librarians, Pardue could only guess at the turnout for their first event, but he numbered initial librarian participation in the hundreds.[31] Participating librarians hailed from all types of libraries, including many from academic institutions. In recognition of their contributions, Yahoo! management contacted Pardue after the event and offered participating librarians a special status as "Yahoo! Answers Knowledge Partners" on their answer board. Considering that Yahoo! Answers ranks second in popularity as an online reference site behind only Wikipedia, this is notable recognition.[32] Participants in "Slam the Boards" maintain a collection of ideas, news, and resources on a WetPaint wiki called "Answer Board Librarians."[33]

The "Slam the Boards" project is based on a reference strategy that Pardue calls "predatory reference," and which he describes as

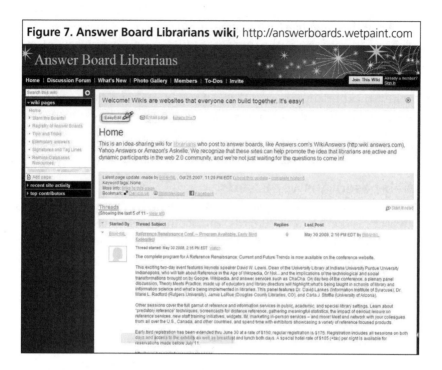

Figure 7. Answer Board Librarians wiki, http://answerboards.wetpaint.com

"*actively finding reference questions, rather than just waiting for them to come in.*"[34] Predatory reference can also take place in other locations on the internet where people go with questions, most notably, Wikipedia. While not an answer board per se, Wikipedia is a Web site that millions of people use to find answers, and a few wise individuals have already begun to build library content and information into the site. Anyone can create an account and begin editing and improving Wikipedia entries and the site enables users to self-identify by a wide variety of professional, personal, cultural, and regional factors. In fact, as of March 2008 over a hundred self-identified librarians were already active in the online encyclopedia, as reflected on the site's "Wikipedian Librarians" page.[35] Many of these Wikipedian Librarians have come together in a united effort to improve the site through an effort called WikiProject Librarians. As the librarian who goes by the name "Helperzoom" explains, "It's time we stepped up and contributed to Wikipedia: not just to its content but to its structures and technologies. This project page is intended to provide a rallying point for these activities."[36] Cooperative efforts described on that page include writing articles, enriching existing articles, linking book ISBNs, and enhancing Wikipedia's organization.

Improving Wikipedia from the inside out is one method of advocacy. A twist on this strategy that provides even more visibility for libraries is placing links in Wikipedia articles to push related library and specific content out to users, as the University of Washington (UW) Libraries has done. Librarians at UW located Wikipedia articles related to their library's digital content, and if those articles did not exist, created them. Then the articles were seeded with links to the UW Libraries Digital Collections Web site. The results indicate that the effort achieved some measure of success in referring Wikipedia users to the UW Libraries' Web site. Over the course of one year, from October 2005 to September 2006, server statistics showed that Wikipedia had referred more than eleven thousand new users to the UW Libraries Digital Collections.[37] By pushing their unique content out on Wikipedia, the UW Libraries are making their collection of over 120,000 digital images, texts, and audio files known to a huge population of potential users.

Answer boards and informational wikis are just two types of information-based Web sites through which librarians can expand their digital advocacy efforts, but they are the major ones at this point in time. The Answer Board Librarians and the UW Libraries are doing great work, but many more must follow the trails they have blazed. Truly successful library advocacy on sites like Yahoo! Answers and Wikipedia demand greater participation from all librarians to make those contributions more visible.

Conclusion

Before we doom libraries to an early grave of irrelevance, we should seriously reassess the boon that emergent technologies offer us. Free, informal, and accessible Web-based technologies are reshaping the way people interact with one another and with institutions. Location and time are no longer barriers to communication and, given the climate of innovation, people have grown to expect more from online services. A static Web site is insufficient to meet the multifarious needs of today's Web consumers. A library's online presence must provide the kind of interactive and relevant mien that will draw in and continuously engage potential supporters. Whereas libraries have in the past relied on passive but tried-and-true methods of information dissemination (such as printed newsletters, card catalogs, Dialog searches, and telephone reference), today's libraries are beginning to piggyback on Web-based resources developed by others (including

Facebook groups, Ning networks, WorldCat Web, blogs, and Lib-Guides) to change the way in which they engage users and assert their value. This puts libraries in a more active role than previously, a role that demands constant participation and contributions.

By building and frequently updating blogs and dynamic Web spaces, by sharing audio and video files, by engaging users on so-cial networking platforms, and by inviting constant feedback and commentary from users, libraries can actively reassert their value. Through these mechanisms libraries can spread the message that the library is about far, far more than books. These online tools can help libraries change the face they show both to the users of the "brick and mortar" library and to the ever-expanding internet user base and can provide an opportunity for libraries to redefine their roles, relevance, and core values. "In an increasingly digital world, the idea of the library has to be somewhere *and* everywhere: real, physical locations as well as ubiquitous access. Neither alone will suffice in meeting the varied and expanding needs of our communities, and neither alone expresses the true nature and usefulness of what a 'library' is and can be (and ought to be and has to be) in the 21st century."[38] The continu-ing challenge facing librarians is to exploit these interactive technolo-gies to become more visible and more integral in a world that has forgotten, in large part, what libraries can offer. Digital advocacy is about going to the places where library patrons find much of their in-formation and pushing out valuable resources, services, and expertise where it now matters the most. When librarians embrace this new role to its fullest, they will find that users are paying attention—and they are ready to join in to redefine what it means to be a library.

Notes

1. Siess, *The Visible Librarian*, xiii.
2. Martin, "The Evolution of the Librarian," 17.
3. American Library Association, Library Advocate's Handbook, 2.
4. Ibid, 14.
5. Bernoff and Li, "Harnessing the Power," 37.
6. Ibid, 42.
7. Wenzler, "LibraryThing and the Library Catalog," 1.
8. See http://www.librarything.com/wiki/index.php/LTFL:Libraries_using_LibraryThing_for_Libraries.
9. Springshare.
10. Armstrong, "Using RSS feeds," 185.
11. Sifry, "The State of the Live Web."
12. Pew Internet & American Life Project, "New data on blogs."
13. See http://www.blogwithoutalibrary.net/links/index.php?title=Welcome_to_

the_Blogging_Libraries_Wiki.
14. Brookover, "Why We Blog," 31.
15. Meebo, "Advertise on Meebo."
16. Gordon and Stephens, "Embedding a librarian," 45.
17. Pew Internet & American Life Project, "Wireless Internet Use, 20.
18. Library Success.
19. Facebook.
20. Alexa Internet, Inc.
21. Charnigo and Barnett-Ellis, "Checking out Facebook.com, 31.
22. Osimo, *Web 2.0 in Government*, 47.
23. Gordon and West, "Data and Desires," 42.
24. Stephens, Web 2.0 and Libraries.
25. Raymond, "Flickr followup."
26. Farkas, *Social Software in Libraries*, 207–208.
27. Information Today, Inc.
28. Bradley, "Education on the Run," 6.
29. Blumenstein, "Librarians 'slam the boards.'"
30. Long, "Longshots #81: Slam the boards."
31. Radford, "Predatory Reference."
32. Heffernan, "The Oracle Collective," 20.
33. See http://answerboards.wetpaint.com.
34. Radford, "Predatory Reference."
35. See http://en.wikipedia.org/wiki/Category:Wikipedian_librarians.
36. WikiProject Librarians.
37. Lally and Dunford, "Using Wikipedia."
38. Janes, "In the Library," 49.

Works Cited

Alexa Internet, Inc. (2010). Top Sites United States. Retrieved January 27, 2010, from http://www.alexa.com/site/ds/top_sites?cc=US&ts_mode=country&lang=none.
American Library Association. (2006). *Library advocate's handbook* (2nd ed.). Chicago: American Library Association.
Armstrong, K. (2007). Using RSS feeds to alert users to electronic resources. *Serials Librarian, 53(3)*, 183–191.
Bernoff, J., & Li, C. (2008). Harnessing the power of the oh-so-social web. *MIT Sloan Management Review, 49(3)*, 36–42.
Blumenstein, L. (2007). Librarians "slam the boards." *Library Journal, 132(16)*, 12.
Bradley, P. (2008). Education on the run. *Community College Week, 20(18)*, 6–7.
Brookover, S. (2007). Why we blog. *Library Journal, 132(19)*, 28–31.
Charnigo, L., & Barnett-Ellis, P. (2007). Checking out Facebook.com: The Impact of a digital trend on academic libraries. *Information Technology & Libraries, 26(1)*, 23–34.
Facebook. (2010). Press Room: Statistics. Retrieved January 27, 2010, from http://www.facebook.com/press/info.php?statistics.
Farkas, Meredith. (2007). *Social software in libraries: Building collaboration, communication, and community online.* Medford, NJ: Information Today, Inc.
Gordon, R. S., & Stephens, M. (2007). Embedding a librarian in your web site using *Meebo. Computers in Libraries, 27(8)*, 44–45.
Gordon, R. S., & West, J. (2008). Data and desires: What users really want. *Computers*

in Libraries, 28(1), 42–43.

Heffernan, V. (2008, June 29). The Oracle Collective. *The New York Times Magazine*, 20.

Information Today, Inc. (2008). Computers in Libraries 2008. Retrieved January 27, 2010, from http://www.infotoday.com/cil2008/default.shtml.

Janes, J. (2008). In the library. *American Libraries, 39(6)*, 49.

Lally, A. M., & Dunford, C. E. (2007). Using Wikipedia to extend digital collections. *D-Lib Magazine, 13(5/6)*. Retrieved January 27, 2010, from http://www.dlib.org/dlib/may07/lally/05lally.html.

Library Success. (2009). Libraries Offering SMS Reference Services. Retrieved January 29, 2010, from http://www.libsuccess.org/index.php?title=Online_Reference#Libraries_Offering_SMS_Reference_Services.

Long, S. (2008, January 9). Longshots #81: Slam the boards. Podcast retrieved January 27, 2010, from http://www.sarahlong.org/podcast/?_episode=81.

Martin, A. (2007). The Evolution of the librarian as advocate: Are advocates born or developed? *Knowledge Quest, 36(1)*, 16–19.

Meebo. (2008). Advertise on Meebo. Retrieved January 27, 2010, from http://www.meebo.com/ads/.

Osimo, D. (2008). *Web 2.0 in government: Why and how?* Luxembourg: European Communities. Retrieved January 27, 2010, from http://ftp.jrc.es/EURdoc/JRC45269.pdf.

Pew Internet & American Life Project. (2005). New data on blogs and blogging. Retrieved January 27, 2010, from http://www.pewinternet.org/Press-Releases/2005/New-data-on-blogs-and-blogging.aspx.

———. (2004). How Americans use instant messaging. Washington, DC: Pew Internet & American Life Project. Retrieved January 27, 2010, from http://www.pewinternet.org/Reports/2004/How-Americans-Use-Instant-Messaging.aspx.

———. (2009). Wireless Internet Use. Washington, DC: Pew Internet & American Life Project. Retrieved January 29, 2010, from http://www.pewinternet.org/~/media//Files/Reports/2009/Wireless.

Radford, Marie L. (2007, October 7). 'Predatory Reference' an Interview with Bill Pardue about 'Slam the Boards.' Second Slam Coming Up on October 10, 2007! In *Library Garden*. Retrieved January 27, 2010, from http://librarygarden.blogspot.com/2007/10/preditory-reference-interview-with-bill.html.

Raymond, Matt. (2008, January 18). Flickr followup. In *Library of Congress blog*. Retrieved January 27, 2010, from http://www.loc.gov/blog/?p=237.

Siess, J. A. (2003). *The Visible librarian: Asserting your value with marketing and advocacy*. Chicago: American Library Association.

Sifry, D. (2008). The State of the Live Web, April 2007. In *Technorati Weblog*. Retrieved January 27, 2010, from http://www.sifry.com/alerts/archives/000493.html.

Springshare. (2010). LibGuides. Retrieved January 27, 2010, from http://springshare.com/libguides/.

Stephens, M. (2006). *Web2.0 and Libraries: Best Practices for Social Software* (Library Technology Reports, 42(4)). Chicago: ALA TechSource.

Wenzler, J. (2007). LibraryThing and the Library Catalog: Adding Collective Intelligence to the OPAC. Retrieved January 27, 2010, from http://online.sfsu.edu/~jwenzler/research/LTFL.pdf.

WikiProject Librarians. (2008). Retrieved January 27, 2010, from http://en.wikipedia.org/wiki/Wikipedia:WikiProject_Librarians.

Advocacy & Academic Instruction Librarians: Reflections on the Profession

Susan Vega Garcia

Advocacy and outreach are the bread and butter of instruction librarians at all levels and in all types of libraries. While the relevant literature concerning academic and research libraries may not use the term "advocacy" as much as the literature concerning public or school libraries does, much has been written on the need to advocate for information literacy (IL) in colleges and universities at all levels—national, institutional, the individual course level, as guest lecturer in faculty classes, and so on. A closely related and equally familiar topic is the need for academic instruction librarians to advocate for IL instruction to others in order to form effective partnerships and coalitions, thus working together to advance IL initiatives. The literature is replete with interesting and influential variations on the "with whom can we collaborate and to whom can we reach out" theme, ranging from the individual patron (such as interested, indoctrinated faculty), multi-user programs (such as student services programs, writing programs, etc.), specific user groups or organizations (including honors students, international students, etc.), inter-institutional partnerships (high school to college, charter schools), and more.[1] Another huge body of published literature concerns advocating for new instructional spaces, the creation of Information or Learning Commons and other student-centered physical spaces. These multi-purpose environments are intended to facilitate student collaboration and foster interpersonal relationship building through relaxing, socializing, multitasking, and even gaming—while surrounded by library services, collections, and support. Anyone needing literature and practical ideas on any of these advocacy and outreach themes can easily search the literature, as well as professional Web sites focused on information literacy, or even tap into helpful email distribution lists such as ILI-L.

But what information do we need to know before we can begin to effectively advocate for instruction at any of these levels? This chapter reflects on the realities and concerns facing the current state of academic library instruction, and advocates for instruction librarians themselves, in the belief that we must first know ourselves as "instruction librarians" in order to understand the nature of our work in the library. Only then can we help shape the perception of library instruction in academic libraries and the way in which it is viewed and supported by our institutions.

What Is It We Need To Know Before We Begin?

First, there are a number of important trends that drive the need for instruction librarians to advocate for ourselves and for change. Foremost among these trends is the continually rising demand for instructional services in college and research libraries. Library instruction in itself is nothing new. However, the drive toward information literacy instruction and constantly shifting technological innovations have increased the need for library instruction, particularly as users grapple with unfamiliar databases and the often unperceived need to understand the wide realm of information choices available to them beyond Google.

Probably no academic library unit reaches more users in a sustained, comprehensive, and transformative way than a robust instruction program of classes, workshops, course-related instruction sessions, online tutorials, web-based guides, and other learning materials. A typical reference transaction might last a few minutes or so, while an instruction class or program is longer, much more comprehensive, and typically designed with a strong focus on student learning outcomes and the assessment of those outcomes. Recent statistics from the Association of Research Libraries (ARL) clearly identify this strong trend in instruction growth at academic and research libraries and note that it is taking place at the same time that reference transactions continue to decline. During 1991-2006, for example, ARL statistics document a continuing downward decline of 41% for reference transactions at 123 ARL member libraries while, during the same period, "participants in group presentations" increased by 83% and the total number of group instruction sessions increased by 64%. The ARL statistics also show that there are a growing number of academic librarians who "are becoming more involved in the instructional process and are increasingly an integral part of the teaching and learning infrastructure at their institutions."[2] Before getting carried away with numbers it is important to note that even though the numbers are showing a downward trend, the number of reference transactions counted by ARL still figure in the tens of thousands for the typical academic library. According to David Tyckoson, 2007-08 president of the Reference & User Services Association (RUSA) of ALA, "Reference statistics are down not because we are doing less to assist our users, but because we historically measured that assistance based on what was the easiest to count."[3]

The Paradox of the Missing Instruction Librarian

If it is not easy to count reference transactions, it is even more difficult to know some of the most basic things about instruction, such as how many academic library "instruction librarians" there are in the U.S. The Instruction Section of the Association of College & Research Libraries (ACRL), the largest section within ACRL, counted approximately 4,000 members in 2008–09, a number compiled by Sarah McDaniel, then-chair, on the Section's introductory web page.[4] It is not necessary to be an "instruction librarian" to join the ACRL Instruction Section but membership is a good indication of strong interest in academic library instruction, regardless of one's actual job title. These numbers do suggest a strong faction of teaching librarians in academic libraries, a sizable group that is worthy of our attention.

Curiously, however, looking at ARL's most recent *Annual Salary Survey*, which includes the most recently published salary statistics for over 12,000 librarians at all member institutions (including several in Canada), reveals the complete absence of instruction librarians from the survey and from all listed positions. Presumably, instruction librarians may be subsumed in ARL's "Reference" category instead, although this is not clearly indicated.[5]

According to *Survey*, the job categories listed correspond with library "activities" rather than specific organizational structures or actual job titles; those submitting their information are urged to choose the categories that make sense for their own individual institutions and the "primary" activities fulfilled by those being described. According to the general instructions for completing the *Survey*, ARL has begun to provide more granularity in defining certain broad job categories such as "Functional Specialist," which is now broken down into eight separate position codes, and "Subject Specialist," now defined primarily as bibliographers who may or may not have other responsibilities. However, there is no explicit mention of teaching or instruction responsibilities as major or minor components of any position's responsibilities, and the category of "Reference" is defined solely as pertaining to "Reference librarians, both general and specialized."[6]

Thus, the absence of an "Instruction" category in the *ARL Annual Salary Survey* not only suggests the traditionally intertwined history of reference and instruction, but also points to what continues to be today's reality– that the typical academic instruction librarian is rarely "dedicated" solely to instruction, and often has major responsibilities in areas such as reference, collection development, and perhaps other more specialized or functional areas. It is difficult to know what types of positions and blended responsibilities academic instruction librarians really have, given the absence of instruction in the ARL Salary Survey and the lack of any other data about the numbers and activities of instruction librarians.

Instruction Librarians: Joint Appointments & Conflicting Demands?

The possibility of multiple and conflicting demands resonates in non-library faculty culture with the "joint appointment" dreaded by many faculty. Ideally, joint appointments comprise an invigorating mix of subject areas and responsibilities with one person fulfilling the needs of two departments or programs but in reality it often puts the faculty member in a position where he or she must awkwardly straddle the duties of two departments and run the risk of having professional work and achievements valued or rewarded differently by one or both.[7]

Are these "joint appointments" any less awkward for librarians? Perhaps so when considering that library positions have traditionally involved a mix of responsibilities, and that academic librarians and organizations have come to see this as a "natural" and necessary element of the job. In addition, these different appointments are likely to take place in the same general location, usually within the same library, with the librarian having the same physical space, colleagues, and administrative structure in both elements of their position. In other words, librarians with such appointments have less "commute" time as they negotiate or transition from one professional identity to the other. But academic libraries also have a tendency to increase the responsibilities of their librarians through committees, task forces, and evolving expectations that the librarians must juggle with their "traditional" duties. How much, then, is too much?

In 2001, Deborah F. Sheesley reviewed recently published research on burnout among instruction librarians. In her results, she noted that three previous studies from the 1990s all found significant levels of burnout among academic instruction librarians.[8] While a number of reasons for burnout are listed, Sheesley offers up a fictional (yet true to life) scenario of an instruction librarian who is overwhelmed by too many days of teaching multiple instruction sessions, eating lunch while attending committee meetings, and working on collection development projects while staffing the reference desk and also attempting also to assist a student—all the while undoubtedly planning the next instruction session.

Sheesley supports the reality of this scenario by citing recent research findings, including a study by Mary Anne Affleck stating that the "role conflict" or "role ambiguity" that librarians experience may cause tensions regarding the question of "whether the librarian's mission is to *provide* information or *teach* library users how to find information"[9] (emphasis added). Sheesley concludes by offering numerous proposed "solutions" and coping strategies from the published research for dealing with burnout. One such solution includes an important observation from Patterson and Howell in 1990:

> "Dedicated teaching librarians deserve a work environment that provides them with recognition and support. Appropriate support includes being rewarded financially, being provided with necessary resources, and *having sufficient work time available for activities connected with teaching*"[10] (emphasis added).

Patterson and Howell concluded, almost two decades ago, that good teaching by dedicated instruction librarians takes time, effort, and thought, an observation that suggests the need for our positions and organizations to be adaptable in order to support this important professional responsibility, and specifically to provide instruction librarians with the *time* for teaching.

Anyone with teaching experience knows that the time spent in class is accompanied by hours of thoughtful advance preparation planning the session, determining learning goals, developing content and assessment aligned to those goals, and structuring the class learning activities and discussions. After the class, additional time is spent on assessment of student work, student learning outcomes, and session evaluation data, plus any necessary follow up meetings or communications with students. Thus, even a one-shot instruction session is likely to take many hours of thoughtful preparation and reflection on the part of a dedicated instruction librarian.

The Aging Workforce

Before examining how the latest instruction-focused positions are being defined, we need to reflect on two other developing trends as they introduce complex opportunities and challenges in academic libraries that seek to meet the increasing demand for instruction. These trends are, the aging of the professional librarian workforce taking place concurrently (and somewhat paradoxically) with the ever-decreasing time span between major information technology innovations. A 2003 report on ARL librarian age demographics conducted by Stanley Wilder found that 63% of librarians surveyed in the *Current Population Survey* in 2000 were 45 years old or over and that librarians as a whole tended to be older than workers in comparable professions.[11] Wilder also analyzed a number of other significant trends related to the aging of the professional librarian population and noted that the percentage of second-career librarians who are both new to the profession and 45 and older at entry has also increased in recent years.[12]

The report includes no data that specifically pertain to instruction librarians—indeed that job title does not appear in the report at all. Perhaps, once again, instruction-related data is folded in with the data on reference librarians. However, Wilder does observe that "[t]he management issue resulting from the aging of librarianship is not retirements; it is how to obtain new entrants in sufficient numbers, quality, and expertise to replace retirees and keep the cycle turning."[13] One of Wilder's conclusions focuses on "demand and replacement assumptions," or, as increasing numbers of academic librarians retire, whether new hires should merely replace those exact same positions or if there exists greater demand elsewhere in the organization to develop new services or explore new opportunities.[14]

A recent survey conducted by *Library Journal* corroborates these conclusions, finding that the average age of librarians polled, some 3,095 library workers from academic, public, and other library types, was 47 years old, and that more than 50% of the respondents were over the age of fifty. Far fewer survey participants (282) were under thirty years of age.[15]

Both Wilder's report and the *Library Journal* survey also mention new technologies. Wilder specifically identifies the growing need to address new technologies as one example of potential new service opportunities,[16] while responses to the *Library Journal* survey point out a stark generational divide in technology use. Of a number of common social networking and communication technologies mentioned (including email use, actively blogging or simply reading blogs, use of IM, posting pictures online, listening to podcasts, or having a Facebook page), only email use rated high among the 50 and older set who responded to the survey.[17] A casual walk through the student computing areas of most academic and research libraries today will undoubtedly reveal that the majority of student users engage in one or several of these activities at any given time of day. What does it mean to have a majority of library workers not only so much older than their largest user group, but, much more importantly, potentially so disconnected from the daily realities of that group, and disconnected as well from one of the major trends driving change in our libraries today?

It may be that factors determining likelihood of response to the *Library Journal* survey might have skewed the sample. For example, it is possible that generational differences may have made it more likely in general for older library workers to respond to such surveys, or perhaps the readership of *Library Journal*, and therefore the likelihood of learning of the survey, might itself trend toward a faithful readership among older librarians while younger librarians read professional blogs instead. Much more research is needed to learn how representative these data might be of academic librarians in general, and specifically instruction librarians. It is obvious, however, that the rising rate of retirements does increasingly present academic libraries with the opportunity to reflect on decisions of filling vacated positions "as is" or redefining those positions to address new growing needs, such as instruction. How are academic libraries responding to this opportunity?

Seeking Energetic, Innovative, Service-Oriented, Technology-Savvy...

If instruction-focused job ads listed from 2007 through mid-2008 in *C&RL News* can be viewed as representative of the most current instruction needs in academic and research libraries, an informal and quick review of those job ads reveals that today's academic instruction librarian positions are very rarely focused solely on instruction responsibilities and most often include a wide variety of responsibilities in different service areas.

The most common instruction-focused job title during this period remains the typical triad of "Reference / Instruction / Subject-area Librarian," followed closely by the even more traditional dyad, "Reference & Instruction." It is interesting to note the order in which these identities are listed; reference service responsibilities are still privileged as the primary responsibility despite national trends. The third most common job title was "Instruction Librarian," which might seem to imply an exclusive focus on instruction—yet job ads found with this job title explicitly detailed full reference service responsibilities, frequently including mandatory evening and weekend reference shifts, as well as specific expectations of general reference service and electronic and IM reference. Surprisingly, even instructional technology positions charged with time-consuming development of tutorials, learning objects, and other online curricular materials carried reference and sometimes even collection development responsibilities. Managerial instruction positions (Head, Chair, Coordinator) listed during this time also included obligatory reference responsibilities with evening and weekend reference service expectations, and sometimes collection development responsibilities as well.

In addition to the common blending of reference plus instruction plus collection development responsibilities, a number of "instruction librarian" positions listed during the period consulted also included responsibilities as varied as supervising staff in other units including Circulation, Interlibrary Loan, and Reserves. Almost all of these positions also stipulated strong instruction-focused expectations in challenging areas such as instructional technology design leadership, instructional outreach to special populations including distance learners and users with disabilities, developing, leading and assessing complex instruction programs, integrating IL into the curricula across the disciplines, development of online curriculum modules, and assisting non-library faculty in the use of technology for teaching, to name the most prevalent.

What about the responsibilities or requirements listed in those job ads? Not surprisingly, the job ads reveal the strong expectation that instruction librarians will teach, closely followed by the expectation that the incumbent will develop, lead, advance, or otherwise coordinate instruction at the program level, which is a full-time job in itself. While it might be expected that only unit leadership positions would include this expectation, this was not the case. Curiously, required teaching experience or teaching ability was mentioned *less often* than the routine requirements of excellent communication skills, ability to work independently and in a team, and stock personal descriptors such as "energetic," "innovative," and "service-oriented." In addition, a large number of instruction-focused job ads gave no specific details regarding the teaching qualifications or teaching responsibilities of the position, though sometimes pointing elsewhere (such as a library Web site) for more information.

These loaded expectations help us understand burnout in very current terms: continuing demands for more instruction programs using ever-changing technologies to reach increasingly diverse and dispersed students, networking with subject faculty and reaching out to students, and being charged with truly challenging long-term initiatives while also working night-shifts and weekends at the reference desk, building collections, and supervising sometimes disparate units and staff. Added to this are the standard expectations of local, regional, and national committee work, and research and publications, plus all the additional expectations of professional development workshop and conference attendance, leadership, and collegiality.

What about Technology Expectations?

A number of the instruction-focused job ads from the period consulted included specific expectations or responsibilities regarding teaching with technology, as would be expected given the increasingly strong trends in rapid technology change and innovations. However, the job ads demonstrate only a general interest at best in hiring instruction staff in these areas. The specific technology responsibility mentioned most often was creation of Web-based guides and other unspecified online instructional materials, followed by the desire for someone to take the lead in investigating and evaluating new technologies and techniques. The need for an individual who is able to provide instructional technology leadership (which is not necessarily the same thing as actual design, creation, and maintenance responsibilities) suggests library staffing needs for supporting the *beginning* stages of instructional technology implementation, as does the need for creation of "Web-based guides," as these are typically among the simplest and most ubiquitous of online instruction materials. More complex Web-based materials are generally known by their more specific names, such as "content modules" or "interactive tutorials".

Very few instruction-focused job ads listed highly specific expectations in teaching with technology, and many softened or deflected creation and development expectations by using phrases such as, "ability to use…," "ability to learn…," "contribute to…" or "participate in design of…" in order to describe teaching with technology needs. Also in many of the job ads reviewed, the phrase "knowledge of…," followed by a scattered potpourri of software and technologies (or the rather vague but safe catchall phrase "knowledge of current and emerging trends") appears to take the place of actual required experience and specific job expectations. What does it mean that technology needs seem to be strongly clustered in the "knowledge" rather than the proven "experience" realm of these job ads? When instruction librarians are hired with technology *knowledge* rather than actual experience, it is important to recognize that acquiring relevant technology skills and learning new technologies well enough not only to use them effectively but potentially to teach others or provide program leadership in their use can represent a significant and often stressful time commitment added to all the other demands on instruction librarians' time.

Building Teaching Relationships

In order to understand why we need to advocate for academic instruction librarians, we need to recognize the highly collaborative nature of the work and recognize that successful collaborations are built on sustained person-to-person interactions. In the best-seller *Seven Habits of Highly Effective People*, author Stephen R. Covey makes the simple yet profound observation that we should aim toward "effectiveness" rather than "efficiency" when dealing with interpersonal relationships.[18] The concept of efficiency suggests a close association with time management, and more specifically, managing and accomplishing tasks in the shortest amount of time possible. Building effective relationships that result in productive collaborations, however, involves networking, interest exploration, identifying shared mutual goals, and devising ways to work together to accomplish those goals. Although it may appear straightforward, networking with faculty is a complex process for many instruction librarians in part because the traditional reference service model expects patrons to come to the librarian, at certain times and certain places (whether in the library, a satellite location, or online) to have immediate questions and information needs answered. An instruction service model necessarily reaches out, assuming that potential collaborators will not always knock on the librarian's door first.

Instruction librarians who are scheduled to provide reference service at a physical desk at night and weekends (expectations that are listed in many current instruction job ads) may thus find their schedules fundamentally out of synch with potential collaborators who are most likely off campus and offline at these times. Similarly, the time off that compensates for the librarian working nights and weekends schedules that librarian to be out of the office during normal weekday work hours, again out of synch with classroom faculty who are most likely to be on campus then. Even when scheduled during the work week and normal business hours, extensive reference responsibilities such as these can be problematic. Thus, for instruction librarians, traditional reference service schedules and expectations have the potential to produce a fundamental misalignment of productive work hours that can interfere with efforts to make meaningful connections with classroom faculty, work that often relies on sustained face-to-face interactions.

In addition, many faculty members at academic institutions still do not have information literacy on their radar. Regardless of whether librarians have faculty status, many classroom faculty members do not consider librarians to be peers or teachers, and thus may not be particularly inclined to initiate teaching collaborations with librarians. On the other hand, instruction librarians who have faculty status may take this apparent equality at face value and expect immediate recognition and acceptance. To their surprise, they may find classroom faculty to be largely unaware of librarians' faculty status and, once informed, largely unimpressed and skeptical.

In academic and research library settings, instruction librarians typically wish our information literacy instruction efforts to reach the largest group of users possible—namely, our students in all their wealth of diversity, including rank (freshman through seniors, graduate students through "all but dissertation" Ph.D. students); college and subject area focus; learning styles; intellectual, emotional, and physical abilities; race, gender, ethnicity, national origin, language, and more.

In order to reach our students, instruction librarians employ many different strategies, but when considering how best to extend instruction into campus classrooms, the perception of classroom faculty as gatekeepers to library and information literacy instruction in their classrooms is not entirely incorrect. The library research literature includes many research articles and practical examples

providing guidance and practical suggestions in building collaborations, frequently documenting individual case studies and success
stories of faculty-librarian collaborations.[19] Often embedded within
many of these success stories is the admission that it takes *time* to
build successful teaching partnerships and effective instruction programs, and that "faculty culture" and the organizational cultures at
the specific institution may play a critical role in the success or failure
of academic library instruction efforts. Indeed, cultural norms may
influence faculty receptivity to librarians as teachers on campus and
within faculty members' classrooms.

For example, in recent case studies of strong instruction collaborations at five very different institutions, the elements of time and
culture emerge repeatedly.[20] In examining the factors behind Earlham
College's long and illustrious success with course-integrated library
instruction, Jennie Ver Steeg notes the unique Quaker cultural values
that shaped Earlham College's apparent campus-wide acceptance of
faculty-librarian teaching collaborations as the expected norm, and
cites Thomas Kirk's observation that "...it takes at least ten years to
develop a library instruction program."[21] Similarly, Sarah Beasley documents five years of an ambitious partnership of learning communities and library instructional teams at Indiana University-Purdue
University at Indianapolis, a unique institutional consolidation that
serves a large population of non-traditional students.[22] Scott Walter
likewise details the organizational culture and collaborative atmo-
sphere of Evergreen State College, and describes a unique rotation
program at Evergreen that involves both librarians and classroom
faculty, bringing "librarians into the classroom and members of the
classroom faculty into the library."[23] Importantly, Evergreen librarians
are granted release time so that they can participate in this classroom
teaching initiative.

Beyond these and other exemplary (though perhaps unique) programs, there are, no doubt, innumerable case studies documenting
smaller successes, perhaps more isolated or finite as examples but just
as successful in their own ways. More research is needed to gather
these from the published literature and examine how the elements of
time and culture are mentioned, and whether trends can be determined. In the meantime, we can reflect on how realistic is it to assume that this kind of collaborative work can be easily accomplished
while squeezed in between numerous multiple responsibilities, with
the constant interruptions and abrupt transitions from one task to the

next that punctuate the professional lives of most instruction librarians?

There are also more sobering studies that analyze reasons for less than satisfactory faculty-librarian collaborations, highlighting cultural differences as chief among the stumbling blocks. In his fascinating examination of faculty culture and what may be seen as a cultural disconnect between faculty and librarians, Larry Hardesty lists a number of reasons why faculty have been and may continue to be resistant to library instruction taking place in their classrooms.[24] Faculty are just as overtaxed as instruction librarians when it comes to multiple expectations and demands on their limited available time, and—similar to instruction librarians—they are not likely to have had much if any emphasis on learning to teach during their graduate studies.[25] According to Hardesty, one of the most important differences between faculty and librarian cultures is that faculty members are likely to focus their teaching goals on subject area *content*, while librarians focus on teaching *processes*—for example, the process of defining an information need, selecting and effectively searching relevant information sources and the process of evaluating research results. For librarians, the *process* often equals the *content* of what is taught, which is quite different than teaching and learning the complexities of 19th century French literature, to give one example. Hardesty also cites faculty members' "professional autonomy" in their course preparation and teaching, and expectations of academic freedom within their own private classrooms as strong factors that may decrease the likelihood of initiating classroom collaborations with librarians.[26] Others such as William Badke (2005) and Paul Hrycaj and Michael Russo (2007) have come to similar conclusions, citing subject-area "turf" issues and feigned or tacit approval of classroom library instruction as long as it is "not in my backyard."[27]

Even when librarians are invited into the classroom, many faculty and students may be more comfortable with the traditional view of librarians as service-oriented individuals who lead users to information and knowledge, but may not recognize the teaching role of instruction librarians, even when examples are right in front of their noses.[28] For one interesting example, Kate Manuel, Susan Beck and Molly Molloy (2005) identified a number of successful faculty-librarian classroom teaching collaborations and explored the attitudes that led those faculty to participate in library instruction.[29] When asked to describe their "best experiences" with library instruction taking place in their own classrooms, almost half (10) of the small local sample of 21 faculty participating in the study identified "in-depth reference assistance" during the class session as one of the "best experiences," strongly suggesting the traditional view of librarians not as an expert *teacher* but as expert *answerer*—this even when the faculty themselves invited the librarian into their classroom to *teach*. Similarly, Jody Fagan (2002) reported on a local study of college students enrolled in a library skills class and their perceptions of librarians.[30] Amazingly, even among this group of students actually enrolled in a library skills class, results indicated that only 9 out of the 45 students (or 20%) identified "teaching or training" as part of librarians' professional responsibilities.[31]

Collaborating with Ourselves

The differences in areas such as terminal professional degrees, on-campus professional titles, as well as our teaching responsibilities in terms of scope, context, duration, credit hours, and intensity are likely to be sticky issues for some faculty and their academic instruction librarian colleagues for some time. Classroom collaborations are of course just one component of most thriving academic instruction programs, along with a number of more independent librarian-led instruction initiatives such as developing one's own credit-bearing IL courses, hands-on workshops, seminars, orientation programs, and online instruction materials of various types. However, it is important to recognize that even in-house library initiatives demand a significant commitment of time from instruction librarians for preparation and development, as well as deep understanding of the library's own organizational culture.

One important reason for this is that academic instruction programs may tend to be led by coordinators whose positions have been explicitly crafted to hold no formal supervisory responsibilities or formal reporting relationships with those librarians who will undertake teaching responsibilities. In academic library circles and particularly instruction circles, one widely-heard maxim has it that coordinators have "lots of responsibilities but no authority." Without frequent validation through administrative support, securing buy-in and accountability from our colleagues (meaning those librarians who must juggle instruction along with many other responsibilities) for ambitious long-range instruction initiatives may be just as challenging as developing external relationships with classroom faculty.

While a few recent ARL SPEC Kits on instruction topics have included organization charts from a small number of libraries showing how specific instruction departments or programs are structured, it would be interesting for future research to examine a larger number of academic library instruction programs and their organization charts to investigate relationships between strong and successful instruction programs and certain types of organizational structures.[32]

Looking to the Future

Where do these interconnected reflections on instruction librarianship lead? Clearly, the strong demand for instruction is growing at academic research libraries but our continued traditional approaches to staffing for instruction may not be the models most conducive for developing and maintaining strong instruction programs. It is likely that the majority of academic librarians who teach are in positions that blend reference, instruction, collection development, and other responsibilities. Current job advertisements show that academic libraries continue to use this traditional staffing model, regardless of job title or division of responsibilities. Reference service has its own history and service expectations, much of which may run counter to the expectations and demands of face-to-face classroom or online teaching and instruction program development. We need to reevaluate our assumption that instruction is a responsibility that can adequately be juggled with other responsibilities, and rethink our current structures of support, reward, and recognition for instruction librarians. This is our charge for advocating for instruction librarians and successful academic library instruction initiatives.

We have seen that teaching well and developing meaningful collaborations and programs demands time—time to learn, time to reach out and network with others outside and within libraries, time to develop curricular materials, time to interact with students and to assess their learning. Time is indeed a precious commodity for librarians who teach, particularly since current job ads suggest strongly that academic instruction librarians are still expected to learn how to teach, how to implement new technologies, how to develop collaborations with classroom faculty, how to manage programs and supervise personnel while on the job, rather than entering their position with much relevant professional experience.

Additionally, as students surround themselves with new technologies that blend educational, social, and entertainment needs, academic instruction librarians are among the forefront of librarians who, regardless of age or interest, simply must also be conversant with these new technologies. They must keep abreast of the more familiar technologies that are prevalent in libraries and the information world. Librarian knowledge and adaptability is certainly more important than age itself, and indeed the ability to stay current with technological changes encourages faculty to collaborate with librarians and helps open classroom doors. Instruction librarians cannot afford to ignore new technologies embraced by patrons. We need to advocate for instruction librarians to have access to continuing learning opportunities, and to encourage risk-taking in implementing new teaching and learning technologies.

More than anything, we need to advocate for changing the mindset and structures of our libraries in order to have an impact on instruction in academic libraries. More research is needed to move from these reflections toward a refocusing not only of our responsibilities but also our professional identities, rethinking the workforce to better address the structure and time demands of our best teaching work, and thereby moving instruction and instruction librarians from the margins to the center.

Notes

1. For a good overview, see Raspa and Ward, *The Collaborative Imperative*. Other recent examples of specific collaborations include Walter and Eodice, "Meeting the student learning imperative," Elmborg and Hook, *Centers for learning*, Riehle, "Partnering and programming," Boff and Johnson. "The library and first-year experience," Deuink and Reinsfelder, "Charting a course."
2. Kyrillidou and Young, *ARL Statistics 2005–06*, 5 (see Table 1 graph for 1991–2006 trend data)
3. Tyckoson, "That Thing You Do"
4. McDaniel, *Welcome to the Instruction Section*
5. Kyrillidou and Young, *ARL Annual Salary Survey 2006–07*.
6. Kyrillidou and Young, *ARL Annual Salary Survey 2006–07*, 89.
7. For examples, Smith, "An Incomplete Picture," C1, Gray and Drew, "What they Didn't Teach You," A40.
8. Sheesley, "Burnout and the Academic Teaching Librarian"
9. Ibid, 448, citing Affleck, "Burnout among Bibliographic Instruction Librarians."
10. Ibid, 450, citing conclusions from Patterson and Howell, "Library User Education."
11. Wilder, *Demographic Change in Academic Librarianship*, 3.
12. Ibid., xv.
13. Ibid., xiv.
14. Ibid., 56
15. Berry III, "Great Work"

16. Wilder, *Demographic Change in Academic Librarianship,* 56.
17. Berry III, "Great Work"
18. Covey, *The Seven Habits,* 169–170.
19. For recent examples, see the many individual essays in Raspa and Ward, *The Collaborative Imperative*
20. Walter, Ariew, Beasley, Tillman, Ver Steeg, "Case Studies in Collaboration," 39–78.
21. Ibid., 46.
22. Ibid., 50–51.
23. Ibid., 56–57.
24. Hardesty, "Faculty culture and bibliographic instruction"
25. A review of the massive literature in the area of how librarians learn to teach is beyond to scope of this chapter, but for one recent example with a very thorough bibliography, see Walter, "Improving Instruction," 363–379.
26. Hardesty, "Faculty culture and bibliographic instruction," 351–352
27. Badke, "Can't Get No Respect," Hrycaj and Russo. "Reflections on Surveys Faculty Attitudes"
28. See, for example, Fagan, "Students' Perceptions of Academic Librarians" Fagan bases her work on an earlier study by Hernon and Pastine, "Student Perceptions of Academic Librarians," and cites that study when discussing the perceived notion of librarians pointing or leading to information rather than teaching.
29. Manuel, Beck, and Molloy, "An Ethnographic Study of Attitudes"
30. Fagan, "Students' Perceptions of Academic Librarians"
31. Ibid, 138
32. Walter and Hinchliffe. *Instructional Improvement Programs,* Snyder, Logue, Carter, and Soltys. *Instructional Support Services*

Works Cited

Affleck, M. A. (1996). Burnout among Bibliographic Instruction Librarians. *Library and Information Science Research , 18,* 169–172.

Badke, W. B. (2005). Can't Get No Respect: Helping Faculty to Understand the Educational Power of Information Literacy. *The Reference Librarian* (89/90), 63–80.

Berry III, J. N. (2007, October 1). Great Work, Genuine Problems. *Library Journal , 132* (16), 26–29.

Boff, C., & Johnson, K. (2002). The Library and First-Year Experience Courses: a Nationwide Study. *Reference Services Review , 30* (4), 277–287.

Covey, S. R. (2004). *The Seven Habits of Highly Effective People.* New York: Free Press.

Deuink, A. L., & Reinsfelder, T. (2007). Charting a Course. *American Libraries , 38* (9), 58–9.

Elmborg, J. K., & Hook, S. (2005). *Centers for Learning: Writing Centers and Libraries in Collaboration.* Chicago, IL: Association of College and Research Libraries.

Fagan, J. (2002). Students' Perceptions of Academic Librarians. *Reference Librarian* (78), 131–148.

Gray, P., & Drew, D. E. (2008, April 25). What They Didn't Teach You in Graduate School. *Chronicle of Higher Education , 54* (33), p. A40.

Hardesty, L. (1995). Faculty Culture and Bibliographic Instruction: an Exploratory Analysis. *Library Trends , 44* (2), 339–367.

Hernon, P., & Pastine, M. E. (1977). Student Perceptions of Academic Librarians. *College & Research Libraries , 38,* 129–139.

Hrycaj, P., & Russo, M. (2007). Reflections on Surveys of Faculty Attitudes Toward Collaboration with Librarians. *Journal of Academic Librarianship , 33* (6), 692–696.

Kyrillidou, M., & Young, M. (2007). *ARL Annual Salary Survey 2006–07.* Retrieved September 25, 2008, from Association for Research Libraries: http://www.arl. org/bm~doc/ss06.pdf

Kyrillidou, M., & Young, M. (2008). *ARL Statistics 2005–06.* Retrieved September 25, 2008, from Association for Research Libraries: http://www.arl.org/bm~doc/arlstats06.pdf

Manuel, K., Beck, S. E., & Molloy, M. (2005). An Ethnographic Study of Attitudes Influence Faculty Collaboration in Library Instruction. *The Reference Librarian* (89/90), 139–161.

McDaniel, S. (2008). *Welcome to the Instruction Section.* Retrieved October 15, 2008, from http://www.ala.org/ala/mgrps/divs/acrl/about/sections/is/welcome/gettinginvolved.cfm

Patterson, C. D., & Howell, D. W. (1990). Library User Education: Assessing the Attitudes of Those Who Teach. *RQ , 29,* 521–523.

Raspa, D., & Ward, D. (2000). *the Collaborative Imperative: Librarians and Faculty Working Together in the Information Universe.* Chicago, IL: Association of College and Research Libraries.

Riehle, C. F. (2008). Partnering and Programming for Undergraduate Honors Students. *Reference Services Review , 36* (1), 48–60.

Sheesley, D. F. (2001). Burnout and the Academic Teaching Librarian: an Examination of the Problem and Suggested Solutions. *Journal of Academic Librarianship , 27* (6), 447–451.

Smith, C. (. (2006, May 26). An Incomplete Picture of Me. *Chronicle of Higher Education , 52* (38), p. C1.

Snyder, C. A., Logue, S., Carter, H., & Soltys, M. (October 2001). *Instructional Support Services.* Washington, D.C.: Association of Research Libraries.

Tyckoson, D. (2008, January). *That Thing You Do: From the President of RUSA,* vol 47, no 2. Retrieved September 25, 2008, from RUSQ: http://www.rusq. org/2008/01/06/that-thing-you-do-2/#more-81

Walter, S. (2005). Improving Instruction: What Librarians Can Learn from the Study of College Teaching. In H. A. Thompson (Ed.), *Currents and Convergence: Navigating the Rivers of Change. Proceedings of the Twelfth National Conference of the Association of College and Research Libraries, April 7–10, 2005, Minneapolis, Minnesota* (pp. 363–379). Chicago: Association of College and Research Libraries.

Walter, S., & Eodice, M. (2005). Meeting the Student Learning Imperative: Supporting and Sustaining Collaboration Between Academic Libraries and Student Services Programs. *Research Strategies , 20* (4), 219–225.

Walter, S., & Hinchliffe, L. J. (2005). *Instructional Improvement Programs.* Washington, D.C.: Association of Research Libraries.

Walter, S., Ariew, S., Beasley, S., Tillman, M., & Steeg, J. V. (2000). Case Studies in Collaboration: Lessons from Five Exemplary Programs. In D. Raspa, & D. e. Ward, *The Collaborative Imperative: Librarians and Faculty Working Together in the Information Universe* (pp. 39–78). Chicago, IL: Association of College and Research Libraries.

Wilder, S. J. (2003). *Demographic Change in Academic Librarianship.* Washington, D.C.: Association of Research Libraries.

Advocacy and Workplace Diversity

10

Janice Welburn

More than a buzzword, *advocacy* has become a way of thinking in a growing number of college and university libraries. Advocacy is a strategy for library administrators and frontline staff to employ grassroots leadership influence tactics with campus administrators, faculty and student groups to create organizational change. Specifically, advocacy promotes collaboration and coalition building between the leadership in libraries and the campus to persuade and influence the direction of campus-level strategic initiatives that affect library priorities, thereby building library organizational capacity. When advocacy and diversity are associated with one another in the library context, much of the focus has been given to outreach and collection development, especially given the changing demographics in the composition of student populations, expanding scholarly canons, and in opening new pedagogical frontiers.

Yet advocacy is less associated with workplace diversity in academic libraries. Although much of the writing on academic libraries has focused on best practices in managing diversity as a workplace issue, little attention has been given to the potential validity of its association with advocacy as a strategy to influence human resource management and decision making. This chapter considers the promise of advocacy in influencing organizational change and development in regards to workplace diversity. From this vantage point, both advocacy and workplace diversity are considered in relation to one another in the articulation of transformative strategies to create, build, and get the most from workforce diversity in academic libraries. The essay considers how these two concepts are defined using research from behavioral and social research and how synergy between advocacy and workforce diversity can result in long-term strategic and structural change, not only in the composition of professional, support, and student staffs but on the aspect of thinking of an academic library as a learning organization.

Defining Diversity and Advocacy

There is a lengthy history to the association of diverse and under-represented groups in higher education in the United States, dating well back to the 19th century and the nation's ambiguity over inclusion of women and people of color in colleges and universities. Yet one might source the present day working definition of diversity used by colleges and universities to the June 1978 Supreme Court decision in *Regents of the University of California v. Bakke.* The Bakke decision affected an important argument on affirmative action that emerged in the 1960s Civil Rights movement and was firmly grounded in historical patterns of social inequality and discrimination as applied to collegiate admissions decisions. Bakke also informs subsequent court decisions and state referenda that have narrowly tailored, if not outright banned, the use of affirmative action measures[1] that purportedly give preferential treatment in an effort to diversify a student population, workplace, fellowship and grant awards, and government contracts.

As Peter Schmidt noted in his review of the legacy of Bakke for the *Chronicle of Higher Education,* "Before *Bakke,* selective colleges regarded race-conscious admissions policies mainly as a way to remedy past societal discrimination against black, Hispanic, and Native American applicants. The *Bakke* ruling declared that justification off limits, replacing a rationale grounded in history with one grounded in educational theory."[2] Using the minority decision of Justice Lewis F. Powell, the legal justification for considering race in *college admissions* might continue on the grounds of educational benefit. Broadening the concept beyond the courts, social inequality is then supplanted by the attraction of diversity as a value not only to college admissions but throughout society and its organizations. Diversity, not historically rooted inequity, has become the basis for engaging communities through access to service and resources, citizen advocacy, and building inclusive work environments.

In libraries, concern for diversity has evolved in different ways in the decades since Bakke. As Winston and Li observed in a paper on diversity and liberal arts colleges, "Generally, these (diversity) programs focus on recruitment and retention of members of under-represented groups, increasing diversity awareness in the workplace, building multicultural collections, and designing and providing library services for users from diverse cultural backgrounds."[3] Although Winston and Li are careful in delineating between each of these dimensions of diversity, they do so against a current with a tendency to intermingle workplace diversity with outreach and services to diverse populations, citizen advocacy and empowerment, and developing multicultural collections. Yet there are distinctive and contextual meanings for workplace diversity, and as the authors found, in practice varying weights are attached by libraries and their respective institutions to the levels of service provided to new and emerging populations, to collection development that is responsive to changes in scholarly disciplines[4], and in personnel and human resource decisions.

As a workplace issue, the impact of diversity is not only associated with who gets hired from availability pools, but in the organization of work itself, decision-making, and organizational climate and development, and its overall performance. Van Knippenberg and Schippers provide a common definition for workplace diversity[5], as "a characteristic of a social grouping (i.e., group, organization, society) that reflects the degree to which there are objective or subjective differences between people within the group (without presuming that group members are necessarily aware of objective differences or that subjective differences are strongly related to more objective differences)."[6] However, van Knippenberg and Schippers also identify the limitations to this far reaching definition, instead offering that the concept of diversity should extend beyond the parameters of demographics and the dispersion of populations to consider more social interactions and nonlinear relationships *between* cultural categories. Drawing from the theorizing of Roosevelt Thomas on managing diversity, Edward Hubbard has proposed that diversity is "a collective mixture characterized by differences and similarities that are applied in pursuit of organizational objectives," taking the form of different dimensions: workforce, behavioral, structural, and business and global diversity.[7]

These approaches are also consistent with Welburn's earlier theoretical position on the relevance of diversity and library and information science education. Welburn maintained that diversity is often treated as a static construct identifying and delineating populations by demographic, linguistic, and sociocultural characteristics. As an alternative, he proposed that diversity must be a substantially more dynamic construct if it is to have any meaning, suggesting that "cultural diversity is not the mere existence of different cultures occupying a single space; it is a dynamic engagement between cultures, their values, beliefs, and ways of knowing."[8] Both van Knippenberg and Schippers' and Welburn's stress on social interaction between different groups shifts the focal point of diversity away from an emphasis on recruiting a diverse work force to workplace development and the incorporation of diversity in strategic planning and goal setting. In doing so, the discussion of workplace diversity becomes re-centered on sociological issues, a concept that has lost its prominence since Bakke, rather than its present emphasis on legal frameworks and identity theory. As DiTomaso, Post, and Parks-Yancy have concluded, "Management research on workforce diversity, however, has not drawn broadly from the core disciplines of sociology and psychology in the development of workforce diversity research, but has focused on only a few topics and issues; most prominently, organizational demography from sociology and social identity theory from social psychology."[9] Consequently, much of the discussion on library workplace diversity rarely challenges underlying *structural* dimensions of diversity and change in libraries, what Charles Tilly called "durable inequality,"[10] the categorical inequality that is long-term, fixed, and cannot be unseated by attempts to individual behavior in the workplace.

If diversity entails social interaction and is also related to broader questions of social inequality, advocacy then is regarded as a methodology used by academic library administrative and staff leadership to mobilize campus-level support for diversity, to place it as a crucial value for institutional viability in the 21st century. *Advocacy* as applied to academic libraries is, as Camila Alire reminds us, "citizen-initiated" and well-suited not only for administrative leadership but for front-line, grass roots action by library staff who assume leadership roles and are in the best position—based on knowledge and experience—to garner campus-level support for libraries.[11] Politically speaking, one might consider as advocacy a form of community organizing that better represents the needs and interests of library users by librarians who work directly with them[12] Yet advocacy also has the ability to move an organization's capacity to forge influence strategies with institutional collaborators[13] to provide incentives to retain and insure the success of librarians as well as faculty, administrators, and other staff in a setting that not only values diversity but actively seeks to employ it as an instrument to eradicate historically rooted social inequality and promote intercultural communication and interaction in the pursuit of organizational development.

In this context, the relationship between workplace diversity as a goal or value and advocacy as a strategy to influence organizational change may have more resonance than advocacy as citizen empowerment in the political sphere. Advocacy becomes a mechanism for addressing the shortcomings found in vision and mission statements and the underlying values and principles of representation in the college or university community. In other words, advocacy presents an organization with bursts of energy to accomplish long-term change not only in hiring, retention, and promotion practices but in the composition of those actively engaged in organizational decision making

In reviewing works published on workforce diversity in academic libraries and in other types of organizations, similar conclusions have been reached. There appears to be a dearth of empirical knowledge about the efficacy and utility of many strategies for achieving diversity in organizations. The most cogent and heavily cited study published in recent years on the subject of diversity in organizations is based on the research of Kalev, Dobbin, and Kelly[14]. Their study is a departure from the small corpus of research available to guide administrators and practitioners working in professional organizations such as libraries, and for three important reasons. First, their paper is one of the very few that examines diversity across a broad range of organizations. Many studies focus on one type of organization or are concentrated on socio-psychological and interpersonal dimensions of team or work group behavior. Moreover, because Kalev, Dobbin, and Kelly's paper is informed more broadly by sociological theory and analysis, it takes full advantage of research on social organization, institutionalization, and social inequality. And, because of the breadth of scope of their research, the authors are able to identify in their analysis patterns in the strategies that a range of organizations employ in their efforts to achieve diversity.

Kalev, Dobbin, and Kelly collapsed seven different types of diversity programs they identified as common in private sector organizations—affirmative action plans, diversity, committees, diversity managers, training, managers' evaluations, networking initiatives, and mentoring programs[15]—into three "mechanisms for remediating workplace inequality rooted in different social science literatures,"

> "One mechanism, based in arguments from Max Weber and organizational institutionalists, is the creation of specialized positions as the way to achieve

new goals. Another mechanism, based in theories of stereotyping and bias, involves training and feedback as the way to eliminate managerial bias and its offspring, inequality. A third mechanism, based in theories of social networks, involves programs that target the isolation of women and minorities as a way to improve their career prospects."[16]

In other words, diversity initiatives identified across a number of organizations can be summarized as those that structure responsibility for diversity in some fashion, seek change through education and advice, and address the "social isolation" of individuals within the organization. These mechanisms can also be divided into those that seek change in either organizational or individual behavior.

Understanding the important distinction between organizational and individual change may be a crucial next step for libraries seeking to use advocacy and influence strategies to address workplace diversity in colleges and universities. As Kalev, Dobbin, and Kelley have noted, there is evidence from organizational sociology that those methods and strategies that attempt to remedy social inequality in the workplace and "structure responsibility" are likely to have greater effect than those that attempt to change the individual. They observed the following:

> "The most effective practices are those that establish organizational responsibility: affirmative action plans, diversity staff, and diversity task forces. Attempts to reduce social isolation among women and African Americans through networking and mentoring programs are less promising. Least effective are programs for taming managerial bias through education and feedback."[17]

This is not to suggest that libraries and other organizations should dispense with diversity training programs and mentoring and networking initiatives. Their work indicates, however, that such efforts are more effective when administrators address underlying structural issues affecting inequality within an organization, and they concluded,

> "Although inequality in attainment at work may be rooted in managerial bias and the social isolation of

women and minorities, the best hope for remedying it may lie in practices that assign organizational
responsibility for change."[18]

Practices in Libraries

Among the most lasting practices in addressing workplace diversity
in college and university libraries are those that are consistent with
goals and initiatives articulated to achieve organizational change.
While a substantial amount of time, energy, and resources have been
expended on training staff to become culturally sensitive and to create networking and mentoring opportunities for diversity hires, these
are less likely to be effective in libraries than confronting underlying
structural impediments to achieving strategic priorities and commitment from library leadership to address those aspects of durable inequality in libraries and on campus. Many libraries have used at least
one tactic intended to address such structural impediments. They
have created positions for diversity officers, formed diversity steering groups and standing committees, developed residency programs,
and collaborated with library and information science programs to
expand the availability pools of LIS graduates from underrepresented
populations that are entering the workforce.

Some academic libraries have experimented with the idea of adding the position of diversity librarian to their organizational structures. These positions often have less of an intention to increase the
number of librarians from underrepresented populations on staff and
create fundamental changes in the workplace as they are primarily
focused on broadening service opportunities to special populations
within the university and surrounding community. At best, diversity
librarians are hired to create synergies wherever they go, between
the library and academic support units, in racial, ethnic, or gendered
communities within the campus, and in outreach beyond campus in
support of collegiate efforts to build campus-community partnerships
and to recruit faculty and students.

Yet few diversity librarians are empowered beyond service to
affect the composition of the library workforce. Their responsibilities
to building organizational diversity are often limited and ex-officio
to hiring and retention practices. If they are responsible for diversity
training, they are more likely than not isolated and ancillary to long-
term growth strategies for changing social inequality within libraries
as organizations. And they are often too junior in the organization to

affect mentoring and build networking opportunities among diverse hires.

Strategically, diversity librarians can be most effective in addressing long-term workplace diversity issues under two important conditions. First, if the aim is to diversify the library workplace, then diversity should be assigned to someone with administrative responsibility in the area of personnel and human resource management and development. This individual should have authority—or at least a strong say—in affirmative action policies, hiring practices, and personnel evaluations. Moreover, a library's diversity officer should ultimately be in a position to monitor and influence decision making on overall human resource management issues, including the development of mentoring and social networks, and hiring student workers, interns, and residents. A diversity librarian that is actively engaged in and has influence on library workplace issues can also be strategically linked to campus-level diversity initiatives, including other diversity officers and committees, as well as campus human resource management. By association with campus-level diversity work, a diversity librarian is better positioned to engage in campus-level advocacy, influence campus strategic goals, and to forge associations with chief diversity officers.[19]

Where an academic library has an internal governance structure, appointing a diversity steering committee can also influence long-term organizational change. Diversity steering committees and groups can be especially effective when they are charged with sincerity by library administrative leadership to ensure that diversity issues are well-reflected in the vision and values of the library, in strategic planning and assessment, and in the implementation of hiring, retention, and performance evaluation (including promotion and tenure decisions) practices. However, it is essential to the viability of diversity committees that they meet several important criteria. Effective diversity committees must be charged as standing committees and not be viewed as supplemental to the governance structure. A diversity steering committee should be understood as a key group charged with addressing fundamental strategic goals regarding the direction of personnel and workplace development, including but not exclusive to those that address diversity directly. Diversity committees must also be diverse in membership and include both new and senior staff reflecting differing viewpoints across culture and points of view. There is a need to include powerful and effective members of an organization whose presence will signal the importance of the committee to staff and campus. Accordingly, the diversity committee performs two important advocacy functions. For one, diversity committees can advocate for inclusive hiring and promotion practices at all levels of library staff. As a part of the governance structure, they have a pivotal role in developing guidelines for orientation and enduring retention initiatives that include mentoring and networking strategies. The charge of a library diversity committee can be aligned with corresponding campus-level committees or committees in other units. In doing so, congruity can be achieved in setting benchmarks and metrics to measure progress in workplace diversity against institutional goal attainment. Diversity committees also have the effect of fostering support for building inclusivity within the library if its membership is perceived of as both committed and influential.

In some academic libraries, underrepresentation has been presented as the basis on which to identify instantaneous methods to make diverse hires. These are often precarious decisions, as many staff may view new staff members as affirmative action hires and not hired for professional expertise or ability. The use of diverse hiring practices should be a strategic practice of bringing people into the organization at all levels. In using diverse hiring practices, it is crucial to consider long-term structural issues, including terms of employment, structural relationships with supervisors and peers, and ultimate goals and benefits to diversifying the organization.

One such initiative has been to promote the concept of the residency program as a method of inclusion and for increasing the number of librarians from underrepresented backgrounds. Although the practice of residency and internship programs has been present since the 1970s if not earlier, the model has, in the past two decades, become a way of increasing diversity on library staffs.[20] Although the majority of residency and internship programs have not been designed for the sole purpose of achieving diversity, a sufficient enough number of diversity-focused programs have been instituted at various college and university libraries throughout the United States to warrant consideration as a method to address underlying structural issues in hiring and retention and influencing workplace diversity.

Residency programs provide an opportunity for participants' immersion in an academic library. Several models have been employed. Some programs begin with internships, hiring individuals while still enrolled in LIS programs. However, many residency programs are designed as a post-graduate experience over a defined period of time. In some instances, residents are assigned to departments according to their stated areas of interest, while other libraries will use a rotation model similar to graduate students assigned to bioscience laboratories so that residents gain exposure to different functions before determining their professional preferences.

There is a significant drawback to residency programs that will likely affect their longevity and effectiveness in affecting diversity as it has been defined in this essay. As Brewer noted there is potential that residents may face the challenge of stigma associated with a program designed specifically to recruit librarians of color. Research on college students has suggested that internalizing stereotypes and stigmas has a profound and detrimental effect on minorities in majority organizations.[21] It is vital for a well planned residency program to reduce stereotyping by structuring programs so that all participants—residents and other staff alike—integrate the program into the library's operations and that alumni of residency programs achieve success beyond the end of their respective programs, either as a retained employee or in placement at another college or university. As Brewer and Winston noted, evaluation of program efficacy is essential to identify and combat the stigma associated with being a resident.

Two other approaches to improving workplace diversity in academic libraries have also gained momentum since the mid-1990s. Library and Information Science educators have been strongly encouraged to expand availability pools of diverse hires by creating initiatives that broaden enrollment in professional master's programs. According to the results of a study of perceptions by librarians of color on the recruitment and retention initiatives of LIS programs, Kim and Sin found that the racial and ethnic composition of LIS Master's programs was much less diverse (11.3%) than Master's programs in general (26.4%), let alone the broader population (31.3%) by the early years of the 21st century.[22] These data not only suggest little progress in recruiting librarians of color despite 30 years of effort, they also indicate that library and information science has been far less successful than other professional master's programs in increasing diversity in the availability pools of new librarians.

There are exemplary models of recruiting for diversity at individual programs in library and information science that can be adopted broadly in LIS education. The University of Arizona's Knowledge River and the Library Access Midwest Program (LAMP) have initiated novel projects to reach culturally diverse populations of potential students, with the financial support of grants from the Institute for Museum and Library Services (IMLS). Other programs have worked in partnership with their graduate schools to secure funding for individual students they recruit by competing for campus-wide fellowships.

Associations have also developed initiatives designed to increase the number of librarians of color in an effort to improve racial and ethnic diversity. The American Library Association's Spectrum Scholars Initiative has, with an infusion of resources from IMLS, created opportunities for students to receive funding for Master's and doctoral degrees and provided leadership training to scholarship recipients. Their initiative has been augmented by the support of the Association of College and Research Libraries. The long-standing diversity initiatives of the Association of Research Libraries, including its Leadership and Career Development Institute and Diversity Scholars program, are also efforts designed to institutionalize resource support and mentoring between LIS programs, member institutions, and the association to increase diversity among new and mid-career academic librarians. Taken together, these programs are beginning to realize a measurable impact by preparing cohesive communities of librarians who form professional networks with mentors and one another.

Both LIS and professional association initiatives have the potential to reshape the racial and ethnic composition of availability pools of librarians to better utilize librarians from diverse populations in college and university libraries. Yet, there is a potential pitfall. Program developers must be acutely aware of the limitations of externally awarded funding that over time will need to be replaced with other revenue streams if they are to have any longevity. Part of the success of the ARL initiative is that it is modeled and fixed within an association that has endorsed a shared responsibility of the program by member institutions. As long as there is both the will and determination among members to maintain their diversity initiatives, programs will grow and prosper, creating clear opportunities for change over time. Careful and sustained long-term coordination between associations, LIS programs, and libraries may also have the potential to lead to longer-term structural changes in entry to the LIS profession and the receptivity of college and university libraries to recruit a diversity of staff from increasingly diverse availability pools of new talent.

It is on this last point that there are also strong possibilities for blending advocacy as strategy-in-action with the objectives of workplace diversity. Purposeful, long-term change can begin by changing the culture of library and information science education and rethinking assumptions and values of our professional associations. As Kim and Sin found in their research, many librarians of color pointed to the need for cultural change in LIS Master's programs that would not only welcome diversity but result in the formation of more inclusive communities intertwining diverse scholarship and curricula in addition to financial support and mentoring.[23] Sustained coalition building between academic libraries, professional associations, and LIS programs—through advocacy strategies—are more likely to result in the assimilation of diversity as a fundamental characteristic of the library profession.

Campus Practices: Setting Strategic Goals

Ultimately, opportunities for college and university libraries to address workplace diversity are associated with campus-level strategic priorities on diversity and inclusion. Despite well meaning, earnest work, libraries are not helped by ineffectual, nonexistent, or unattainable metrics of success in achieving campus-level diversity. It is, therefore, crucial that college and university librarians identify the locus of campus-level efforts on workforce diversity, whether a Chief Diversity Officer, Affirmative Action compliance officer, campus committee, or administrative or faculty initiative, to create strategic partnerships and to influence strategic goals on equity and diversity.

Identifying specific areas of organizational learning and development will help to address and change inequality in the workplace as the library interacts with the campus. First, the leadership role of the library must be explicit in goal setting and the integration of the practice of developing workforce and workplace diversity must also be closely articulated to campus planning. Given that much of the research on workplace diversity has focused on teams or work groups, there is substantial evidence to suggest that there is also a need for close articulation between individual and unit level goal setting, that there can be effectiveness when teamwork is associated with team diversity.[24] Success achieved by the library as an organization is heavily dependent upon the internal integration of diverse staff in units and cross-functional work teams and, more specifically, intra- and intergroup behavior. Ely and Thomas observed that among perspectives of diversity and work group behavior that work, an integration-and-learning perspective has its greatest effect as it "links diversity to work processes—the way people do and experience work—in a manner that makes diversity a resource for learning and adaptive change."[25] Not only are work processes highly functioning and diversity is valued, but outcomes of efforts at the level of the unit or team create an opportunity for advocacy through team leadership within the library and between the library and other campus units that are concerned with the long-term retention of diverse hires.

Ideally there should be perfect alignment between individual, unit-level, library wide, and campus strategic goal setting. Perhaps the greatest concern at the campus level is whether or not public rhetoric on diversity by college and university administrators will actually translate into action. Advocacy from libraries on workplace diversity will have its greatest effect when librarians work with others on campus to turn public discussions into policy and practice, with the necessary resources allocated to achieve desired goals. Then, the concept of advocacy as applied to workplace diversity is well manifested in campus-level discussions, when librarians join their campus colleagues and students to advocate for and translate their own engagement on diversity into campus-wide realities.

Conclusion

There is an indirect relationship between the present discussion on advocacy and workplace diversity and a quotation from Jeffrey Pfeffer's collection of essays, *What Were they Thinking? Unconventional Wisdom About Management*. In "No More Excuses,"[26] Pfeffer identifies three ways that leaders can "break through the excuses that seem so common in organizational life":

- "The first and most basic principle is not to accept reasons for why things that need to be done can't be."
- "The next thing to do in the process of getting people to go beyond reasons why important things won't work or can't be accomplished is to articulate a vision that can inspire the effort required to overcome seemingly impossible obstacles."
- "...lead by example."

Although these three statements can be universally applied to any leadership situation, they are compelling enough to be relevant to the discussion of how college and university library leaders—whether administrative or from the front line of service and operations—can advocate to promote long-term, structural changes in workplace diversity. Although advocacy has generally been associated with service to special populations in colleges and universities, it has the capacity to be used to persuade and influence colleges and universities and their libraries toward long-term structural realignment of the kind of social inequality that colleges and universities have been slowly addressing. By establishing advocacy as a strategy for achieving workplace diversity, success will be achieved in retaining and promoting as well as recruiting, in assigning decision making responsibilities, using diverse teams to manage processes.

Moreover, advocacy when associated with workplace diversity presents itself as a strategy for coalition building across our profession, between libraries, library and information science programs, and professional associations, to increase diversity in availability pools of new and mid-career librarians and to pursue changes in professional cultures that retain and promote a diversity of librarians. Diversity may be seen as a threat to the cohesion of a library as an organization, and advocacy may be dismissed as a political strategy, tainted by an impulse of activism or community organizing. Yet advocating for workplace diversity may address an overriding communitarian concern to redress inequality, which has been seen as both permanent and unyielding. Advocacy, then, becomes a vehicle of building interdependence and interaction within the library and between the library and other campus units in an effort to collaboratively influence broader institutional agenda on hiring and retention practices.

Notes

1. Although the concept of affirmative action was in full use before President Lyndon Johnson's Howard University commencement address of June 4, 1965 ("To Fulfill These Rights"), it is often cited as an articulation of the historical sociology for affirmative action, specifically in the following passage:
   "You do not wipe away the scars of centuries by saying: 'now, you are free to go where you want, do as you desire, and choose the leaders you please.' You do not take a man who for years has been hobbled by chains, liberate him, bring him to the starting line of a race, saying, 'you are free to compete with all the others,' and still justly believe you have been completely fair... This is the next and more profound stage of the battle for civil rights. We seek not just freedom but opportunity—not just legal equity but human ability—not just equality as a right and a theory, but equality as a fact and as a result."
   http://www.lbjlib.utexas.edu/johnson/archives.hom/speeches.hom/650604.asp
2. Schmidt, 'Bakke' Set a New Path to Diversity."
3. Winston and Li, "Managing Diversity in a Liberal Arts College," 205

4. See for example Rodrigues, "Rethinking the Cultures of Disciplines."
5. In this chapter, workplace diversity is distinguished from workforce diversity. While "workforce" diversity refers to a macro perspective on diversity across organizations, workplace diversity provides a view of what goes on inside of an individual organization or institution.
6. Van Knippenberg and Schippers, "Work Group Diversity." 519
7. Hubbard, *the Diversity Scorecard*, 8
8. Welburn, "Do We Really Need Cultural Diversity"
9. DiTomaso, "Workforce Diversity and Inequality," 474.
10. Tilly, *Durable Inequality*
11. Alire, "Advocating to advance academic libraries."
12. "Political Representation"
13. Kipnis, Intraorganizational Influence Tactics. See also, Simmons-Welburn, "Perceptions of Campus-Level Advocacy."
14. Kalev, "Best Practices or Best Guesses?"
15. Ibid, 590
16. Ibid, 591
17. Ibid, 602
18. Ibid, 616
19. The campus chief diversity officer (CDO) has the potential to advocate for substantial institutional transformation. As Nancy "Rusty" Barceló, the CDO at the University of Minnesota, has observed" "In creating these positions, institutions not only illustrate their renewed commitment to diversity but, more importantly, assert that diversity will be 'at the table,' informing policy in formal ways at key meetings with senior officials. These positions also enhance the coordination of diversity efforts within a campus and with external communities… (it) indicates an acceptance of diversity as a reality of this century, and an acceptance of the opportunity to bring diversity from the margins to the center of the campus." Barcelo, "Transforming our Institutions."
20. Brewer, "Post Master's Residency Programs"; Cogell and Grunwell, *Diversity in Libraries*; Brewer and Winston, "Program Evaluation"; Brewer, "Implementing a Research Library Residency Program."
21. Sidanius, et. al., *The Diversity Challenge*
22. Kim, "Increasing Ethnic Diversity"
23. Ibid.
24. See for example the research by Ely and Thomas
25. Ely and Thomas, "Cultural Diversity at Work"
26. Pfeffer, *What Were they Thinking*, 135–137

Works Cited

Alire, Camila. "Advocating to advance academic libraries: The 2005–06 ACRL President's focus," *C&RL News*, Vol. 66, no. 8 (September 2005) http://www.ala.org/ala/acrl/acrlpubs/crlnews/backissues2005/september05/advocatingtoadvance.cfm (last accessed July 10, 2008)

Barcelo, Nancy "Rusty. "Transforming Our Institutions for the Twenty-first Century: The Role of the Chief Diversity Officer." Diversity Digest 10, no2, (2007): 6

Brewer, Julie. "Post-master's residency programs: enhancing the development of new professionals and minority recruitment in academic and research libraries." *College and Research Libraries* 58 (November 1997): 528–37.

Brewer, "Implementing a Research Library Residency Program," Synergy: News from ARL Diversity Initiatives, no. 2 (http://app.e2ma.net/campaign/c954cfadf699bb 98dc59e2c4d617f7a1#Brewer) Last accessed July 15, 2008

Brewer, Julie and Mark Winston. "Program evaluation for internship/residency programs in academic and research libraries." College and Research Libraries 62, no 4 (July 2001): 307–15.

Cogell, Raquel V and Cindy A Gruwell. Diversity in Libraries: Academic Residency Programs. Westport, CT: Greenwood Press, 2001

DiTomaso, Nancy, Corinne Post, Rochelle Parks-Yancy. Workforce Diversity and Inequality: Power, Status, and Numbers *Annual Review of Sociology*, Vol. 33 (August 2007): 473 –501

Ely, Robin J and David A. Thomas. "Cultural Diversity at Work: the Effects of Diversity Perspectives on Work Group Processes and Outcomes." Administrative Science Quarterly 46, no. 2 (June 2001): 229–273.

Hubbard, Edward E. The Diversity Scorecard: Evaluating the Impact of Diversity on Organizational Performance. Oxford : Butterworth-Heinemann, 2003

Kalev, Alexandra, Frank Dobbin, and Erin Kelly. "Best Practices or Best Guesses? Assessing the Efficacy of Corporate Affirmative Action and Diversity Policies." *American Sociological Review* 71, no. 4 (August 2006): 589–617.

Kim, Kyung-Sun and Sei-Ching Joanna Sin. "Increasing Ethnic Diversity in LIS: Strategies Suggested by Librarians of Color." *Library Quarterly* 78, no. 2 (April 2008): 153–177

Kipnis, David, Stuart Schmidt, and Ian Wilkinson. "Intraorganizational Influence Tactics: Explorations in Getting One's Way." *Journal of Applied Psychology* 65, no. 4 (1980): 440–52.

Knippenberg, D.L. van and Michaela Schippers. "Work Group Diversity." *Annual Review of Psychology* 58 (2007): 515–541.

Lyndon Baines Johnson Library and Museum. "President Lyndon B. Johnson's Commencement Address at Howard University: 'To Fulfill These Rights,'" June 4, 1965. http://www.lbjlib.utexas.edu/johnson/archives.hom/speeches. hom/650604.asp. (last accessed March 9, 2009)

Pfeffer, Jeffery. *What Were they Thinking? Unconventional Wisdom About Management.* Cambridge, MA: Harvard Business School Press, 2007.

"Political Representation," *Stanford Encyclopedia of Philosophy* http://plato.stanford. edu/entries/political-representation/ (last accessed July 10, 2008)

Rodrigues, Raymond J. "Rethinking the Cultures of Disciplines," *Chronicle of Higher Education*, April 29, 1992. (http://chronicle.com) (last accessed July 10, 2008)

Schmidt, Peter. " 'Bakke' Set a New Path to Diversity for Colleges: 30 years after the ruling, academe still grapples with race in admissions." *Chronicle of Higher Education*, June 20, 2008. (http://chronicle.com/weekly/v54/i41/41a00103.htm) Last accessed July 10, 2008.

Sidanius, Jim, et. al. *The Diversity Challenge: Social Identity and Intergroup Relations on the College Campus.* New York: Russell Sage, 2008.

Simmons-Welburn, Janice, Beth McNeil, and William Welburn. "Perceptions of Campus-Level Advocacy and Influence Strategies among Senior Administrators in College and University Libraries." Paper presented at the ACRL 13th National Conference, March 29–April 1, 2007, Baltimore, Maryland.

Thomas, David A and Robin J. Ely. "Making Differences Matter: a New Paradigm for Managing Diversity." *Harvard Business Review* 74, no 5 (September/October 1996): 79–91,

Tilly, Charles. *Durable Inequality*. Berkeley, CA: University of California Press, 1998.

Welburn, William. "Do We Really Need Cultural Diversity in the Library and Information Science Curriculum?" *Journal of Education for Library and Information Science* 35, no.4 (Fall 1994): 328–330.

Winston, Mark and Harping Li. "Managing Diversity in a Liberal Arts College Library." *College and Research Libraries* 61, no. 3 (May 2000): 205–216.

Academic Libraries and Graduate Education: Advocating for Points of Confluence in the Graduate Student Experience

11

William Welburn

Urban sociologist Elijah Anderson's paper, "The Cosmopolitan Canopy," offers useful insight into sociocultural conditions in cities that is also pertinent to understanding colleges and universities. Using Louis Wirth's portrayal of urbanism and its role in the emergence of the modern city, Anderson has argued that the city "is more racially, ethnically, and socially diverse than ever, with profound cleavages dividing one element from another and one social group from another."

> As the urban public spaces of big cities have become more riven by issues of race, poverty, and crime, much of what Wirth described as urbanites' blasé indifference seems to have given way to a pervasive wariness toward strangers, particularly anonymous black males …In places such as bus stations, parking garages, and public streets and sidewalks, many pedestrians move about guardedly, dealing with strangers by employing elaborate facial and eye work, replete with smiles, nods, and gestures geared to carve out an impersonal but private zone for themselves.[1]

Like cities, today's college and university campuses are also more culturally and socially diverse than ever before, with subcommunities separated by cultural and disciplinary differences that create a similarly fractured environment. Yet Anderson's fieldwork has also revealed subtle points of confluence in cities, where populations converge under what he refers to as a "cosmopolitan canopy." For Anderson, locations of intercultural engagement in cities occur in such varied public or semi-public locations as public markets and jazz clubs. They are, in his words, "heterogeneous and densely populated bounded public spaces within cities that offer a respite from this wariness, settings where a diversity of people can feel comfortable enough to relax their guard and go about their business more casually." The cosmopolitan canopy enables "people of different backgrounds the chance to slow down and indulge themselves, observing, pondering, and in effect, doing their own folk ethnography, testing or substantiating stereotypes and prejudices or, rarely, acknowledging something fundamentally new about the other."[2]

The need to identify and cultivate such points of confluence in colleges and universities has no less significant meaning then it does for the city, given the breadth and depth of diversity found in academic environments. Not only is the persistence of division evident in analysis of campus demographics but also among disciplines, the social and cognitive differences of students, and other less visible aspects of diversity. Nowhere is the existence of diversity more sharply observed than in *graduate* education, and in particular among the professional desires and goals of graduate students. If points of confluence serve to unite otherwise disparate groups, then can the intellectual space afforded by college and university libraries serve as the cosmopolitan canopy much needed within the campus?

The essay that follows attempts to offer justification for libraries to seek out and engage in collaborative advocacy[3] with other academic and research units within the campus to create points of intellectual and social confluence. Specifically, the essay examines the potential for such intra-institutional engagement between libraries and graduate schools with hopes of improving the quality of academic life and community for graduate students. It begins with an effort to identify and review several salient trends in graduate education that have a direct bearing on the formation of partnerships between libraries, graduate schools, and other campus units. These trends are juxtaposed with three promising focal points for collective advocacy. These focal points may serve to strengthen the academic and professional development of graduate students as they prepare to meet broader societal expectations with advanced scholarly and professional knowledge.

Trends in Graduate Education

> Research libraries will be called upon to (1) support scholarship in an educational environment characterized by increasingly fluid boundaries between disciplines, departments, and curricula, and (2) provide services to a new type of student—one that

many folks now refer to as the "millennials." Their
capacity to do so will, in fact, make possible the new
forms of scholarship/research that may characterize
21st-century knowledge production.[4]

So observed Susan Ortega and Carol Lynch as the presented a
keynote address before a 2007 ARL/CNI forum on graduate education in the 21st century. Both the changes resulting in interdisciplinary teaching and research and enrollment of graduate students
steeped in emerging technologies are crucial starting points for
collaborative advocacy. Ortega and Lynch offer a succinct analysis of
important trends in graduate education, juxtaposing broader societal
developments with the campus as a microcosm of that society. For
these veterans of graduate education administration, there are several
key factors that capture the trends in graduate education: changes in
research and scholarship, the nature and structure of graduate student
learning experiences, and the challenges of educating future generations of students with increasingly varied cultural identities, socio-
economic characteristics, and educational and academic interests.
The factors can be parsed to include demographics and discipline,
technology and delivery of teaching and scholarship, interdisciplinarity, and financing and accountability.

Demographically speaking, graduate students are more diverse
than ever. Throughout history, the expansion of graduate education
in the United States has been consistent with the diversity of those
students seeking educational opportunities beyond the baccalaureate degree. Graduates of Historically Black Colleges and Universities
across the Southern United States have attended Master's and doctoral degree programs in leading universities in Northern, Mid-Atlantic,
and Midwestern states for over a hundred years. After World War II,
students from outside of the United States, especially from nations
emerging from colonialism and hegemonic governance systems,
enrolled in advanced programs reflecting national and transnational
interests in developing new or revised political and economic systems
and scientific enterprises. Yet in recent years the global sociocultural
milieu has created an important occasion to change the fabric of
graduate education. By 2005, nearly 2.2 million full time and part
time students were enrolled in graduate programs in the United
States, up from 955,000 in 1969. Moreover, the gender balance has
shifted substantially among students choosing to pursue graduate

degrees. Although some disciplines continue to be heavily subscribed by male students, by 2005 more than 1.3 million (or approximately 60%) graduate students were women, up from 1969's reported female enrollment of 366,000 (or 38%).[5]

The racial and ethnic distribution across graduate student populations has also changed in recent years. In 1976, one in ten graduate students (134,500 students) was from a U.S. minority population. However, by 2005 the number of U.S. minority graduate students grew to 22.7%, or 475,000 students, with substantial gains realized from African American, Latino (a), and Asian American populations. White student enrollment also increased from 1.1 million to more than 1.4 million; however, the proportion of white students actually declined from 84.4% of the graduate student population to 65.3%. Changes in these figures also reflect an increase in the number of international students enrolling in graduate programs in the United States.[6]

Graduate education in the United States has also been heavily redefined by the increasingly international character of the graduate student populations found on college and university campuses. While U.S. graduate programs have attracted students for many years from many different countries, by the first decade of the 21st century, the impact of the interest by international students and their countries in pursuing graduate study in the United States has changed the constitution of students enrolled in graduate programs. As an National Science Foundation study, while 10.2% of those students receiving doctoral degrees in the United States between 1960 and 1964 were temporary residents, by the late 1990s, that number had risen to 22.9%, with a significant increase in the number of permanent residents enrolled in U.S. doctoral programs (from 2.8% to 7.9% during that same period). These numbers vary significantly by field of study, with the greatest increases reported in scientific disciplines.[7]

More than numbers, the changing demographics of graduate education have also changed educational experiences substantially. Multiple languages are spoken within single campuses, exhibiting increasingly complex ethos of academic interests and achievement, social interactions, and cultural subcommunity growth and development affecting not only the future composition of faculty, industry, and government and public service, but the very experiences of all students—undergraduate and graduate alike—seeking higher learning.

Beyond characteristics of the graduate student population, the differing academic interests of students have altered the way in which learning and scholarship takes shape in graduate schools. Tracking trends in *doctoral* enrollment and degrees earned may serve as an important bellwether on graduate education; however, a significant number of students enroll in Master's and post baccalaureate graduate and professional certificate programs. The Master's degree in particular may be an important indicator of the degree to which professional requirements and the market value of higher education have shifted to post baccalaureate study and degree attainment. According to the National Center for Educational Statistics, 91% percent of the graduate degrees awarded in 2005 were awarded to students enrolled in Master's programs, with large concentrations in Education, Business, and other professional fields.[8] The number of Master's degrees awarded has grown from 21% of the overall number of undergraduate and graduate degrees awarded in 1970-71 to 28% in 2005, while the percentage of doctoral degrees awarded has remained relatively unchanged during that same period. In other words, the credentialing of U.S. workers and employees worldwide with advanced degrees has experienced its most significant growth at the Master's level.[9]

Two Cultures / Blurred Genres

These increases in the number of people enrolling in graduate programs, and especially among Master's degree programs, have created stresses and strains on learning, pedagogy and changes in the design and delivery of programs of study. Two important features of graduate program development entail differences in values and definition of the purpose of graduate education. First, ever since C. P. Snow resurrected a 19th century debate over a gap between scientific and humanities worldviews in his published lectures, "The Two Cultures," higher educators have debated the importance of such distinctions in contrasting disciplinary traditions in scholarship and learning. Although Snow's ideas are highly contested,[10] the distinctions between sciences and the humanities continue to be evident across disciplines. Graduate student training, and the resources that accompany graduate education, have been clearly divided by the requirements of research and publication, training in teaching, and in available funding to support graduate education. The persistence of the image of the solitary English doctoral student alone in the library stacks between his research and teaching multiple sections of composition and the Chemistry student spending long hours—well beyond a 20-hour per week research assistantship—working on her mentor's heavily grant-supported laboratory serves to illustrate difference in individualized and collaborative scholarship and financial support between humanities and scientific disciplines.

Yet such images may also conceal an increase in hybridity and interdisciplinarity that blurs the surface-level differences among disciplines. More opportunities for interdisciplinary research and learning, for example, enable graduate students across the humanities, social sciences, and sciences to find points of confluence on substantive if not methodological grounds. The end results are likely to be that of a scientific community more cognizant of writing and communication and a humanities community trained in the ethics of human subject research or engaged in the digitization and computer based analysis of information.

Consistency in teaching and scholarship across otherwise disparate disciplines has been encouraged by opportunities to advance interdisciplinary research and program development between traditional disciplines and among international studies programs and in new fields of scientific advancement and cultural understanding in areas as far reaching as mathematical biology, computational linguistics, bioinformatics, and gender studies. Interdisciplinarity, by the opening of the 21st Century, has become a driving force in graduate education as the translation of faculty interests in collaborations and exchanges of ideas across disciplines that have spurred graduate student collaborations and the advance of new programs of study spanning the boundaries of scientific, social science, and humanities branches of learning. Such collaborations have helped to offset the effects of disciplinary isolation.

Although there is still some merit in revisiting C.P. Snow's contribution to understanding traditional disciplines gaps, his thesis never fully anticipated the seriousness of a greater gulf only alluded to in the "Two Cultures." There is an even more pronounced distinction between basic or traditional graduate education ultimately leading to the doctor of philosophy degree and the emerging power of professional education. As Paul Starr has carefully documented in his study of the rise of medical education and the medical practice, the field of medicine developed over a period of a hundred years as an enterprise that commands not only an elevated status but also a substantial investment and expenditure of resources within campuses with the programmatic and financial support of state, federal, and nonprofit agencies.[11] Since the middle of the 20th Century, professional Master's programs, including recent enthusiasm over the concept of the Professional Science Master's degree, enroll a major share of students enrolled in graduate programs, all with an eye toward the market value of degrees in everything from human resource management to bioenergy to creative writing.

The goals of basic graduate and professional education cannot be assumed to be identical. While doctoral graduate training involves the pursuit of original ideas and cutting edge scholarship, professional education more often than not entails *praxis*, or the application of theories and concept in real world situations faced in professional practice. Moreover, professional education involves training in accordance with sets of ethics or codes of behavior that govern social interaction between working professionals and their respective clientele. The lines of distinction between the communities of doctoral and professional education are grey and their relationships are complex. Most professional studies programs have formed advanced programs for doctoral-level research, where theories from core disciplines are routinely used and transformed by professional values and practice. In some instances, similar programs exist within a single campus, such as the teaching of economics in liberal arts and business schools, and the most distinguishing characteristics have to do with the applications of concepts to professional activities.

Consequentially, observable differences between basic graduate and professional programs pose challenges to goal congruity for graduate education. Many policies have been formed and services implemented from the vantage point of doctoral education, while many of the nation's graduate students are enrolling in Master's programs. Resource needs and requirements may vary; yet, financial and human costs are substantially higher for doctoral students given the length of time and dedication needed to pursue doctoral study. Likewise, more Master's students and some doctoral students are pursuing their degrees part-time and are only partially engaged in the life of the university. Their needs may often be expressed through remote access to classes, libraries, computing centers, and advising services. Such situations are likely to require institutions to restructure approaches to support and access to resources based on distance and virtual models of teaching and service.

The "New Human Environment"

The presence of part time and online students in graduate education is but one component of the trend in the way that technology has and continues to affect education and scholarship. As Marshall McLuhan is often quoted as saying, "Any technology tends to create a new human environment."[12] There are a number of different ways that technology has affected graduate education and its students. For one, the opportunities to pursue advanced degrees virtually through online study and *blended* learning opportunities are critical to understanding how graduate education has grown in recent years. Students prepare using multimedia lectures and participate in synchronous and asynchronous discussions without regard to geographic boundaries. The opportunities for sharing ideas are improved by the mix of geographic localities of students enrolled in distance courses. Conversely, for the very same reasons, community building is difficult and equal access to resources is unevenly distributed within the distance learning environment. Resource support presents both opportunities and challenges to the well-structured virtual learning environments in that they have the capacity to go beyond emulating traditional classroom settings and take full advantage of different forms of communicative technologies to socially network, simulate, digitize, and provide remote access to a wealth of information to augment new or revised learning models. Other uses of technologies serve graduate student communities by making it feasible to establish and grow social networks and sub networks of disciplinary or interdisciplinary communities, enabling an exchange of ideas and shared access to research across disciplinary, institutional, and geographical boundaries. Some graduate students have embraced the idea that there are benefits to social networking technologies such as blogs to communicate within and between scholarly communities and to advocate for open access.[13]

Nowhere has the adoption of Web-based information technologies been stronger than in the migration of theses and dissertations from print to electronic environment, thanks to advances in the development of software for portable document format (PDF) and markup languages.[14] Electronic theses and dissertations (ETDs) have been actively developed by universities in North America and Europe since the mid-1980s and by 2008 have become adopted in Europe, the United States, South Asia, Africa, and Australia as a method of access and preservation of graduate theses and dissertations. The ETD has become the preferred method of access and delivery for the UMI / ProQuest Dissertation Publishing Program, and many universities are choosing to add them to their institutional repositories.[15] Because of advances in technology, ETDs also have the potential to augment text with sound and visual media.

ETDs present both opportunities and challenges for universities seeking to offer them as either an option or as a requirement. ETDs stand to broaden access to students' research, much of which will not likely appear in published form. Moreover, they provide an opportunity for an electronic submission and review process, thereby eliminating not only the physical deposit of thesis work but enabling interaction between students and their advisors and departments as well as graduate school thesis examiners prior to the electronic transfer of the final product to the library, institutional repository, and to UMI / ProQuest or other external repository. Since the speed of digital access to thesis is greatly enhanced by ETD initiatives, useful controls are also fostered by the very same technology to enable students to exercise their authors' rights to embargo their work from premature release for specified periods of time.[16]

Perhaps the most significant challenge posed by ETD technology involves the preservation of intellectual property rights in a digital environment. Placing an embargo on students' work to prevent premature release is intended to offset or allay students and their advisors' concerns about future publishing opportunities by insuring the student authors' rights during subsequent book and journal publication negotiations. More challenging, however, is the widespread use of copyrighted materials in theses and dissertations that suddenly becomes substantially and more immediately accessible with Web access. The convergence of technology and intellectual property presents educators with a new human environment replete with dilemmas concerning effective training on issues associated with copyright and the meaning of fair use, not only in the dissemination of an electronic dissertation but in the classroom as well, where many graduate students are teachers as well as students.

Financing and Accountability

Finally, given the cost of education, the financial constraints to accessing graduate education are of real concern not only to higher education but to government and policy makers and to the broader society. What the next generations expect from graduate education will likely reflect broader societal issues and priorities and will be inextricably tied to the capacity for all who seek and are prepared for graduate education to obtain access.

According to reports by Kenneth Redd of the Council of Graduate Schools, "From 1995 to 2004, the cost of graduate education increased more than 60%," and that funding in the form of fellowships and scholarships, grants, and assistantships cannot keep pace with the demand for access to graduate education. Acute among the differences in funding are gaps between scientific disciplines and professional degree programs and substantial increases in borrowing for education. Heavy reliance on loans means that an increasing number of students are increasing their overall indebtedness to pursue advance degrees. The growth rate in indebtedness, the author speculated, may affect attrition among graduate students as well as their choices of as part time or full time students.[17]

The cost of pursuing higher education has caused great angst among educators and policy makers, students and families. These costs are further exacerbated in graduate education. The vortex created by the cost of education and options for online or virtual learning over residential enrollment and participation in graduate education, and higher education in general, may have a long term effect of forging a two-tiered system of postsecondary education—those who are on campus and those who are not and, therefore, subject to differing standards and measures of accountability. It is entirely plausible that such a two-tiered system may also further divide those disciplines that can afford to fund students and those that cannot or will not do so. Further, if specific demographic student subpopulations are concentrated more heavily in disciplines where little opportunity for funding exists outside of loans, as Redd has observed, the long term consequences might also slow increases in the overall diversity of students receiving advanced degrees. This may function as a canary in the coal mine for the larger population seeking entrance into fields where opportunities for funding are generally scarce, as well as for Master's students who have fewer funding options.

How Libraries and Graduate Schools Can Respond Together

The practice of advocacy involves the degree to which practitioners can influence individuals or groups into action.[18] In social care, advocacy helps to form networks of interdependent agencies that serve the good of those individuals in need.[19] Librarians and graduate educators can respond together through a partnership that not only blends these approaches but considers advocacy as a shared practice.

Through collaboration, libraries, graduate schools, and other agencies within a university can work together toward common goals, evoking influence strategies to provide necessary resource support to graduate students and programs. This form of advocacy as an outgrowth of partnerships between campus units is referred to here as *collaborative advocacy*.[20]

There are clear prerequisites for successful collaborative advocacy that will likely have the most impact on graduate students. For one, the organizational structure of graduate education focuses on the centrality of the graduate program and the relationship between faculty and students from admission to graduation. Influence in graduate education is achieved through resource support and the formation of new concepts and models in learning. This occurs where there are clear benefits to mastery of knowledge and pursuit of original and applied research goals, enhanced support from new information technologies, and opportunities to create space for individualized and collaborative study.

A second, more obvious prerequisite carries deeper implications. Students enrolling in undergraduate education are, for the most part, admitted to the institution and are free to roam their college or university in pursuit of the right major. However, graduate students are usually admitted to a single program and their relationship to their educational objectives is typically defined within their program of study only in association with broad institutional parameters. Program requirements, research methods and training requirements are distinguished by discipline and program objectives, and most graduate students' energies are concentrated within a single area or subarea of study. In the face of such traditions, students are crossing disciplinary boundaries and, together with their faculty, are creating new opportunities for interdisciplinary scholarship in research and the formation of interdisciplinary programs and research centers. The leadership role of graduate deans and administrators varies from campus to campus; however, all possess a strong commitment to removing the obstacles that inhibit interdisciplinary research but program development.[21]

A third prerequisite considers market driven forces that shape the creation of new programs and discontinue others. Responsibility-Centered Management (RCM) has forced some institutions to streamline their degree programs and consider the market value of new initiatives. Among Master's programs, a number of new initiatives are built around the demands from industry and government. Many Professional Science Master's programs have been created around partnerships with industry and integrate internships into the overall required program of study. Conversely, RCM and market-driven initiatives have forced institutions to carefully assess the efficacy of troubled or low enrollment programs and individual courses.

Taken together, these three prerequisites are drawn from broader set of issues that drives collaboration between graduate schools and other partners within their institutions. Both faculty and graduate students are more likely to identify with their respective departments, schools, and colleges, thereby limiting the line authority of graduate deans. Graduate deans are able to exert influence through policy setting and resource allocation because these and other prerequisites for collaboration are largely out of their hands. Given these constraints, strategies that are advocacy-based and focused on influence, persuasion, and collaboration on academic support services are likely to be more effective than those that attempt to impose top-down decisions.

Understanding the Information Needs of Graduate Students

Libraries and graduate schools have numerous points of confluence. Three are identified for further discussion. They are information needs and requirements of graduate students across a broad spectrum of academic and professional interests, tangible resource support for the pursuit of graduate study, and the desire to find or create physical space that overcomes disciplinary and cultural boundaries.

Thus far we have identified some of the implications of several important factors that affect graduate education, including variations in the makeup of graduate student populations and their disciplinary foci, as well as the distinctions drawn between research and professional-focused goals in graduate education. While services in higher educational institutions have usually been designed to navigate differences among students across academic dimensions, it may be more useful to focus on points of confluence during the development of a collaborative advocacy strategy supporting graduate students. Three specific issues should be considered in assessing information requirements of graduate students. Given demographic considerations, graduate students speak *in all languages*, reflecting both cultural and disciplinary backgrounds and characteristics. Language is a tangible demonstration of the web of cultural plurality that is most evident among graduate student populations. Here points of confluence need to be formed, where culturally diverse communities find common ground and mutual interests in the pursuit of knowledge through scholarship and learning.

Beyond demographic points of confluence, there are commonalities across disciplines. As John Unsworth has noted, *scholarly primitives* may be particularly useful in shifting focus toward converging information needs of graduate students. Unsworth used the idea of primitives "to refer to some basic functions common to scholarly activity across disciplines, over time, and independent of theoretical orientation. These 'self-understood' functions form the basis for higher-level scholarly projects, arguments, statements, interpretations—in terms of our original, mathematical/philosophical analogy, axioms."[22] While his comments are primarily directed toward defining research in the humanities, the concept that there are universal considerations in research—from discovery to representation—is significant enough to provide guidance on information requirements spanning disciplinary boundaries.

Studies of the information needs and requirements of graduate students constitute a relatively small research thread; however, important themes have emerged from a few key studies. Graduate students continue to treasure personal contact with faculty, fellow students, librarians, and others they feel possess relevant information. Accordingly, the need to provide support for students in research-based degree programs is compelling. While accessing information has been deeply affected by Web-based resources using common search engines, such information has not supplanted the use of online and print resources accessible from libraries. Some studies that have given insight into how graduate students interests move from general Web searching to the use of library databases, taking into account variance by discipline. A University of Minnesota study noted the differences among disciplines in sources of information, where graduate students in the sciences were heavily reliant on online resources, while students in the humanities and social sciences continue to value libraries and their print collections in their research.[23] There is also a growing interest in setting the information requirements of graduate students within the context of scholarly communication.

According to a 2007 report of a study of Association of Research Libraries' member institutions, 29 institutions surveyed (53%) had not yet targeted scholarly communication activities for graduate students. However, 22 (40%) and 4 (7%) targeted specific disciplines had begun to engage in programming and Web-based tutorials for graduate students. The opportunity presented here calls for a broadened engagement between libraries, graduate schools, and research administrators in educating graduate students on a full range of issues that include authors' rights, intellectual property, academic integrity, an research conduct.[24]

These studies point to a need not only for continued research into the needs of graduate student, but to possible points of collaborative advocacy between libraries and graduate schools. There is an ongoing need to foster support, including technological support, for the mentoring relationship between students and faculty and social networking between students to ensure the continuance of invisible networks for information sharing. Moreover, graduate administrators' understanding of evolving issues affecting libraries, including emerging information technologies and issues in scholarly communication, can serve as focal points in collaborative advocacy during the process of institutionalizing changing practices in scholarly communication and managing intellectual property and the conduct of research.

Supporting Resource Needs through Collaborative Advocacy

The concerns about the information needs of graduate students leads to a second opportunity for collaborative advocacy, to combine efforts to promote institutional resource allocation to advance basic graduate and professional education programmatically, and to provide the necessary resources for high quality graduate educational experiences. Next to financing higher education, the specific issues that are likely to dominate graduate education involve securing fiscal, human, and technological resources. Much of the public attention in higher education in the past few decades has focused on undergraduate issues. Without sacrificing those vital issues concerning academic progress and engagement of undergraduate students, issues affecting graduate students have begun to move to the foreground of discussions about the short-term future of higher education. Areas of increasing importance are likely to include a concern for a range of intellectual property issues, most importantly having to do with authors' rights and a reevaluation of the meaning of fair use as it is practiced in the digital era. A growing number of institutions are, through offices of research, libraries, and graduate schools, developing workshops, documentation, and tutorials directed primarily at graduate student audiences to further their understanding of intellectual property issues and protect them from legal entanglements over the use of their work and the works of others.

Other areas of collaboration that involve the use of institutional resources pertain to involve collaborative implementation of various technologies designed to enhance access, communication, and preservation of students' research and creative work. Electronic theses and dissertations' projects have involved close association between the staffs of graduate schools, libraries, and computing centers to insure effective preparation and transmission of thesis work through the thesis review process, preservation in digital repositories, and access by designated communities of interest. ETDs constitute but one area of collaboration for which the need to advocate for resources to support graduate students is imperative. What is also apparent is a need to engage students who are "not bound by traditional modes of research exchange…students are using all the technologies at their disposal to engage in scholarly discourse—including blogs, wikis and tagging tools." Yet graduate students must also balance, if not temper, enthusiasm with full recognition of the hegemony of enduring traditions in scholarly communication that protect authors' and publishers' rights and rigorous academic peer review bound by disciplinary conventions.[25]

Creating the Space

Finally, the need to create or invest in physical and virtual spaces continues to be an ongoing concern in creating the proper environment for graduate education. As has been noted in studies conducted at New York University and the University of Minnesota, graduate students continue to need space not only for work and study but for intellectual engagement with one another.[26] In a virtual context, social networking is presented as a mechanism for reaching all graduate students and encouraging the creation of subgroups devoted to specific academic, social, or cultural interests. Additionally, creating physical space for engagement and collaborative activities, or for independent work in collaborative environments such as scholarly commons and technologically enhanced centers for teaching and research support, can be crucial to building communities.

Conclusion

Elijah Anderson's cosmopolitan canopy is situated to foster engagement across demographic, cultural, and socioeconomic boundaries. In the circumstances of social exchange in everyday life, people converse about "what they have in common with other human being, regardless of their particularity."[27] Placed in the context of graduate education and given the argument that graduate student communities are loosely structured yet yearning for points of confluence, it follows that efforts toward building community among graduate students will require greater collaboration between units within institutions of higher education.

This essay attempted to identify key trends affecting communities of graduate students throughout the United States and their implications for forging a response from graduate schools and libraries to address the quality of graduate educational experience. Given the enduring scarcity of resources in higher education and traditional emphases on undergraduate education and the needs of undergraduate students, strategies employing collaborative advocacy between librarians and graduate administrators will likely have the greatest effect on institutional strategic planning and resource allocation.

Notes

1. Anderson, "The Cosmopolitan Canopy," 14–15
2. Ibid, 15, 25
3. The term collaborative advocacy is derived from Spicer, *Organizational Public Relations*, 247–267
4. Ortega and Lynch, "The Changing Nature of Graduate Education"
5. 2007 Digest of Educational Statistics
6. Ibid
7. *U.S. Doctorates in the 20th Century*
8. 2007 Digest of Educational Statistics
9. Ibid
10. See, for example, Gould, The Hedgehog, The Fox, and the Magister's Pox, which observes shortsightedness in Snow's thesis. Gould, The Hedgehog, The Fox
11. Star, The Social Transformation of American Medicine
12. McLuhan, The Gutenberg Galaxy
13. See "Working with the Facebook generation"
14. ETD Guide
15. ETD Repository and Submission
16. Surratt, ETD Release Policies
17. Redd, "Financing Graduate Education"
18. Todaro, "The Power of Persuasion"
19. Levy, Jean and Malcolm Payne. "Welfare rights advocacy in a specialist health and social care setting: A service audit." British Journal of Social Work 36, no. 2 (February 2006): 323–331.
20. Bartunek, Foster-Fishman and Keys, "Using Collaborative Advocacy"
21. It should be noted that the concept of interdisciplinarity is not unfamiliar to higher education. Since World War II, area studies programs flourished with

support from U.S. governmental agencies and private foundations, and since the late 1960s, many institutions developed racial/ethnic and gender studies programs with a presence in graduate education. While the appearance of interdisciplinary scientific programs is quite recent by comparison, much of the present day discussion of interdisciplinarity is focused on new and emerging scientific collaborations. In the humanities and social sciences, evolving programs include areas as widely diffuse as film or cinema studies and social inequality.

22. Unsworth, "Scholarly Primitives"
23. Marcus and Williams, "Assessing Graduate Student Research Behaviors"
24. Newman, Blecic, and Armstrong, "Scholarly Communication Education," 14
25. "Working with the Facebook Generation"
26. Covert-Vail and Mandel
27. Anderson, "Cosmopolitan Canopy," 29

Works Cited

2007 Digest of Educational Statistics. Washington, D.C.: National Center for Education Statistics, 2008.

Anderson, Elijah. "The Cosmopolitan Canopy." *Annals of the American Academy of Political and Social Science* 595 (September 2004): 14–30.

Bartunek, Jean M., Penny G. Foster-Fishman and Christopher B. Keys. "Using Collaborative Advocacy to Foster Intergroup Cooperation: a Joint Insider-Outsider Investigation." *Human Relations* 49 (1996): 701–733.

Boeke, Cindy. "IPRES 2006 Conference Report: Digital Preservation Takes Off in the E-Environment." 12, no. 12 (December 2006).

Covert-Vail, Lucinda and Carol A. Mandel. "NYU Graduate Student Academic and Research Experience." *ARL Fall Forum.* Washington, DC: Association for Research Libraries, October 12, 2007.

ETD Guide (The Guide for Electronic Theses and Dissertations). http://em/wolobppls/prgwoloETD_Giode#Omtrpdictopm (accessed February 2, 2009).

Gould, Stephen Jay. *The Hedgehog, The Fox, and the Magister's Pox.* New York: Harmony Books, 2003.

Levy, Jean and Malcolm Payne. "Welfare rights advocacy in a specialist health and social care setting: A service audit." *British Journal of Social Work* 36, no. 2 (February 2006): 323–331 .

Marcus, Cecily and Karen Williams. "Assessing Graduate Student Research Behaviors: Humanities, Social Sciences, and Sciences." Washington, DC: ARL, October 12 2007.

McLuhan, Marshall. *The Gutenberg galaxy; the making of typographic man.* Toronto: University of Toronto Press, 1962.

Newman, Kathleen A., Deborah D. Blecic, and Kimberly L. Armstrong. *Scholarly Communication Education Initiatives.* SPEC Kit 299, Washington, D.C.: Association for Research Libraries, 2007.

Ortega, Suzanne and Carol Lynch. *The Changing Nature of Graduate Education: Inputs and Outcomes.* ARL/CNI Forum on Enhancing Graduate Education, Washington, DC: Association for Research Libraries, 2007.

Redd, Kenneth. *Financing Graduate Education: Current Trends, Future Concerns.* http://cgsnet.org/portals/0/pdf/FinancingGradEd.pdf, Washington, D.C.: Council of Graduate Schools, December 2006.

Spicer, Christopher. *Organizational Public Relations: a Political Perspective*. Mahwah, NJ: Erlbaum, 1997.

Starr, Paul. *The Social Transformation of American Medicine*. New York: Basic Books, 1982.

Surratt, Brian E. *ETD Release Policies in American ARL Institutions: a Preliminary Study*. http://www.tdl.org/documents/ETD_Release_Policies.pdf, Washington DC: ARL, 2005.

Thurgood, Lori, Mary J. Golladay, and Susan T. Hill. *U.S. Doctorates in the 20th Century: Special Report*. Arlington, Virginia: National Science Foundation, 2006.

Todaro, Julie. "The Power of Persuasion: Grassroots Advocacy in the Academic Library." *C&RL News* 67, no. 4 (April 2006).

Unsworth, John. "Scholarly Primitives: What Methods do Humanities Researchers Have in Common, and How Might Our Tools Reflect This?" *Humanities Computing: Formal Methods, Experimental Practice*. Prod. Kings College. London, May 13, 2000.

Vireo. *ETD Repository and Submission*. http://www.tdl.org/publications#etdvireo (accessed February 15, 2009).

WG Trusted Repositories . http://nestor.cms.hu-berlin.de/moinwiki/WG_Trusted_Repositories_-_Certification?action=show&redirect=WG+Trusted+Repositories (accessed February 15, 2009).

Working the Facebook generation: Engaging student views on access to scholarship. Washington, DC: SPARC, January 2008, http://www.arl.org/sparc/meetings/ala08mw/.

Advocacy in Higher Education Environments: No More Excuses

12

Julie Todaro

Those of us in higher education spend a great deal of time searching for "teachable moments." But the teachable moments we search and prepare for and then exult in—if and when they arrive—focus on research questions and answers, scholarly pursuits, critical thinking, choosing from among alternatives, pursuit of lifelong learning, cultural exploration and—if we're lucky—we get to lead and/or experience our constituent in the discovery process.

The most important teachable moments of all, however, are the moments we spend illustrating 'who we are' as well as 'what value we bring to the educational setting' and—in general—the importance of research and information in the life of the student in the pursuit of the successful educational experience. This process of illustrating or *advocating* for the library by connecting our internal constituents and decision makers to who we are and what we do and why we do it—with a focus on value—has become or some say has always been, one of the most important things we do or should do. The problem is that we don't always learn *advocacy* in educational curriculum, we don't include *advocacy* in job descriptions, we seldom include *advocacy* in our goals or performance plans and we seldom have strategic plans for advocacy. We do have opportunities for learning and implementing legislative advocacy at the state, regional and federal levels, but our "local" advocacy—within institutions and on campuses is not part of job descriptions typically—exclusive of the highest levels of library administration.

Given this reality, academic librarians need to acknowledge they have only base line knowledge of the process, limited training, little experience, a lack of knowledge of the target audience, an uncertain commitment, a lack of political acumen, a lack of knowledge of the umbrella institution's budget processes, disagreements on what the message is, unreal expectations of who delivers the message and—finally—little time to advocate in general as well as little time to integrate the concept into the life of the organization. Yet, advocacy within institutions may be the single most important thing that we do in our professional lifetime. What is a librarian to do? The answer is partially found by assessing the negative, countering with the positive and—most importantly realizing we have no more excuses.

Assessing the Negative / Countering with the Positive

We have only base line knowledge of the advocacy process.
Library and Information Science education for librarians, educational programs for library assistants, curriculum for library supporters and higher education master's and Ph.D. programs have very little content on advocacy. Typically found in the general educational core and—as targeted follow up—in 'type of library' curriculum, legislative advocacy is the primary focus on legislative policies that are often the infrastructure of professional activities, resources and services. Much time is spent on teaching basic and advanced knowledge on specific policies such as copyright and Internet access, however, little time is spent on how to convince others of the correct application and role of these issues in contemporary libraries and—specifically—academic libraries within their higher education institutions.

When recommending who educates whom on what, it isn't even clear who should teach application and role, however, the increasing number of educational packages in professional development or continuing education format—when specifically linked to library education content—has to be the answer. Building in those curriculum links, however, have to be systematic and consistent *and* provide a process for library educators to vet development and C.E. content for the best match. So is the answer for library educators to design and deliver their own curriculum through master's programs? Possibly, however, broader packages addressing the variety of target audiences including those who don't attend library education programs must be considered. In addition, finding the perfect one-size-fits-all program for library students and library supporters as well as professionals in—for example IT and media programs is not easy. There is a realization that what is being taught is not complete and the vetting and consistent linking of curriculum to content offerings is not adequate.

We have limited training.
Obviously related to the "base line knowledge of the advocacy process" Library and Information Science association conference and workshop content, continuing education offerings, consortial training

and internal higher education or academic library training has very little content on internal advocacy in general. Also lacking is training on application and roles as discussed previously. And although there is much advocacy training content for library supporters in the legislative process, "training" and "professional development" are not designed or focused specifically for training employees to speak up and speak out within their higher education environments. Training in this area for all employees, supporters and other related professionals who work in or support libraries should include:

- Identification of best practices
- Application of best practices to institutional and association training programs
- Design of a full institutional program that strategically provides advocacy training content that includes basic awareness/basic knowledge, persuasion techniques in logical formats, presentation skills and abilities and a commitment to integrating training into the institution and the academic library.
- Training for all levels of employees
- Training for other professionals in the academic setting
- A match of pedagogy to the advocacy content area with a broad method of delivery

We have limited experience.
It stands to reason that without educational or training curriculum on application and role, librarians, library employees, library supporters and other related professionals in higher education arenas lack the skills and thus the experience in advocating for library needs. When faced with a "lack of experience" problem, the answer is not just educating on content but:

- Focusing on best practices where experiences have been successful and then matching targeted techniques to organizations
- Identifying individuals with advocacy strengths and pairing them with inexperienced individuals to form teams. These teams could look for advocacy opportunities
- Designing more specific content that might include written scripts for advocacy encounters such as scripts for circulation desk assistants to use with constituents at circulation exchanges.

We have an uncertain commitment.
Although many may assume "everyone who works in a library values the same things," this assumption is not borne out in reality. The strength of organizations comes from—among other things, a diversity of individuals, thoughts, and belief systems. Not everyone comes to the academic setting with the desire or the commitment to the advocacy process. Convincing others to value you and your expertise and persuading others to give you needed resources is often seen as the responsibility of the library or even college or university administration. As this is the case in so many academic environments, educating all groups on the broader advocacy process must include:

- Clear definitions of roles and responsibilities, including specific activities for each role
- Discussions of how different levels of advocacy *set the stage* for higher level advocacy
- An identification of specific areas of need, design of scripts and identification of specific times and opportunities for advocacy efforts to have maximum impact
- Building discussion of commitment into organizational documents including job descriptions, interviewing and hiring decisions, orientation, and training and education in ongoing core functions such as reference, classroom faculty relationships, and—in general—all customer service and public communications.

We lack political acumen.
Librarians, library employees, library supporters and related professionals are not educated for, trained for, nor typically expected—at all levels—to be proficient politically. In fact, throughout library education and professional development, continuing education and organizational orientation and training there is little curriculum on the politics of libraries or even the politics of non-profits or specific to academics surviving a political tidal wave on higher education. Those areas, however, are exactly where we need further education. Higher education has always been and is becoming increasingly more political with each growth period and with each set back. Although not viewed as a competitive arena, the university and/or college campus is often best conquered by the strongest "politician" in the best sense of the word.

Building political and library advocacy skills into education and training must be part of all curriculum Individual specific roles and responsibilities or levels of internal advocacy must be determined to illustrate who sets the stage, who provides background, who advocates in the general sense, and who actually advocates for the libraries specific needs. Not everyone is political nor should everyone be political but providing levels and specific responsibilities goes a long way to making sure all are involved but within individual expertise and comfort zones.

We lack knowledge of the umbrella institution's budget processes.
Higher education environments are complicated business environments with a blend of non-profit and profit business practices. To successfully advocate for library needs, administrators and selected other groups such as targeted middle managers in institutional and instructional technology, must have an in depth understanding of the budget processes within the institution and between the institution and its funders. Curriculum and professional development and/or C.E. should include—for the academic librarian administrator—higher education coursework and content designed by and delivered by higher education entities rather than library-specific associations. Instead, our library associations and educational entities should identify what content exists and direct us to the content. Using higher education content—on budgeting for example—provides the learner with not only budget content but with context and perspective. In these cases it is not up to the presenter or educator to show how the context relates to libraries. Instead, the learner should apply and interpret the context to be a more effective advocate. Learning about how higher education thinks about money is as valuable to us as which budget forms to use. This is also true of assessment data used to justify budget requests. External content on what higher education is required to do and how they are required to track and present data is critical to the success of the academic library's decisions on what they want to assess and how they want to use their own data in justification and accountability exercises? Justifications?.

We have disagreements on what the message is.
A roomful of librarians and library administrators—much less—of library supporters or related professionals—will not agree on what the most important message is at any given time. And that is okay. As

in other areas, academic librarians walk the line between articulating and applying their own message within the institution and piggybacking their message on the message of the higher education environment in which they reside. A balance can and should be achieved between the two messages. Connecting or aligning library and information setting messages with the umbrella institution is a political necessity. The crafting of the library advocacy message (terminology, vision, articulation of needs, design of scripts, etc.) begins with an examination of the advocacy message of the parent institution and a review of other successful departmental messages.

We have unrealistic expectations of who delivers the message.
In a perfect world, I want all of my staff, all library supporters and all related professionals to be working together to advocate for the library within the institution. I want the institutional technology associate vice president to come to me to partner and use our data to justify the need to increase bandwidth or to prepare the IT budget requests for technology trade out schedules for hardware. These collaborations sometimes occur and sometimes do not. Librarians may ask themselves "why didn't they think of the library?" or "why weren't we included in the discussion?" It is unrealistic to expect that one breakthrough will be all that is needed and that it will persist through time. Realistically, educators come and go, administrators come and go and make their own agreements and decisions, often without the input of librarians. However the broader the advocacy training and the more consistent and far reaching the involvement, the more likely the message will not only leave the library and permeate the campus/institution but—most importantly—stay out in the campus/institution environment.

We have little time to advocate in general as well as little time to integrate the concept of advocacy into the life of the organization.
Advocacy training must be integrated into organization documents and all primary and secondary processes. Training must also be integrated into the timing and life of individuals within the library organization. The more organized the process, the more integrated into core processes and the more scripts written, the more likely it is that advocacy will become an integral part of each individual's work making it easier to identify advocacy opportunities and timing activities for highest impact.

How do we decide on our target audience, that is, how do we choose to whom we advocate?

Part of the advocacy process—and obviously one of the most critical parts of the process is to identify and match target audiences to scripts and specific activities within the process. Examples include:

- Science faculty need to remain active and vocal supporters of subscriptions for online journals therefore librarian/science faculty relationships and communication are critical and content can be built into departmental or task force presentations and information literacy.
- Institutional technology managers view the library as partners in the design of 21st century university/college environments and therefore, identified librarians (specific technology skills and interests) are placed on specific institutional committees.
- Identifying the targets should include:
  - Determining what message needs to be conveyed to what group and when.
  - Academic librarians should spend significant time designing a strategic plan for integrating advocacy that includes:
  - A "six degrees of separation" approach for identifying existing supporters, possible supporters, converting naysayers needed to move forward, etc.
  - Matching message to the motivation of each targeted group
  - Identification of existing data available for approaching targeted groups
  - Identification of new data needed for approaching targeted groups
  - Rationales connecting data to target group motivation
  - A match of who –within the library—might approach the targeted groups with the message/rationale/data

What Else Do We Have to Have to Do?

Setting the stage for the higher education community is just as important as setting the stage for library groups. This stage setting involves the design of ongoing, systematic opportunities for educating the higher education community on 21st century higher education and library and information settings; the role we play in knowledge management; the role we play in student engagement;

the role we play in higher education and assessment; the role we play in the pursuit of research and scholarship; our role in preserving the culture of the institution; the role the brave new digital world relationships play and the role that in-person relationships play.

So…my guess is you thought that the identification of the critical teachable moment would be the identification of the successful advocacy exchange, but instead, it is convincing academic librarians that there are no more excuses and that they need to know how to advocate and must advocate…that's the teachable moment. We have no more excuses.

An Afterword

In *Three Cups of Tea*, the bestselling book about Greg Mortenson's humanitarian mission to build schools for girls and boys in Afghanistan and Pakistan, there is an enduring lesson for practitioners of advocacy, one of the challenges associated with making a difference. For Mortenson, the lessons he learned were focused on the continual process of understanding the very cultures and communities he aimed to help before he could advocate for money needed to build schools. We are well advised to heed this message as we argue for libraries or seek to influence policies and decision making.[1] One must stand on firm ground and understand the cultural nuances of colleges and universities, their libraries, and the information needs of their communities before engaging actively in advocacy on their behalf.

There are several key elements to this argument as it has been associated audaciously with the life work of Mortenson in geographically and politically uncertain regions of Central Asia. The common theme of the essays found in this volume all point to the complexities of the webs spun in college and university campus communities. There is hardly a living, breathing college or university in the United States that in 2010 resembles itself in 1960 due to an array of social, cultural, and technological changes. Many of our colleges and universities are seeking stronger engagement with multiple publics, spurred not only by calls for greater accountability and transparency of higher education by citizens but also by a desire to contribute to the good of society.[2] An increasing number of academicians have found value in communicating ideas more broadly than their own disciplines, and institutions have gains in social capital by developing service learning opportunities for students, community clinics, and partnerships with governmental and nonprofit agencies.

As the nation's populations become more diverse, questions surrounding the sociodemographic makeup of the communities of students, faculty and staffs of colleges and universities have also challenged assumptions about access to postsecondary education. Increasingly, the assumption about the difference between K–12 and postsecondary education as one of *right and privilege* appears to no longer hold as a stronger relationship evolves between occupation and educational attainment. Closely related to the sociodemographics of academic communities are expansions in scholarship and the external funding generated to support new directions in research and creative activity. Related to changes in scholarship are new and continually emerging information and communication technologies that have shifted us from analog to digital thinking. And related to technological change is a shift in managerial thinking toward client-centered restructuring, organizational learning, and the empowerment of staff in decision making and governance.

The essayists in this volume were challenged to think long and hard about the meaning of advocacy. Independently from one another, essayists' thoughts coalesced on these themes as they sought to understand the application of advocacy through their respective frames. They will likely contribute to ongoing discussions and begin new ones among staff and administrators and in professional circles across the landscape of America's academic libraries.

Not only was Greg Mortenson successful in carrying a message of education and peacemaking from a misunderstood part of the world to the West, his personal advocacy has led to new and revised understandings of how to interact and provide necessary resources for social change. Effective advocacy as explored by the authors in this volume rests upon an ever changing social and cultural milieu affected by these and other trends. If academic libraries were ever the warehouses of books as supposedly perceived by many of our constituents[3], the real challenges of advocacy leadership, whether from managers, frontline librarians, or supporters and collaborators, will likely be to continue to persuade decision makers and influence policy and constituents on their understanding of the *integral* role of the academic library as the nation's colleges and universities respond as institutions of higher learning.

Notes

1. "Advocacy refers to the totality of an organization's efforts to argue its position and influence the outcome of public policy decisions, through both direct and indirect techniques," Advocacy, *Encyclopedia of Activism and Social Justice*, ed. By Gary L. Anderson and Kathryn G. Herr (Thousand Oaks, Calif. : Sage Publications, c2007), p 41.

2. For further understanding of the influence of public engagement in college and universities, see the Community Engagement Elective Classification created by the Carnegie Foundation for the Advancement of Teaching, http://classifications.carnegiefoundation.org/descriptions/community_engagement.php, (last accessed March 12, 2010)

3. Johann Neem, "Reviving the Academic Library," *Inside Higher Education*, 19 November 2009 http://www.insidehighered.com/views/2009/11/19/neem (last accessed March 12, 2010)

About the Contributors

Camila Alire is a long time advocacy trainer. She is library dean emeritus at University of New Mexico and Colorado State Universities. She received her MLS from the University of Denver and doctorate in Higher Education Administration from the University of Northern Colorado. In 2008, she was elected President of the American Library Association for 2009–10.

Paul Bracke is Associate Dean for Information Technology and Resource Services and Associate Professor of Library Science at Purdue University.

D. Scott Brandt is professor of library science and associate dean for research in the Purdue University Libraries, where he is responsible for overseeing research programs, interdisciplinary collaborations, and extramural funding. As a Provost Fellow at Purdue University, he works half time in the Office of Vice President for Research on projects related to research integrity and retention.

Memo Cordova is a Reference and Instruction Librarian at Boise State University's Albertsons Library. Memo received a BFA (Graphic design/illustration) from Boise State University in 1991 and a MLIS from the University of Washington in 2003.

Ray English is Azariah Smith Root Director of Libraries at Oberlin College. He is a long-time member of the SPARC Steering Committee and has served as its chair since 2006. He was also a primary founder of the ACRL Scholarly Communication Program.

Heather Joseph is the Executive Director of SPARC, The Scholarly Publishing and Academic Resources Coalition, a library organization that working to create a more open system of scholarly communication. She also serves as convener and spokesperson for the Alliance for Taxpayer Access.

Kim Leeder is a reference and instruction librarian at Boise State University, where she divides her time between reference, teaching, outreach, and exploring new ways to leverage technology to inform and educate her university community.

Scott B. Mandernack is Head of Research and Instructional Services at Marquette University, where he coordinates, directs, and promotes reference and research services, information literacy instruction, e-learning and instructional development, library diversity services, and a funding information center.

Beth McNeil is associate dean for academic affairs in the Purdue University Libraries. She is the co-author of Fundamentals of Library Supervision, with Joan Giesecke (2005) and co-edited *Human Resource Management in Today's Academic Library* with Janice Simmons-Welburn (2004).

Julie Todaro is Dean of Library Services at Austin Community Colleges. She has written extensively on a range of issues affecting academic libraries, including advocacy and persuasion.

Susan Vega-Garcia is Associate Professor and Head of Instruction Programs at Iowa State University, where she is also Race and Ethnic Studies Bibliographer.

Scott Walter is Associate University Librarian for Services and Associate Dean of Libraries at the University of Illinois at Urbana-Champaign, where he holds appointments in the Graduate School of Library and Information Science and the College of Education. He has published widely on topics including education librarianship, information literacy instruction, and professional education for academic librarians. He received an M.L.S. and M.S. in History and Philosophy of Education from Indiana University, and a Ph.D. in Higher Education Administration from Washington State University.

Janice Welburn is Dean of the Raynor-Memorial Library at Marquette University. She co-edited *Human Resource Management in Today's Academic Library* with Beth McNeil (2004).

William Welburn is Senior Advisor to the Provost on Diversity Initiatives at Marquette University. He received a Ph.D. in Library and Information Science from Indiana University.

Jean Zanoni is the Associate Dean at Marquette University Libraries and has responsibility for human resources, facilities, assessment initiatives and grant writing and external funding activities.